Author Biographies

The Teachers of Light

Also known as the Elders, the Teachers of Light are a group of Archangels and Ascended Masters working together for the spiritual evolution of all of humanity and Mother Earth. They have orchestrated this course and are the primary authors of this book. The Collective includes Archangels Metatron, Michael, Uriel and Zadkiel, Lord Melchizedek, Yeshua, Mother Mary, Mary Magdalene and others. They give you their wisdom, support, powerful tools, energetics and initiations in present-time. Their desire is to create a new pathway into a full state of consciousness and the Living Light Body.

Jim Self

Jim is one of the few international teachers, authors and speakers actually working at the leading edge of the current planetary Shift of Consciousness. He provides solid, up-to-date information and practical energy tools to help us keep pace with the transition we are in.

Jim lives in both the material third-dimensional world and within the higher realms of consciousness. As an entrepreneur he has successfully built and sold two corporations, and he is the founder and current board chairman of a third. Since childhood he has had the ability to recall his experiences within the sleep state. This awareness has expanded into relationships with the Archangels, Ascended Masters and

Teachers of Light. The tools and information presented in this book are a co-creation with these Great Beings.

Roxane Burnett

Roxane was a successful art director and manager for two major corporations for many years prior to taking the leap of faith and starting her own design firm. In the evening she taught the tools presented in this book and was soon faced with the decision to jump off another cliff – to teach and coach full time. She has never looked back.

Roxane is the co-founder and Chief Operating Officer of Mastering Alchemy, and has co-authored, with Jim, *Spirit Matters* and *What Do You Mean the Third Dimension is Going Away?* She presents the successful webinar series *Female Alchemy* and has been offering tools for developing intuition and personal management tools to individuals, businesses and professional women's groups since 2000. Roxane has appeared on television and radio and has been featured in international publications.

What people are saying about A Course in Mastering Alchemy

In February my full-time job ended. We were only a few months away from signing a mortgage for our new home (in a city we had moved to so I could take the job) and the birth of our second child. Instead of focusing on worry and fear I focused on the material in A Course in Mastering Alchemy, setting my intention and creating what I want. We are now in the new home with a beautiful child, and I am building a healthy consulting business working with loving and caring people. Life is spectacular. I am enjoying the work very much.

Rodney, Ottawa, Canada

A Course in Miracles says that it is designed only to take you to the front gate of Love. A Course in Mastering Alchemy opens the gate and allows entrance.

I am far more aware of being 100 per cent about service to self and 100 per cent about service to others. I am trusting my inner wisdom and allowing myself to be directed from the inside out.

RB, New York, USA

After all these years of being not all here (scattered), and being on autopilot, I feel like I'm *finally* behind the wheel and driving this bus! It feels *really* good and liberating! Journey on!!!

Alice S, Newfoundland, Canada

I have been teaching yoga for some 17 years. Coming back to the grounding and the breathing, as you instruct it, and the centring has made a profound shift in my practice.

The vibrations of the Living Word exercises are fantastic. I used "Certainty" yesterday in my physical yoga practice and was able to move my body in a way that was not doable until then. As I felt uncertainty coming in I just went back to the vibration of Certainty and my body kept opening up more and more. The positive vibration of Certainty overcame all of my lower-level vibrations that for the past 20 years have kept me out of the pose.

Thanks again! As you can tell I really enjoy this new aspect of the journey!

Steve P, New Mexico, USA

I have been practising T'ai Chi, Chi Kung and Reiki for many years now. While I have become adept at circulating and sensing energy, I have always been like a leaf in the wind, unable to hold still in a storm and unable to move in the stillness. I find your tools to be a gift from heaven, for I am now learning how to hold my centre – to be myself – in any circumstance, and how to be conscious throughout the day. Thank you.

Caroline, California, USA

I am having a *blast*. This is Wisdom Teaching at the highest level! I could *not* be more excited. It's *hard* to go slow. I feel like a sponge for this experience. And I'm not having any trouble with any of it, conceptually nor experientially. People wonder why I've got this smile on my face all the time *and* I don't take everything personally any more – a *great* thing for me.

My circular breathing has become automatic. Sometimes I do become the breath, only the breath. I feel *so* happy, confident, capable, gracious, and *know* who I am! And I carry that Rose with me all day long!

Thank you so much for deciding to incarnate onto the Earth at this time. You are truly a blessing.

Juliann, Wyoming, USA

Hello, I have been listening to and practising your amazing material for some time now. So from the depths of my being I want to say, "Thank you". I am practising most days and my life is certainly improving in ways I never imagined. My vibrational energy has clearly been raised up. More and more and for longer periods of time I am able to stay in the centre of my head and look out and be with what is in front of me. Wow, absolutely awesome!

As my vibration has risen up, my thinking is clearer and my business is improving. And as this occurs I am helping more people. As a result more money is appearing.

Paul J, New York, USA

"Wowie zowie!" is what I have to say about how this work changes family dynamics. I am on such a different level with my kids since doing this work. There is nothing missing and much to be gained by staying in that 5-D space.

I visited my kids for Mother's Day and have never had such high-level conversations or participated in a family project before. Most times my son-in-law finds very little to talk with me about, and almost never generates the conversation. But this time we were all completely present, full of love for each other and involved the whole four days. It was nonstop conversation and excitement.

SS, Illinois, USA

I'd like to share a story with you. Two young boys at school today got into a scuffle that quickly progressed into a full-on fight. One of them kept violently lunging at the other and needed to be held back so he wouldn't seriously hurt the other child.

After several people tried to intervene in various ways and a large degree of struggle took place, I remembered the Grounding Cord and thought I might see if that would help this aggressive child. I went over to him and put my hand on his shoulder (he was still being held and was fighting to go after the other boy), I told him he was going to be okay and very intentionally grounded him and myself along with him. After about 30–45 seconds of doing this, I told him he was going to be let go and he had to stand up and not run away. He was let go and amazingly he did just that. Then I gently took his hand and we both walked calmly and quietly out of the room so that I could talk to him about the incident with less of an audience.

It was an incredible experience! This young boy was completely transformed in a matter of seconds. Miracles really can happen when we believe that they will (and have tools)! Thank you, thank you, thank you! You really are helping to change the world.

Sonia D, United Arab Emirates

In the last few weeks I have had really long-time issues simply dissolving in an easy and loving way. I am overwhelmed – doors have opened. It is as if I could ask myself, "Why was that an issue anyway?"

And this week I have more than once consciously experienced what you described as "one part of me feeling the old way of reaction and frustration, and another part of me now taking over; knowing that it is time to breathe and use the tools, leading me to a very mature win–win solution with everybody involved having their space". Thank you so much.

Sonja M, Switzerland

This work has been *huge* in my life for many reasons. I am definitely calmer, more content. A year ago my husband transitioned and I had to put both our dogs down within nine months of each other. My three kids don't talk to me any more. People don't understand why I'm not falling apart; the old me would have. Instead I'm moving on. I sold our home and downsized into the most adorable condo, I have a new car and a new dog and cat who add so much joy to my day. I notice I go outside more, I breathe in beauty, I feel happy. Actually, I'm happy all of the time.

I notice synchronicity more. I have a knowingness and certainty, colours are brighter, I see more waves and flashes of light. My dreams are lucid. I've experienced the answer coming before the question is asked.

Thank you from the bottom of my heart for guiding us on this journey. I *know* without a doubt this is why I am here.

Gail B, Colorado, USA

A month after this coursework has come to an end, I still feel different. My world feels different. I am more calm, more internally aligned. As a matter of fact, from where I stand today, I know for certainty, within every fibre of my being, that my life has been all about the tiny, almost imperceptible progression of steps leading up to this "auspicious" course.

I can feel the success of accomplishment doing what we all agreed to do as a collective. A responsibility of sorts, a solemn oath, perhaps, has been fulfilled. I feel a sense of freedom and a "yes, we did it!"

I have taken this journey in A Course in Mastering Alchemy very seriously. I so much desire and intend the current energetics to be my perpetual space, developing even more mastery through eternity. Tall intent, yes, and as you have reminded us often, "It starts with an intent."

Susan L, Massachusetts, USA

I don't know how many lifetimes I have dreamt about this opportunity – to rise humanity, the Earth and myself. I'm infinitely grateful to you, Jim, to Archangels, to Masters and everyone from higher realms of Light for guiding us and helping us to remember who we are.

I'm opening every lesson with excitement and curiosity. I'm enjoying watching how everyone around me (who is left) changes in my presence. Getting calmer, less dramatic. Enjoying the "Happy" within, the smile in the heart. Thank you.

Amrit, Massachusetts, USA

I "happened" to be in Orlando during the nightclub shootings. The day before the shootings, I "happened" to do the Christed Matrix lesson.

I realize that I actually have no emotion about the shootings whatsoever. (This could sound weird to my 3D friends.) I am having strong thoughts from the chaotic collective but it's not real to me personally. It's almost like a movie, with everyone acting out their own fears and dramas and lessons.

With us doing all of the brain changing in these lessons, I am really feeling the division in the two realities. I have never felt so calm and balanced and am really amazed at how quiet I feel. Even in all of this chaos and emotional energy, I am okay. There is a sense of freedom in this. I understand that this is really part of our work. To become this quiet in the chaos.

AV, Florida, USA

Tools to Shift,
Transform
and Ascend

A Course
in Mastering
Alchemy

Jim Self and Roxane Burnett

WATKINS
Sharing Wisdom Since 1893

This edition first published in the UK and USA 2018 by
Watkins, an imprint of Watkins Media Limited
19 Cecil Court
London WC2N 4EZ

enquiries@watkinspublishing.com

10 9 8 7 6 5 4 3 2

Designed and typeset by Donald Sommerville

Printed and bound in the United States of America

A CIP record for this book is available from the British Library

ISBN: 978-1-78678-014-0

www.watkinspublishing.com

In Appreciation and Gratitude

To the wonderful Teachers within the realms of the Archangels, Lords of Light and Ascended Masters, for your guidance in co-creating a pathway to step out of unconsciousness and help us remember who we are on our journey Home.

To Joan Walker, for her assistance in bringing forth these elegant communications.

Contents

Preface

Welcome to what's possible.

This is a course and a journey to personal power and ascension that has never before been offered to humanity. The Archangels, Ascended Masters and other Teachers of Light who bring it to you asked that the conversations and classes they teach with Jim be transcribed and shared with humanity in book form. They asked Jim and Roxane to be their scribes.

Jim has been in communication with these Teachers since childhood. He has the ability to distil and simplify their transmissions in a way that allows their tools and information to be understood and practised by all. Dedicated students transcribed the lessons and Roxane, in collaboration with the Teachers, compiled and edited them to create this step-by-step path in written form.

How this book works

The Teachers of Light chose the most fundamental and transformative aspects of A Course in Mastering Alchemy to include here. The full online course is three years of focused, intentional coursework and live interaction with Jim and Roxane.

This book is divided into four parts; each one includes excerpts from transcriptions of channelled conversations and classes with the Teachers of Light.

PREFACE

Part 1: Introduction

In the first part of the book you'll discover the meaning of alchemy, meet the Teachers of Light and find out their intention with this course. You will also learn about the Fall of Consciousness and how humanity has got to the chaotic place in which it now finds itself.

Part 2: Creating the platform to receive

Here you will be taught how to create a platform to receive the tools and wisdom from the Teachers of Light. You'll find out how to build your personal power field, understand what the dimensions are, and begin to anchor new choices for your life. You'll learn simple, practical, foundational tools to master your emotions, thoughts and actions. This is the mastering of alchemy.

Part 3: Gifts from the Teachers of Light

With a strong and stable platform in place, you will be able to receive and practise the 14 key energy tools that will allow you to be the master of your life at every moment.

Part 4: Your Living Light Body

Should you choose to continue on this path, the Teachers explain what the Living Light Body is and offer the activations of the seven layers of the Light Body that will allow you to begin to experience its higher vibrational fields of Light. You will experience the lightness of being as you become one with Creator and All That Is.

PREFACE

What to expect from this course

Although simple, the lessons in this book hold profound energetics that can be felt and experienced viscerally. The Teachers have embedded energy and wisdom within their words. This is not a study for the rational mind, but instead an experience for the part of you that yearns to reconnect with who you are and with Creator.

Each lesson builds upon the previous one. If you choose only to engage in one or two sections of the book, you will still receive much more than written words. If you study and practise only the tools in Part 2, your life will change in powerful ways. The noise, stress and drama of the third-dimensional world around you will fall away. Carry on through all the lessons and you will continue to experience greater success, peace of mind and spiritual transformation.

How best to benefit from this course

A college course takes a complex subject and breaks it down into smaller areas of study. For example, when you study mathematics you take classes in individual topics such as algebra, geometry, trigonometry, etc. Likewise this course is divided into lessons, each one containing elements that will expand your understanding and perspective of the world and create new possibilities. The results are measured in the feedback you receive as you observe how you've changed and how the world around you responds to your demonstration of greater certainty, grace, happiness and personal power.

We suggest you don't skip around through these lessons. (There is a reason why you learn addition before multiplication.) Work your way through the lessons in order. Return to past lessons often to review what you've already learned. Take notes of your observations and any questions you might have. You'll be surprised at how often the answers appear before you.

Also included in this book are links to supplemental online resources, including audio recordings, videos and PDFs. These are not essential for your understanding but will enhance the lessons in the course. These additional resources are available in a private classroom only accessible by readers of this book. You'll find links to these online resources throughout the book.

Many terms on this path may be new to you. We've included a glossary of special terms at the end of the book, which we hope will be a valuable reference.

Your journey on this path

This is a course unlike any other. It is orchestrated by the Teachers of Light specifically for those who are committed to becoming who they came here to Earth to be. You are not small or insignificant. You are a big player and have an important contribution to make to your Soul, humanity and the Earth. This course is provided to experience the adventure you came here to master.

We wish you many blessings on this grand journey to who you are.

Jim and Roxane

Part 1

Introduction

Lesson 1

What is this course?

In a conversation I once had with Archangel Metatron, he told me that he, and other Teachers of Light, would like to create a unique pathway upon which no human has walked. Ever. He said this pathway would be an experiment, and the participants (you) are the subjects of the experiment.

He explained that this pathway would allow each individual the opportunity to become fully conscious in his or her personal evolution and ascension. This pathway would provide all of humanity existing in the third dimension with an opportunity to know themselves as fifth- and multidimensional beings of Light. Simultaneously humanity would assist in returning the Earth to its intended state of being.

Then Metatron asked, "Will you join us in creating this pathway"?

Imagine yourself sitting in the presence of a great being of Light and being asked this question. How would you respond? I was stunned, then immediately overwhelmed, scared and shocked. I felt small. I wanted to step forward and say "Yes" but needed to run away. All these thoughts and emotions occurred within one split second.

"Why would you ask me?" I replied.

Metatron answered, "Because we are you and you are we. Here in the nonphysical we know all of the possibilities and probabilities of what is possible. The creation of the third dimension and the Fall of Consciousness are creations of physicality that can only be re-created or changed within the physical. It is you and humanity who are the spirits having a physical experience. You have the physical form. We do not. It is only you, in human form, who can change the experiences of the third dimension and what the Fall created."

It was then that a strange but wonderful awareness began to unfold: a calm certainty; a knowing; a sense of presence. There was no doubt or fear but instead a sense of self that I had experienced during fleeting moments of my life as passion, purpose and excitement. These were experiences and understandings that had often been pushed aside by the external world's demands.

I looked at Metatron and we smiled. The journey began.

What is the purpose of this course?

The Archangels, Ascended Masters and other Teachers of Light have specifically orchestrated A Course in Mastering Alchemy to expand our understanding, consciousness and ability to use the new energy tools they offer. These new tools can assist us in stepping into the higher dimensions.

The course within this book has often been compared to Helen Schucman's *A Course in Miracles* (1976). Both courses share these aspects:

1. They reveal that *everything* involving time, space and perception is illusory.
2. They demonstrate that perception is continuously fuelled by what it originated from – separation, fragmentation, judgement, fear and lack – in this third-dimensional, time–space dream.
3. They provide practical experiences and exercises designed to expand one's understanding and consciousness of who we each really are.

A Course in Mastering Alchemy, however, differs from *A Course in Miracles* in three important respects:

WHAT IS THIS COURSE?

1. The Archangels and Ascended Masters *actively* participate in constructing and teaching this pathway. What you are about to read is more than words on a page. Energetics (combinations of vibrations and frequencies) have been fully embedded in every lesson. Many readers are able to viscerally feel the Teachers' presence and wisdom as they read and absorb their words. For others, this opens the door for their own communication with the Teachers.

2. There has been a significant leap in consciousness over the last few decades. The new energies, technologies and tools that are now available to us in the higher dimensions could not be received or integrated in the 1980s and 1990s. Hence, a large proportion of the information, exercises and tools shared in this book is completely new and has never been taught before.

3. Nothing is as powerful as a deeply felt experience. A Course in Mastering Alchemy is a deeply experiential body of work. Unlike other courses and seminars, it doesn't merely seek to change a reader's perception through speaking to his or her mind, or offer the reader a momentary escape from reality by briefly encapsulating them in a "marshmallow wave of love and light" that can rarely be sustained. This course and pathway is unique in that each experience builds on the one before to transform the participant from the inside out, moving them from a place of conditioned responses to a place of expanded consciousness, where discernment, consideration and choice become a way of life.

The purpose of this interactive book is to provide you with as much information and as many practical experiences as possible to assist you on your journey. This book is not the full pathway laid out by the Teachers. It is an in-depth instructional experience drawn from most aspects of the journey. This book is not a quick read but instead an absorbed experience.

A Course in Mastering Alchemy will help you to:

- Become conscious of the rules, structures and limitations of the third and fourth dimensions.
- Recognize that much of who you believe you are actually has very little to do with who you are.
- Learn how to step out of the unnecessary concept of suffering and build a structure that allows you to experience wellbeing in your life.
- Re-create yourself so your mental and emotional bodies begin to become one again.
- Begin to experience yourself differently as a sovereign being who is no longer at the mercy of conditioned thoughts and emotionally charged reactions.
- Discover new awarenesses and choices that were not available to you before.
- Build and live within your Living Light Body.

How was the course created?

Every conversation I had with the Teachers and every class we taught together was recorded and transcribed. This book offers you many of the substantive tools and teachings that were received during that time. The exciting journey you are about to embark upon is a distillation of my collaboration with the Teachers. And, thanks to technology, I have been able to supplement the information in this book with online resources such as recorded lectures, meditations, videos and animations. To access this online classroom, simply visit www.masteringalchemy.com/book.

The Teachers' wisdom and information was received in three ways.

1. Information was received, remembered and brought back from the higher realms of consciousness within the sleep space (the time when the physical body is fully at rest).

2. The Teachers gave clear instruction during the day and while I presented the material to others. (Communication with the Teachers is always available during the conscious, daytime walking-around space. Ask – and listen – and you shall receive.)
3. Many of the conversations with the Teachers were brought forth and recorded with the assistance of Joan Walker.

Each lesson builds upon the previous one. It's important to approach these lessons as you would any course of study. Although it is possible to skip around and between the lessons, slowly working through them in order will offer you the best benefit. The Teachers have designed this pathway, this course, very deliberately and for a clear outcome: your personal evolution.

What can you expect from the course?

This work is different from any other work you've done. While it is simple, it is not necessarily easy. Some assembly is required. Success on this pathway requires you to create and hold a clear intention to become fully conscious and know yourself. It requires learning to hold your attention in present-time (the now moment) while being aware of your thoughts, words and actions.

The primary purpose of this work is for you to realign, rewire and remember who you have always been. You see, you already know everything that you will read here; you've just forgotten it. As you actively engage in this course, you will begin to remember what you already know. You will remember and experience the Living Light Body that is available to you – it's simply covered and hidden by that bushel basket we call life in the third dimension.

A Course in Mastering Alchemy culminates in the building and activating of your Living Light Body. This is far simpler than I thought it would be when I began this work. As you walk this path with me, and the many who walked before you, you will discover personal abilities and possibilities you never imagined; from developing and honing your clairvoyance to having a personal relationship with Metatron, Yeshua, Anna and the many other Teachers of Light. You will discover how to enjoy your daily life while walking through the fearful chaos of the world. You will become able to change the outcome of any situation by quietly holding your attention on your intention and shifting the energy.

This journey is not about mental information. It's about participation, experiencing and making the decision to become bigger, stronger and more capable. It requires a new level of maturity, responsibility, focus and integrity. It's about you stepping up, remembering who you are and stepping away from who you are not. You have played the third-dimensional game very well, and you have succeeded beyond your wildest imaginings, even though you may not be aware of it.

My task

My task in this adventure is not so much as a teacher but more as a tour guide; pointing out the landmarks, road signs and scenery along the way. Just as the Teachers shared their wisdom with me, I will provide you with information about what you might find if you choose to open the many doors on this spiralling staircase we are going to be journeying upon together.

Your task

Your task on this journey is simply to enjoy yourself and to remember who you are. As you engage in this work, everything else will fall into place. Much information will be provided along the way, much more than you expect to receive at this moment. Much energy will be felt, seen, experienced, released and moved.

WHAT IS THIS COURSE?

This is the journey you came here to experience. This is the journey to go Home. It's time to meet the Teachers.

Online resources

Question: What is the Archangels' intention for this path and what is Jim's role in it? (05:26)

To access the online classroom,
visit www.masteringalchemy.com/book

Lesson 2

Who are the Teachers of Light?

The Teachers of Light (also known as the Elders) have guided this project: this book and course.

There exists a sacred place known as the Sanctuary of the Pink Diamond, a place where you can connect with Creator (the source of all creation) and All That Is (all the creations of Creator). Within the Sanctuary there is a table where you can meet, create and communicate with the Teachers of Light. This table is your table, in your Sanctuary. It is a place of great reverence. The only thing that prevents you from sitting at this table is your attention held upon the noise, fear and doubts of the third-dimension reality outside of you.

The Teachers of Light work together as a collective to unravel the Fall of Consciousness and realign the Earth back into its original twelfth-dimensional state. They work together to uplift humanity into a fully conscious state of alignment with All That Is.

During the years I've spent with these great beings, their personalities, intentions and commitment to humanity unfolded. Although it is possible to research each of their names and read about what others know of them and experience with them, the way you will experience the Elders is unique to you. The Teachers suggest you refrain from researching and simply feel and get to know them as they are introduced in this book. You'll have a more authentic and personal experience if you do.

According to some schools of thought, specific colours, tones, rays, appearances, past lives, locations and job descriptions belong to each Archangel, Ascended Master or Teacher. A handy, well-organized spreadsheet listing such associations would indeed make it very easy and comfortable for the rational mind to fit the material into its conditioned boxes of understanding. Before I met the Teachers, I too wanted a tidy spreadsheet of colours, words and sounds. When I asked for this, the Teachers smiled. They then offered a pathway full of knowledge, wisdom and insight. What they give to humanity encompasses much, much more than what has been described in the Talmud, Christian Gnostic texts, New-Age books and the Internet.

A common agreement between all of the Teachers is their commitment to noninterference. Just like the Prime Directive of the United Federation of Planets in *Star Trek*, this guiding principle prevents the Teachers of Light (and starship crews) from using their superior powers and wisdom to impose their own values or ideals on humans (and less evolved civilizations). The Teachers have agreed to refrain from telling us humans what to do and only rarely make suggestions. Fortunately, they do have the unique and powerful ability to patiently show us an image, turn of phrase or concept that, if we are paying attention, can direct us to what our next steps are. They are very, very patient and will repeat a concept or tool several times until we finally "get" it. Amusement (with humans) is a common trait they all have, which is fortunate for them and for us. Their amusement keeps us all moving forward together in this project.

Below are my experiences and understandings of a few of the Teachers of Light who have participated in this project. The descriptions are meant to be simple introductions; the Teachers are much more than this. Your relationship with the Teachers will be uniquely yours and will continue to grow and evolve as you do.

LESSON 2

Archangel Uriel

Archangel Uriel is a grand storyteller. He was the first archangel I met. He beautifully explained the Fall of Consciousness and how humanity got in the situation we are now in. Uriel is artistic in both the words and visuals he presents to your inner sight. He guides your journey into the higher realms and appears to us as a gentle and kind companion.

Archangel Metatron

Ever the scientist and teacher, Archangel Metatron steps forward during the activations of many of the layers of the Light Body to explain the integration of the sometimes complicated energetics. Understanding the depth of wisdom that Metatron provides requires an audio recorder and time to listen repeatedly. Metatron is often the communicator on behalf of Creator.

Archangel Michael

Archangel Michael is a lead representative of the angelic kingdom. Michael made his first appearance to me during an experience within the Sacred Heart where he, and the angelic kingdom, stood in partnership with the animal and Elemental kingdoms. The first Ray of Creation is given to us by Michael. He is the type of leader who sits quietly at the back of the room, waiting and watching for the perfect time to add a gem of Light to the group's creation.

Archangel Raphael

In this project Archangel Raphael contributes teachings relating to the activations of the Living Light Body and how to integrate the new energetics smoothly into the density of the human body. Raphael is also our supportive, encouraging cheerleader on this journey.

Lord Melchizedek

Melchizedek is one of the Lords of Light. He is an overseer of this project, bringing tools and concepts to humanity to uplift us into higher levels of consciousness. He doesn't get involved in a personal way or as a presenter but instead coordinates all of the Teachers of Light. He often appears in a triad with Michael and Metatron. Melchizedek seldom speaks as an individual.

Archangel Zadkiel

Archangel Zadkiel explains the steps of this project well. He is able to simplify the activations on this path in a way that is easy for us to understand, remember and utilize. Zadkiel helps us understand and practise with many of the Rays of Creation. Zadkiel is very involved in helping us release our limiting beliefs and programming by providing strategies and tools.

Yeshua

Also known as Jesus, Yeshua represents and shows us how to have a physical body and reside in the higher dimensions simultaneously. He reminds us of our purpose for embodying upon the planet and how we can now do what he was unable to when he was incarnate. With the element of Love, Yeshua is here to assist humanity to step into the higher realms of consciousness, where he and the other Teachers reside.

Mother Mary

The mother of Yeshua, Mary embodies and teaches nurturing, understanding and compassion. She is a leader and teacher with great authority. Mother Mary represents the feminine aspect of Creator. She works toward the possibility for each of us to be that also.

Anna

As Yeshua's grandmother and the mother of Mother Mary, Anna teaches the wisdom and the power of discernment. She shows how masterful leadership can demonstrate itself. Today she would be a diplomat to the United Nations. She, along with Mother Mary and Mary Magdalene, offers activations and transmissions that can help bring the balanced, unified feminine and masculine creative energy into your own daily spiritual life.

Mary Magdalene

Unbridled, unrestricted enthusiasm is where Mary Magdalene lives. Together and aligned in the triad with Mother Mary and Anna, Mary Magdalene offers the energetic or raw adolescent curiosity and passion that balances well with Mother Mary and Anna. She is all about wildly creating what is possible and especially what is considered impossible. She seldom speaks as an individual.

Kuthumi

Kuthumi is an Ascended Master. He is a most attentive friend and Teacher. He prepares us for the other Teachers to present their activations and transmissions. Kuthumi is conscientious and clearly a world navigator and teacher. He has deep familiarity with the third-dimensional adventure and can phrase concepts in a way we humans can more easily grasp.

El Morya

Within this course and project, Ascended Master El Morya's commitment is to Earth, her inhabitants and their ability to coexist peacefully. El Morya works closely with the Elementals and the elements. He rarely teaches in this course; however, he has a strong presence in the Collective as a peacemaker, mediator and way-shower.

Meeting the Teachers of Light

As you meet each of these kind Elders, I encourage you to approach them as new friends who have entered your life to participate in a new adventure with you. They are no better then you. They are simply walking a step or two ahead of you on this path, like an older sibling or grandparent. They have stepped through a doorway and are holding the door open for you to enter the realm of possibilities.

Although important and powerful, this journey doesn't have to be serious. In fact, being serious will get in the way of what you can experience here. The last thing the Teachers want is for you to idolize them or be separate from them. Each night you sit at the table with them, discussing and laughing and enjoying each other's company. Soon you will be able to remember the creative fun you have together. The Teachers are your friends and family. They will assist you to consciously remember who you are.

Please enjoy meeting and creating with the Teachers of Light. The journey they offer leads us to the Living Light Body.

Lesson 3

What is alchemy?

In an early conversation with Archangel Metatron, he described alchemy as "changing the frequency of thought, altering the harmonics of matter and applying the element of Love to create a desired result." It's a way of living your life with awareness and intention, returning to a conscious relationship with Creator. Alchemy is transforming the density of your physicality into the Living Light Body.

Changing the frequency of thought

Thoughts are electrical and emotions are magnetic. This is a very important concept. When a thought is coupled with an emotion, the combined energies become electromagnetically charged. The energies become amplified and set in motion.

Let me explain this in a simple way. You may have seen those big junkyard cranes that lift up buses, trucks and cars and move them around. Effectively this type of crane is composed of a block of steel, which has magnetic properties, hanging on the end of a chain. When you take a length of conductive wire, wrap it once around the block of steel and then plug it into an electrical outlet the steel becomes electromagnetic to the power of one. In other words, it becomes a magnet, albeit a weak one. But when you wrap that wire around the block of steel ten times, or a hundred times, or a thousand times, the force of the magnet increases exponentially. It becomes a very strong magnet that holds a tremendous amount of power.

Exactly the same thing happens within us with our thoughts and emotions. Many of us have been taught that we have four bodies, a spiritual body, a mental body, an emotional body and a physical body – known as the four-body system. When you are in a state of ease, feeling happy and unstressed, just enjoying the world around you, you are in your spiritual body.

Now let's say that you're walking down the street, enjoying the spring flowers, and someone comes up to you and says, "You have a very funny nose." The mechanics of what unfolds next could be something like this: you drop from your happy spiritual body into your mental body, relinquishing your seniority and self-ownership. You think to yourself: *I don't like this. That's not a nice thing to say. What do I do with this? Why did they say that? What does it mean? Is this something I should worry about?* You begin mentally to analyse why someone would say this to you, running it over and over again in your mind.

Instantaneously, without any conscious thought or awareness, you then drop into your emotional body. These thoughts generate an emotion that doesn't feel very good – *I don't like this. It doesn't feel good. I feel hurt. Maybe I'm not going to be liked. I'm not good enough. I'm not appreciated. I'm never going to succeed. Oh my, this is a big problem.* And right there the emotion of "off balance" now has an electrical thought wrapped around it: *I am not okay. I'm ugly. What are they going to think of me? I'm never going to amount to anything.* And the more you wrap the thought around the emotion, the more powerful your emotional response becomes, just like that electromagnet. The more you ponder, the more you give up your seniority, and the more uncomfortable you get. You become embarrassed. You don't know what to do with this feeling. You can't talk about it to your friends. Out of desperation, to get this feeling and the thoughts that accompany it out of your field, you put it in a place of unconsciousness by burying it in a box called denial.

But thoughts don't just go poof! and disappear. They all get stored somewhere. Those unacknowledged thoughts and feelings (*I have a funny nose.*

I don't like myself. I'm not accepted. I'm not attractive. I feel so ugly. I'm never going to succeed.) are still alive and vibrating in your unconscious. It is as though you are carrying a huge billboard on your back that reads, "Kick me." The Law of Attraction responds by giving you more of the same.

The Law of Attraction

How you hold your attention (consciously or unconsciously) is very, very important because it draws to you exactly what you focus upon. For example, the longer you hold on to the unconscious belief *I'm not okay, I'm not okay, I'm not okay*, the more it continues to grow and affect your daily life. It continues to be fed by the Law of Attraction, and it continues to be experienced. You so strongly don't want this painful thing to happen again that you hold it out in your future and paste a big red flag on it that says DANGER! Remember, the Law of Attraction does not distinguish between what you want and what you don't want. It simply gives to you what you hold your attention upon.

It cannot be stressed enough, if your reaction (emotion) to a thought is strong, the magnetic charge behind it increases. If your reaction is negative, it may result in an angry outburst that you later regret, or you may withdraw, allowing that destructive energy to build inside of you, causing dis-ease. If your reaction is positive (amused, pleased, neutral, for example), your mental, emotional and physical bodies will be at ease and you will have a sense of wellbeing.

Changing how you feel changes everything. If you choose to think higher thoughts and feel lighter emotions you will raise your vibration significantly, and you won't find yourself gravitating back into the old repetitive behaviours and thoughts of the third dimension. Often when you interrupt a long-standing pattern (breaking the circuit of the electromagnet) the energy flows backward and forward along your timeline, changing the energy all the way back to the first time the painful thing occurred. The energy is reset to the present time, allowing you the room to move freely again.

So you see, you can change the frequency of your thought to create a different result. When you change the frequency of your thought by applying the tools the Teachers of Light offer us, you can transform fear and reaction into love and ease.

Altering the harmonics of matter

Altering the harmonics of matter is not complicated, but to do this successfully it is essential to understand and master changing the frequency of thought. Learning to observe without reacting and allowing your feelings to be more fluid and at a higher vibration is necessary to the process.

Let's start simply. Thoughts have density. Once dense enough, thoughts materialize. If you're continuously holding negative thoughts, soon they will become dense and drop into matter. Often these "densified" thoughts show up in the world of form as physical illness or emotional/mental imbalance. Other times they appear as uncomfortable events or situations. Therefore changing those thought forms is the first step in altering the harmonics of matter.

Changing the harmonics of matter requires changing the frequency or tone of thought. To begin with, transforming your version of an ugly thought can be challenging. It has taken many years to build and anchor this negative thought in your life, so be patient and allowing with yourself.

How to accelerate your awareness

Notice how you speak, and the words you choose to use in conversation with others. By choosing words that feel better in your speech, and in your mouth, you will begin to become more aligned with wellbeing, as well as less restricted in your choices. Consciously choose more interesting words – words that feel good as you speak them. It will be the speaking of these words that will move you into the fourth dimension with ease and balance. Choosing these words will also allow you to change the direction of conversations more artfully before they start veering toward fear, worry and problems. This is a very enjoyable skill to develop.

Applying the element of Love

Love is an interesting and very, very misunderstood word in the third dimension. Love, in real terms, does not and cannot exist in the third-dimensional state of reaction and resistance. Love is open-ended, fluid, expansive, radiant and powerful, whereas the third dimension is rigid, restrictive, conditional and reactive. Love, as a feeling, and a powerful creative tool, only begins to be present and available to you in the fourth dimension.

Love has no end. Love is beauty. Love is your inner smile. Love is the power that moves the wind and pushes the ocean waves. Love is what holds the planets in their orbits. But, most importantly, Love is the creative expression within each of us that creates. Love has no sword. Love does not apply force and it does not restrict or limit possibility.

As you become masterful at changing the frequency of thought from the heavy absolutes of the third dimension to the alternate possibilities and new choices of the fourth, you will begin to find a joy within your heart. This joy carries with it new possibilities of more enjoyable outcomes for all. You will begin to become conscious of this ever-expanding element of Love. When you start to recognize and experience the higher forms of Love in the fourth and higher dimensions, you will be able to apply these forms of Love to your creations.

So what are the higher forms of Love and how can you begin to experience them? Like many things in the higher dimensions, there are few third-dimensional words that adequately describe them. Beauty is perhaps the easiest example to help you start to experience and anchor this Love.

Beauty is a fourth-dimensional experience. It is experienced using the third-dimensional senses of the physical body (for example, a sunset looks beautiful, music sounds beautiful, and so on), but it moves within and through the spiritual body. Beauty is an inner sense or feeling rather than an observation.

Higher forms of Love can only be accessed when you already exist in the higher levels of consciousness. Higher Beauty is the recognition and appreciation of the grandness of All That Is. It may occur while you appreciate a lovely waterfall, but it is not about what you see with your eyes. It is expansive and not physical. For example, have you ever had a moment when you felt expanded and part of everything – a moment of such unification that you were unaware of your physicality? Those moments, which can occur during a great meditation or while listening to music or being in nature, are moments that you can remember, re-create and anchor in order to begin to experience and apply the elements of Higher Love.

Creating a desired result

As you play with and practise the three aspects of alchemy that Metatron offers, you will create your desired result. You will become aware of the way of life that is now available to you. You will begin to trust and open your heart again. You will become conscious of that inner smile that resides within

Online resources

Video: The Law of Attraction (10:36)

To access the online classroom,
visit www.masteringalchemy.com/book

you. A huge awareness will return to you, and you will begin to rediscover your connection with All That Is. You will experience compassion, co-creation and cooperation. You will begin to find alignment and your inner smile will start to take over your life. You will rewire yourself and reawaken. You will reclaim that bigger, grander part of who you are.

This is where the true magic of this course lies – in the re-creation of yourself, in the building of your Living Light Body.

Lesson 4

Why now?

There is a change under way in humanity and the Teachers of Light and All That Is are very excited about it. The Teachers of Light have told me that many Great Beings (with and without physical bodies) are watching humanity and are surprised (and wowed) by the direction we are taking to uplift not only ourselves and our planet but also all planets and all form. However, most of humanity is not aware of this change or its contribution toward it. This course has been given to us to clarify and establish a timeless set of tools that will fully anchor our potential and create a firm connection with All That Is in order that this evolution steps up and continues in a smooth manner.

This Shift of Consciousness is so far-reaching that our limited imagination cannot begin to grasp the magnitude of the changes we are now experiencing. As part of this transition, almost everything we've taken for granted is falling away or reconfiguring. The rigid frameworks that once dictated the way nations, cultures and individuals experienced themselves in our third-dimensional societies are unravelling. This Shift is not only altering our consciousness, it's also changing the world around us. It is affecting every aspect of life on the planet: our political, social and economic structures, the environment, the weather, every institution, wars, how we view our relation-ships, our work, every thought we think and every feeling we feel. It is altering time, our memory, our DNA, the wiring of our physical and emotional bodies, our beliefs, our perceptions of good and bad and right and wrong, and, most especially, our awareness of what's possible. Every day it seems as though there is more injustice, fear, chaos and conflict in the world. For many, such observations are disturbing and upsetting. It isn't easy to watch as families around the globe are being killed or the coral of the oceans is dying. This Shift will occur whether we pay attention to it or not. Humanity and the planet are changing whether we resist it or assist it. So the question is: how will you choose to move through this Shift?

Although you may not recognize it, the Shift is providing new under-standings of how we can once again live in harmony with each other, the Earth and All That Is. Together we are becoming a global community. The third-dimensional structure of duality – black and white, East and West, right and wrong, us and them, good and bad, and male and female – is changing. On the one hand, many dividing lines are becoming less distinct. On the other, we are watching extremism, division, separation and fear all around us. We are moving from the third-dimensional experience of separation and extremes to a way of life that allows for greater possibilities, connected communities and an expanding sense of ease and wellbeing. However there is a period of transition between where we currently exist and this new Heaven on Earth. And this transition will sometimes be rough and uncomfortable. If you observe any segment of culture today, whether it be religion, politics, education or relationships, you may notice that separation and division are more prevalent. Racial tensions, human rights problems, wars, fear and bullying have dominated the news and the attention of many. Things seems to be getting worse, louder and less kind.

To reach that Heaven on Earth, everything that is of a lower vibration must be brought up to the surface, out into the light of day and released. This is why such a high degree of conflict exists in the world right now. As unpleasant and uncomfortable as it is, this increased unrest is a good sign that the imbalances are leaving, soon to be replaced and uplifted.

Worrying about the conflicts and wishing them away does not make them go away. These responses are the very source of what draws the fear and discomfort to you. The Law of Attraction applies here. You will become much more aware of how the Shift is affecting you and how to move smoothly through the changes by quietly observing, creating a point of balance and releasing the imbalanced issues within yourself first. This is the pathway through the seams of the transition to find ease and wellbeing. The Teachers of Light designed an interactive course to make this transition smoother: the purpose of this book.

Why is this Shift happening now?

This Shift is happening now because we have asked for it to occur. It's also happening now because we have accomplished what we came here to achieve. You see, the game of the third dimension has been fully played out, and played out very successfully. It's now time to bring everything to completion and return Home to the heart of Creator. Everyone is going Home to the higher dimensions, but not everyone is going Home on the same timeline or with the same ease and grace. Going Home is precisely what the Shift is all about.

The Shift is clearing away all that we (individually and humanity) are not. It's clearing away all that we hold our attention upon that has nothing to do with who we are. This Shift is assisting us in rewiring our spiritual connections and realigning ourselves so that we can finally remember all that we are. However this is not going to happen without some attention on our part. To complete the third-dimensional experiment we signed up for, we now have the opportunity to put our "selves" back together again. Learning to put yourself back together, rebuilding your Living Light Body, is your journey Home. This task is possible, but attention is required.

Is this something to be happy about? Yes!

Could you be excited? Yes!

Is it simple? Yes!

Is it going to be easy? Not exactly . . . but it does not have to be difficult either.

How this transition might be affecting you

As exciting and as wonderful as this transition is, it's also creating difficulties for many people. These difficulties are occurring as the pace of the Shift quickens and we continue to hold tightly to our third-dimensional beliefs and habits. Judging others and ourselves, resentment, competition, prejudice and fear are only a few examples. There are many. These habits and beliefs are choices that belong to the dense, noisy third dimension and they must be released. As long as we continue to hold these limitations, and argue over "rights" and "wrongs", as long as we believe in lack and see the world through a filter of "us and them", we will experience the uncomfortable effects of the Shift within our physical and emotional bodies. What's going on here is that as we argue for our limitations and hold on to old beliefs that no longer support us, we are creating a resistance or blockage within our four-body system that is causing us discomfort.

As I mentioned earlier, the third-dimensional reality as we know it is shifting. Your awareness is expanding and it is becoming far more aligned and balanced as you move into a higher consciousness. But you can't take your baggage with you. Humanity is waking up, and as it does the old structures that have supported duality, maintained separation and controlled the masses with fear are beginning to crumble.

Just as this Shift is occurring globally, it is also occurring internally within each individual regardless of his or her beliefs, religion, commitment to spiritual growth or lack of awareness. Signs that you are being affected by the external conflicts include internal imbalances, worry, anxiety, physical illness and stress. You may notice yourself being more impatient and easily irritated. You may find yourself withdrawing from others. You may notice you're questioning thoughts and feelings that you have always experienced but never paid much attention to before now. You may notice that the lifestyle you've enjoyed for many years is no longer satisfying.

What if there was a way to allow the cultural agreements to crumble without us feeling lost? What if people really could come together for each other instead of fighting wars? What if you could make a difference and smooth out the inevitable transition so everyone could step into the fifth dimension?

What if . . . ?

Whose thoughts are these anyway?

Our thoughts create our beliefs, our beliefs create our habits and our habits create our lives. In other words, our thoughts, no matter how unconscious, create our reality. However, many of the thoughts that we think and the beliefs that we hold are not even our own; they were given to us by our mothers, fathers, teachers, ministers and the third-dimensional reality outside of us. It's not that our parents, or anyone else, set out deliberately to mislead us. In most cases it was because they loved us and wanted the best for us. Their guidance was very specific: *Do this, don't do that. This is good and right, that's bad and wrong. Talk to these people and not to those people* . . . You get the picture. These caring adults were simply passing on to us what their parents and their parents' parents (along with most of the rest of society) had taught them to accept as the "truth".

Growing up many of us may intuitively have felt that what others accepted as the "truth" did not feel "right" or congruent to us, but consensus opinion is a powerful thing. It's not easy to stand against the crowd or argue with the grown-ups or our loved ones. Hence many of us learned to "fit in" – to repress our intuitive senses and dumb down our feelings. In the process we became numb. This is why so many people today are unhappy but have no idea why. It's because they have lost touch with their own inner guidance system, that internal spark that wants to scream, "Yes, this is who I am!"

As we each begin to awaken, seek our own truth and walk our own unique path, we begin to realize that there is much more to who we are than the outside world would lead us to believe. As we look within ourselves, we begin to realize that we are multidimensional spiritual beings who are able to align with a Higher Truth. As this transformation occurs, a new recognition is revealed: *It is our personal truth that creates happiness and adds simplicity to our path.*

Few have experienced this Higher Truth. But now this truth is an expanding presence sought by many. Because of you and many others, a new consciousness is unfolding! The third-dimensional world that was once defined by the old truths, old structures and old beliefs of those around us is no longer working. That third-dimensional game is being dissolved. You have an important role to play in this transition and you have a great deal to contribute. The Teachers of Light want to make this transition easier for you.

Online resources

Question: Is the unhappiness all over the world part of this massive shift? (04:47)

Question: What is an example of "baggage"? (04:19)

To access the online classroom,
visit www.masteringalchemy.com/book

Lesson 5

The Fall of Consciousness

A master of any discipline knows that to create with ease and inspiration there must first be a platform upon which to stand: a platform that is stable, solid, comfortable and supports the goal. For example, before cooking a fine chef will clear the kitchen, assemble her tools and focus her full attention upon her art. Her passion and purpose is to embody the highest level of mastery possible. A fine chef radiates certainty, power, presence and graciousness. She understands where the ingredients came from and their cultural history. She appreciates what they can become and how they, and she, can become transformed.

Our journey also requires establishing a solid platform upon which we can stand to transform ourselves, all humanity and Mother Earth.

I once asked Archangel Uriel what I thought was a simple question, "What are the Rays?" I expected a simple answer and a tidy spreadsheet. What I got was not a simple answer, but instead the story of the Fall of Consciousness.

What is the Fall of Consciousness? How did it occur? When was it? Who was involved? How has it continued to unfold to this day? Archangels Uriel, Zadkiel, Michael and Metatron told me the following story.

Uriel began by explaining, "There was no war. There were no bad guys. There was no angel that betrayed Creator and ran off with all the knowledge. It did not happen that way."

A long, long time ago, Creator wished to know Itself more fully. So Creator reached into Itself and created many new aspects of Itself, including the Holy

Spirit, the I AM Presence and the Christed Light. Creator also reached into Itself and created an infinite number of beings known as creator gods.

Creator sent the creator gods out to explore and create new possibilities. To assist the creator gods, Creator developed and provided a blueprint and gave it to them to use. Thrilled, the creator gods created.

Using this blueprint they created magnificent creations with the Light of Creator. They created universes, new aspects of consciousness and realms of thought and wonderment, all new and all very exciting. This went on for a very long time (although time as we know it did not exist). At some point during the process something unexpected occurred. Somewhere in All That Is, a creator god did something new and unintentional. Instead of following the blueprint, which said put blocks one, two, three and four together in this sequence, this creator god stacked the blocks differently. They were stacked three, one, two and four instead. At first no one noticed this change and this new pattern began to weave into and appear in many other creations. Eventually this new way of creating was noticed. This discovery caused tremendous excitement among the creator gods. This was a brand new experience, something that had never been present before.

The creator gods went back to Creator and asked for the ability to create even bigger and grander things. Creator agreed and gave them a new blueprint, one that was greatly expanded, containing many, many more aspects of Creator's Light. This became known as the "Will of Creator", also known as the first Ray of Creation. This Ray contained the intention of Creator and everything was in total alignment with Creator's intention. This first Ray was vast. One of the components it contained excited the creator gods very much. It was called "free will". Up until that point free will was not available. The creator gods had always followed the original blueprint, the one Creator had given them. Now, with free will, the creator gods created with both the Light of Creator and their own light, separately and in combination. Equipped with these new tools, the creator gods went out and created in the most amazing ways. That was their job and they loved their job.

Creator also created the Archangels and the angelic realm. The Archangels, according to Uriel, had a very specific purpose: they were created to be, in simple terms, the spectators and audience of the great creations the creator gods were creating. Their job was to go to the great theatres, in a manner of speaking, and enjoy the performances. That was their job. They did their job well and they loved their job.

Creations continued and continued. The creator gods not only created more, they also had the capacity to create more creator gods. The creator gods created more creator gods, and those creator gods created more creator gods, and so the process continued.

The creator gods loved their creations. Some of the creators gods were so excited and thrilled with their creations that they began to use more of their own light to create rather than the pure Light of Creator. As these creator gods continued to create more creator gods, this experience of creating with their own light was passed on to their creations. At first this was not noticed.

As this unfolded, small ripples and wobbles began to appear in the creations. This was observed by many of the original creator gods and Creator Itself. The newer creator gods didn't have the same level of wisdom, knowledge and experience as the creator gods before them. Many of these younger creator gods were enamoured with and loved their creations. Employing their free will, they began to use more of their individual light. Their creations contained less and less of the Creator's Light, less of the intention of Creator and much more of their own individual intention. These newer creator gods were very excited and they were having so much fun with their new abilities that they didn't really concern themselves with this.

This growing number of creations made without the full, original Light continued to be noticed by Creator and the older creator gods. These newer creator gods had free will so it was not the place of the Creator to take away or stop their creations. To bring about a correction and assist these creator gods to return to the use of the blueprint, two new Rays of Creation were given to all of the creator gods. Because there was free will, it was only suggested that they be used, not required. These new Rays provided opportunities to expand All That Is.

The second Ray of Creation was drawn from the first Ray. The second Ray holds all colour. (Colour, until then, had never been experienced.) It also holds the capacity to step energy up and step energy down, much like an electricity transformer. The second Ray brought about many more possibilities of creating in larger and smaller ways, and in more refined ways.

The third Ray of Creation holds frequencies and sub-frequencies in many different configurations and arrangements – known as energetics. Within the third Ray these energetics consist of electricity, magnetism, adhesion and the power held within the atom. These are enormous building blocks of constructive energy that hold all possibilities.

The first, second and third Rays are used during all steps of the creative process. These three Rays were given to the creator gods to expand and add to All That Is. It was also hoped that these new tools would encourage the creator gods to see more clearly the ripples they were creating and return to use the Light of Creator more fully.

Unfortunately mutations and distortions continued to appear in creations. A point was soon reached when many of the newer creator gods were using very little of Creator's blueprint. Uriel explained that at this point a line was drawn and Creator said something very simple, "If you wish to create with Creator's Light, all is available to you on this side of the line. If you are going to create with your own light then you no longer have access to the Light of Creator."

Many of the creator gods understood the importance of what was being offered and they returned to create within Creator's Light and the Rays of Creation, but many did not. There was no conscious intention to create distortions and ripples, but some of the creator gods were so enamoured with their own creations that they chose to continue to create with their own light.

By this time the distortions and mutations had the capacity to replicate and regenerate on their own. The distortions self-organized and did not follow patterns of Light held within the Rays. They had a mind of their own, in a manner of speaking, mutating into expanded distortions with even less Light. These distortions began to have a great impact not only on creations but also all creator gods.

The more the creator gods created outside of Creator's Light, the more distortions and mutations were in their creations. More wobbles and ripples appeared. This continued to be of concern to Creator and all those using Creator's Light. Creator saw the potential of this pattern spiralling wildly out into darkness. Therefore, more Rays of Creation were offered, with the continuing purpose to neutralize the mutations and distortions and contain the disruption, as well as add to the expansion of possibilities within each creation itself. Every new Ray that was created and given worked really quite well . . . until it didn't. The mutations and distortions continued to create and spin off more distortions and more mutations. (Distortions and mutations have no consciousness. They are like a virus or a machine that continues to duplicate and replicate.)

Simultaneously within the aspect of the Creator known as the Holy Spirit, there was a new thought being thought. The thought was a new form of creation never before experienced. Physicalness! Up until then in All That Is, all creations were nonphysical. Nothing had density. As this new thought began to take form, this density became available. This density was much less dense than the gases with which we are familiar today. This thought took aeons to evolve.

As the second Ray of Creation was being used, it was discovered that Light could be stepped down and compressed into density. This opened up a completely new realm of creation. The Great Beings of Light, the avatars and Elohim could now experience themselves in form. This density continued to be stepped down and compressed into all manner of form, and eventually into density such as rocks, oceans, trees and much more.

As creation continued to expand and evolve, another remarkable creation came about. Twelve living centres of consciousness were drawn from the

Christed aspect of Creator and placed throughout All That Is within the density of physicalness. Each of these centres held the Love and Light of Creator. The purpose of each of these centres was to reflect this Love and Light back to the beings who inhabited or visited those centres. Consequently many in the Archangelic realm, the avatars, the Elohim and all the Great Beings of Light, enjoyed these centres of Christed Light as a reflection of themselves in Oneness with Creator.

Earth is one of these very special centres of Light. To assist in this reflection of Love and Light, a simple life form was created and placed upon Earth. The purpose of this life form was to absorb the unique aspects of Love and Light held by the beings who inhabited or visited Earth and reflect them back to them as beauty in form. These reflections became the air and the waters, the flowers, trees and mountains. These simple life forms are known as the Elementals.

Many of the creator gods, as well as others who were aligned with All That Is, came to this Christed centre called Earth. And as the Fall of Consciousness progressed many of these great beings became unknowingly contaminated by the mutations. The physical creations that were being made on Earth began to hold more distortions and less of Creator's Love. As a result of this long and intense infiltration of mutations and distortions, Earth could no longer continue to reflect the Christed Consciousness and Love back to those upon her surface. Her inhabitants no longer received her Light and Earth fell, losing its Christed Light and Love. Earth fell into greater and greater density and distortion. Earth fell. One centre of Light out of the 12 fell. This event created an enormous ripple throughout All That Is. Earth had been, until this fall, a jewel of creation and a significant passageway available to all. As this collapse of Light occurred, many of the Great Beings of Light, the avatars, Elohim, Angels, Archangels and many, many others were consumed and caught within the Fall, increasing the density of the Fall.

The Great Beings of Light petitioned Creator to create a floor or limit to the Fall; a point that if reached would stop the descent. If Earth were to fall past that limit it would not recover. With this request, a new creation within density was brought forth. Known as Metatron's Cube, it was an intricate geometric construction of consciousness, Light and sound that had the capacity to do many things. In this case it created a point where Earth could fall no further. The result was known as the third dimension.

The third dimension was rigid, structured and very dense. There was no flexibility. This dimension had very specific limitations and could sustain and support very little Light, yet there was consciousness held within Earth. Earth existed in this state of severe constriction, separation and limitation for a very long time.

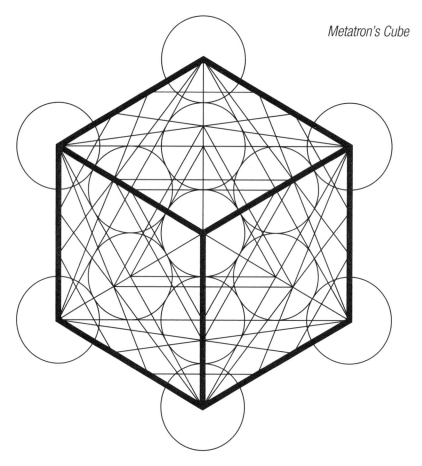

Metatron's Cube

THE FALL OF CONSCIOUSNESS

The Fall of Consciousness overwhelmed so many of the Great Beings of Light that the Archangelic realm petitioned Creator to expand their purpose. They asked that instead of simply watching the creator gods create, it become their primary function to stop the Fall of Consciousness. Their purpose was to reverse the damage caused by the mutations and distortions and free all who had been affected. The Creator granted this request.

Eventually, and over a very long period of time, the remaining consciousness of Earth was able to create enough of a stabilization that the rigidity of structure was removed from the planet. The possibility of Earth falling further into darkness no longer existed. Long after the rigidity was removed, the inhabitants began to create new considerations and new thoughts that were outside the previous limitations. Where before there was only rigidity and no flexibility, now there began to be other possibilities. This change unfolded very slowly. There began to be more awareness and flexibility. Opportunities and different levels of consciousness returned to the planet but the possibility of returning to be a centre of Christed Light was not available to Earth. The Fall had left the planet and its inhabitants in a detached state of unconsciousness.

More and more aspects of consciousness were infused into the planet and became anchored. After a long time the possibility of seeding a new species on the planet began to be considered. This is the point where most of us have an understanding of a "beginning". This new species was called Lemurian. The Lemurians did not have physical bodies but were instead less dense, airy forms. They were simple beings that held Light, and Light consciousness began to live more fully on the dense Earth. The Lemurians were not you. They held a Light consciousness and were the first step of the Great Experiment of returning Earth to its Christed state and returning all to full consciousness.

All through this unfolding the Rays of Creation continued to be offered. With each new Ray, great creative possibilities unfolded but they were not successful in permanently stopping the distortions and mutations that continued to expand and grow. This continued for many tens of thousands of years. Then in the year 2003 something very, very exciting occurred. A new

Ray of Creation was co-created by Creator with many Great Beings of Light, led by Archangel Michael. This Ray contained an element that had never before been used in the creative process. Within All That Is, this element was found here on Earth. The element in this new Ray is the love that humanity holds for humanity. That simple, pure, unique vibration of love was put into this new Ray and activated. It began to permeate many, many aspects of what had been contaminated by the Fall of Consciousness. The new Ray worked. And it continued to work. The growth of the mutations and wobbles and distortions slowed down.

In the third dimension these mutations and distortions are vibrations that you know as anger, jealousy, resentment, rudeness, deceit, domination, control, incest, rape and "isms" such as sexism and racism. All of these ugly feelings and ugly thoughts are the mutations and distortions that play out within our lives today. These feelings and thoughts are all wrapped in, and based on, fear and separation.

To this day the Fall of Consciousness has begun to reverse its influence. For the first time ever the distortions and mutations – the darkness and fear that have permeated many aspects of Creator's creation – are reversing. They are weakening and slowing down and the Christed Light of Creator has more and more room to expand, grow and reach out. This is all because of you. You are the Great Experiment. The Christed Light was placed as a tiny spark of Light deep within your Sacred Heart to be found, grown and brought forth.

The Fall and the process of reversing it has gone on for a very, very long time. There are many places in All That Is that have no Light in them at all. I once said to Uriel, "Won't it be a challenge for this darkness to be brought back into the Light?" I could feel Uriel's smile.

Uriel said, "Those dark patterns and beings who are without Light are not the challenging ones. They will be easy to work with when the appointed time comes. The ones that are most challenging are you. You see, you have free will and you have choice. You hold the single spark of Creator's Light within you. And because you have free will, we will not interfere with your choices. You must choose for yourself. The dark beings were created without free will or choice."

The Rays of Creation, their process and their creative power, are now very much moving throughout All That Is. This incredible process came about because of you, whether you know it or not. It was because of you. The mere fact that you are on this planet at this moment is a testament to how big and significant you truly are.

How is it that you participated?

Simple. You raised your hand and screamed out, "Me – choose me! Send me! I'll go."

If you have read the stories in the book of Revelation in the Bible, you will know that they describe multiple paths that could have been chosen in the process of getting humanity to a decision point where we either choose to follow the mutations or we choose the Light of Creator. Many, many times throughout humanity's history, we fell back into the darkness and we didn't have the strength or will to step away from the distortions and wobbles. It was easier simply to give up and fall.

The year 1987 was different. Again the momentum brought us to a critical moment of decision. Did we (humanity) agree to let the momentum continue and simply fall back into darkness and wait until aeons pass so we could try again? This was the question put forth to you as a Soul, whether you were in a physical body at that time or not. In 1987 we all took a type of vote, and all the Souls and all the beings on the planet together decided to see if we could change what was in motion. Our purpose in making this change was to bring the Christed Light back to the planet. It was a wild consideration. This was a Light that had not been experienced for hundreds of millions of years. Fifty-one per cent of us said, "Let's go for it." We didn't know if it would even be possible. We had no role models and we didn't know the steps required. But we passionately committed to go forward.

Since that time many grand beings have been born onto this planet. The children who were born after that auspicious moment in 1987 are "big" beings who carry with them a vibratory field of Light that is stimulating to those who came before them. These grand beings come from many Christed places. Many of them have never been on this planet before. They have arrived with a strong intention.

In 1987 we began to hold a level of possibility that had never before been held. Because of that possibility, and because of our passion and love for humanity, a transformation is occurring. How do you love one another? As you look around, it may not be very apparent as we all play out our life games, but in fact it is very apparent. Because of what occurred in 1987, many potential predicted catastrophes were averted.

In 2000 an entirely new energetic and the new element of Love were brought onto Earth, and in 2003 Michael brought a new Ray that began to end the distortions. This was all because of you. This new Ray is now operating in All That Is. All universes and all sectors of this universe are now fully engaged in the Shift of Consciousness.

In 2007 an event occurred that made it possible for the presence of the Christed Light to begin to return to the planet. That possibility began to grow and unfold and reveal itself. On the 11th November 2011 there was a grand collective focus of energy all over Earth. There were many people who were able to hold that Christed vibrational pattern and others who were able to call it forth to re-anchor the return of the Christ into Earth. And it was anchored. A new high vibration of Love has begun to radiate into the waters of Earth. Every drop of water within all life on this planet today is now growing, radiating and reflecting this Christed Light. The third dimension is now falling away. Earth has begun to return to its fully Christed status. It now reflects its vibration of unity back into humanity and all Earth's inhabitants.

As of the 11th November 2011, you are not the same person that you were. On that date (11–11–11) there was a change. That change is very strongly anchored within the hearts of everyone on Earth and it is growing, slowly in some and very rapidly in others. Metatron, Uriel and Michael believe that Earth is now beginning to vibrate in harmonic resonance with the other 11 centres of Christed Light in All That Is. All who have been affected by the loss of Light and the Fall of Consciousness are now returning Home to the heart of Creator.

A major milestone in this unfolding occurred in 2012. On the 12th December 2012 (12–12–12), many people all over the world believed a great opportunity was going to unfold. The Shift of Consciousness was to begin. On that day a new formation of creation was brought into form. The vibrational configuration of Metatron's Cube, which had held Earth in the restricted configuration of the third dimension, was reconfigured into a fifth-dimensional geometric alignment. The third dimension was eliminated.

What? Wait!

Nothing has changed you may be thinking right now. My house, my chair, my job, my kids are right here. Yes, you are correct. However, your house and chair are not the third dimension. They are form. Form exists in the physical dimension. The third dimension was built as rigid duality and reaction. It adopted fear as a foundational belief. The fifth dimension, however, is built around the belief and structure of wellbeing. It does not hold fear, judgement, doubt or reaction. I will further explain this in future chapters but here is the challenge: humanity as a whole only knows what it knows. It only knows the third dimension. Humanity does not pay attention to the other choices it has because it continues to live with the noise, drama and reactionary beliefs of the third dimension. We seldom re-examine our beliefs. They continue to drive our actions as if they were truths. We continue to do what we have always done. Although the third dimension was eliminated in 2012, most of us live as if it still exists and we don't look for what else is possible.

At 12 minutes after 12 noon on the 12th December 2012, Metatron spoke very clearly. "The door to the third dimension is closed. No child born after this moment will live in the third dimension. They join humanity with an intention and agreement to live in the higher dimensions with the ability to walk through the third dimension unaffected. These new children come to assist with the ascension of Mother Earth without the previous third-dimensional templates of fear and separation."

These new children will experience themselves differently than those born before them. This new awareness will come forth for all to experience but those born before 12–12–12 will be slower to grasp what is now available to them. They will, however, be very aware of the shifting sands under their feet and they will all have a choice to make. Many will choose the fears they have always chosen. Fears based on limitation and separation. Others will see opportunity and possibility. This Shift will be in transition for some time as each of us gains the new perspective. Although the new children will appear different to many of us, they will, with you, bring about Heaven on Earth once again.

This is Uriel's and Zadkiel's story, Metatron's and Michael's story. It describes a shift or change that they and other Great Beings of Light held as an intention and believed was possible. In addition to being only a small piece of an amazing story, this is also a personal process. If you would pause right here and feel the story, what you will feel is a crystallized aspect of Light that sits in your Sacred Heart. It's in the form of geometry known as the star tetrahedron. This small but brilliant Light has always been there, but until the 11th November 2011 it hadn't held the capacity that it currently holds. The presence of this spark, which grows ever brighter within you, is what enlivens this great Shift in Consciousness. What you feel is the unification of All That Is, now magnified within the Christed Light.

If you pause, exhale and feel the energies in this story, you will begin to have an idea of what the Unified Field of Consciousness holds for all of us. You will touch and begin to integrate the ability to experience yourself within that Unified Field. Here there are no mutations, no distortions, no fear or distrust.

Here you are Home.

Archangel Zadkiel comments on the importance of Earth

Your planet Earth is very valued in the scheme of things, as it is of the Christed realm. It is now returning to that state. At the time of the Fall, there were certain frequency patterns and knowledge that were lost or intentionally removed. This was because of the state of consciousness and the dimensional reality in which the planet and its inhabitants resided. Many things will be given in the coming transmissions that are designed to reinstall the knowledge and energetics that were once available before the Fall of Consciousness.

Your planet was created to be one of 12 that were intricately one with the Office of the Christ. This made your planet very valuable to those who wished to experience form on a planet of Christed consciousness. Of all the created universes these 12 planets were interspersed throughout creation for a purpose. That purpose was to allow Christ Consciousness to be fully present in form.

The sector in which Earth resides has been in a fallen state for aeons. Even though it was in a fallen state, planet Earth was able to maintain a certain degree of consciousness of its Christed origin. As it was able to raise itself up, many avatars and many Christed beings came to assist in reconfiguring those energetics. This set the paradigm for others who were in a fallen state to recoup a higher level of consciousness. Earth has always been regarded as a way-shower in that regard.

Because of its value, there were many Rays that were installed at various times on planet Earth to assist in this process. The 12 Rays of Creation, which we are giving you knowledge of, were a very intricate part of bringing the Christ Consciousness, in its fullness, back into physical form on planet Earth. As this planet raises in that consciousness, it sets a paradigm for other planets and other beings to follow.

Some of these 12 Christed planets are in fallen universes and some are not. Some planets retained the original state and were not affected in any way by those who were not able to maintain the higher levels of consciousness. It is from those unfallen realms, as well as the Christed realm itself, that much assistance has been given, and continues to be given. This is so all planets might be reconfigured and brought into full consciousness of their original states. This was why the 12 Rays were given to the Earth plane. This is why Earth has been given many beings who came from the Christed realm to raise the consciousness to such a degree that certain thought forms could be accepted and used.

As we continue our exploration together, it will become very obvious to you why this pathway is given and how it assists in bringing back your Earth, and all form that resides on planet Earth, into the Christed state of consciousness.

Online resources

Question: Where does Atlantis fit into the story of the Fall? (08:57)

Video: What's that bag over your head? (10:30)

To access the online classroom,
visit www.masteringalchemy.com/book

Part 2

Creating the platform to receive

Lesson 6

What are the dimensions?

This course is designed to help you move easily from the noise and confusion of the third dimension into your Living Light Body of the fifth dimension. To understand and experience life in the fifth dimension, however, it's important first to understand what the third- and fourth-dimensional games are and how they affect your present experience. With some basic information about what dimensions are, everyone has the ability to evolve their consciousness and move gracefully and joyfully into these higher vibrational realms.

Dimensions are states of consciousness that are available to anyone who vibrates in resonance with the specific frequencies inherent within each dimension. You could think of each dimension as a box or game with a unique set of rules as to what is and is not possible to experience within that dimension. These dimensions each have their own characteristics and ways of thinking, feeling and interacting. They also each have unique structures, qualities and aspects that contain a variety of experiences.

Without a clear definition of what experiences are possible within each dimension, it becomes difficult to move around comfortably, let alone master your life. By knowing the differences between the third, fourth and fifth dimensions you can deliberately choose to live the life you wish to live, rather than simply reacting to the life that shows up on your doorstep each morning.

LESSON 6

The third-dimensional box

The objects that surround you are not the third dimension. The third dimension is a state of consciousness. The objects in the environment that surrounds you (trees, cars, people, chairs, etc.) are aspects of form. The Earth is made of form. However, form and the third dimension are not the same. Form is part of the game. Form has shape, mass, texture and weight, and it is the result of density. Form exists in the third, fourth and the fifth dimensions. Form is what allows you to move around in the game having experiences. Form is the staging, props and backdrop that allow you, as the lead actor, to experience the fullness of the play you call "My Life" in your physical form.

Our thoughts and our emotions are also aspects of form. Although they do not appear to have physical density, the thoughts you think and the emotions produced as a response to your thoughts are experienced as form. Heavy or ugly thoughts produce a dense response or emotion. Light, airy, beautiful thoughts produce a very different feeling or response. For example, if you accept someone's opinion that you've done something "wrong", or are blamed for something, you might find yourself walking around with a heavy, uncomfortable feeling of guilt or self-blame. That ugly, dense feeling of guilt is called a "thought form". How you choose to observe and hold that thought form influences your state of mind, your emotions and even your physical health. It determines how successfully – or unsuccessfully – you create your life.

Most of us have been playing this third-dimensional game over the course of many lifetimes. As a result we tend to think it's the only game available to us. Nothing could be further from the truth. The third dimension is a box of rigid, inflexible beliefs. It is very dense and operates within a specific set of rules and structures that solidly hold many thoughts and emotions in a fixed reactionary state. We have access to the third, fourth and fifth dimensions simultaneously; however, due to our habits and rigid beliefs, most of us never recognize that we have the opportunity to choose differently. We stay in the third dimension by unconscious default.

WHAT ARE THE DIMENSIONS?

The third-dimensional box is structured in duality, linear time and separation. It's our rational mind that keeps this engaged. Everything is conditional and choice does not exist in the third dimension. The third dimension is a reactionary state of either this or that. Much more becomes available when we recognize our fourth-dimensional state of choice in present-time, but until then the third dimension is our only choice. The reactionary nature of the third dimension also produces another condition of the third dimension: fear.

In our spiritual quest to fully explore All That Is, in this fallen state of consciousness, we went deeper and deeper into density, choosing to incarnate many times upon the Earth to experience who we truly are, and what living life is all about. We, as enthusiastic spirits, wanted to know and to experience everything possible – and we still do today. To maximize our third-dimensional experience, and to get an even bigger sense of our individuality within this third dimension, we chose to forget the higher aspects of ourselves. As a consequence of this limited perspective and perceived sense of separation, we lost our way and, like abandoned children, we began to experience the energy called fear. This state of fear created further rigidity and limitations, such as doubt, anxiety, uncertainty and self-judgement, making it more difficult for us to move freely and comfortably through life. As we continued to explore and play in this rigid third dimension, we began to take on many uncomfortable attributes, including disease, victimhood, guilt, loneliness, lack and resistance. As odd as this may sound, you chose to do and experience this. And, in spite of what you may think today when you look in the mirror, you have been very successful at playing this third-dimensional game.

Fear is the most powerful emotionally charged thought of all. It is cohesive, sticky, solid and very popular in the third dimension. Fear is by far the densest thought form and it can sneak into every aspect of living. Thoughts of fear are super-charged with emotion, and these emotion-packed thoughts are like powerful magnets. They transmit signals to the universe and the universe (remember the Law of Attraction) automatically responds. If fear is an aspect within your point of attention, and in your belief system, it will unquestionably hold you in a very uncomfortable third-dimensional reality. You will not be able to move into the higher realms of consciousness until you change those magnetic attention points. Becoming conscious of your fearful and destructive thoughts and feelings will disrupt the hold they have over you and disrupt the vortex of the third dimension. Unconscious beliefs and repetitive habits will begin to release so that new choices can become available to you. Fear becomes simply another choice and not an automatic fixed result.

Many people who cling to fear have created a default system or a structure that gives them a false sense of security. (For example, they may believe that they will be safe if they just go inside their home and close the door.) This reaction has closed down our ability to expand and grow, re-merge with our Soul and remember our Higher Selves. Too many humans have stopped living their passion as they argue for their limitations within a web of fear.

Duality or contrast

Understanding the rules and structures of the third dimension will allow your transition through the grand Shift of Consciousness to occur more comfortably. Duality, also know as contrast, is a predominant structure of the third dimension. Before the Fall of Consciousness, contrast was created to provide us with a variety of experiences to choose from, such as hot and cold, large and small, bright and dull, fast and slow. If everything were blue, for example, there would be no contrast. Once yellow is introduced along with the blue, we have contrast and the opportunity to choose what is best for us.

With the Fall of Consciousness came judgement, resistance, limitation, lack and separation. These all empower the state of fear. Through fear we learned to differentiate between "us" and "them", and we learned to resist and reject "them". The dual concepts of good and bad, right and wrong and should and should not created a rigid, unforgiving structure that does not allow for flexibility or choice. This third-dimensional belief system restricted our thoughts and emotions, creating structures that are conditional with extremely limiting beliefs in "never" and "always". These are rigid thought forms that offer us very little opportunity for flexibility, change, ease or wellbeing. Pain has become anchored in this rigid belief system of heavy thought forms. There is no concept of good and bad or right and wrong in the fifth and higher dimensions. There is no judgement, separation or competition. There is nothing to fear, resist or argue about. There are simply many choices that give us more ways to experience and know ourselves through contrasting possibilities.

Linear time and reactionary present-time

Another powerful limiting aspect of the third dimension is one of the most pervasive and unquestioned beliefs that affects and structures our lives. This is linear time. Linear time is the belief that time, and therefore our lives, flows in a certain, absolute pattern of past, present, future. This belief is the default assumption of mass consciousness. Most of us think and act as if it's true because events appear to validate this group agreement. However, this belief is incorrect.

Third-dimensional time was not created as a straight line of events with a beginning, middle and end. It's actually a continuous loop consisting of past and future, with a single identified point known as the present moment (or present-time). It's here where we can take the opportunity to make new choices based upon past experiences and future desires. Far more often, however, we make decisions by reacting to situations with the emotions of fear, doubt or lack of self-worth. Our decisions about the future are based upon the painful past or an uncertain, worrisome future. Our third-dimensional lives become a series of reactionary experiences of resisting what we feared, rather than allowing what we desired. We begin dragging the past with us into the future. Many of us waste a great deal of our energy ensnared in an endless cycle where our past haunts our future, and our future echoes our past. This loop becomes a flow of thoughts and experiences that we label positive or negative, good or bad, right or wrong. We then connect strong emotions to those experiences. Either we embrace them and hope they happen again (but are afraid they won't) or we resist them and hope they never happen again (and worry they will).

In the third dimension there is a small sliver of the present-time, known as reactionary present-time. In reactionary present-time (remember the Law of Attraction again) we step into the future that we've created by focusing upon and resisting what we fear. We then find ourselves reacting to what we strongly, emotionally and loudly swore we never again wanted to experience. In short, we take our past experiences and project them into our future. We then step into that experience in a future present-time moment to feel that pain all over again. We create our future experience and what we draw into it by our emotionally charged reactions to our past and present-time situations.

Let me give you two examples. First, let's say that as I was growing up, wise and loving grown-ups told me that I would be successful and have a happy life if I were to become a lawyer or doctor. As a child, however, this scenario did not feel correct in my gut (my internal guidance system). And as a child, I did not have the words, much less the permission, to disagree with the grown-ups. I had no logical reasons to help explain why this picture didn't feel good inside. So I agreed or simply went along with the plan. I took that past information from the grown-ups and placed it out in front of me. I followed that belief into the future and lived by it, unquestioningly. I went to college, got a degree and a debt, got a house and a spouse. I created the life the now long-gone grown-ups told me I should in order to be happy. But I'm not.

Second, and this is perhaps a more important example, let's say that I once had a relationship that was the best of the best . . . until it was not. My lover left me, telling me I was a terrible person, I would never succeed, I was not nice and I did not have anything to offer to create a successful relationship with them. I was hurt, felt rejected and I went into a deep state of grief. Although

I tried to get over the experience, I could not let it go, nor could I understand how I could be such a terrible person. Eventually I made the decision that I was okay, at least on the surface, and I never ever wanted to meet someone like that again, because I did not want to be hurt ever again. So I screamed to the universe, "God, never let this kind of experience happen to me again. If a person of that type ever comes anywhere near me, please warn me and put up big red flags so I don't get hurt again."

Can you see how I took an uncomfortable experience from my past and placed it squarely into my future like a bright neon sign, and then I added super-charged emotional pain, fear and avoidance in order to protect myself? And because the universe and the Law of Attraction adore me, and it is the universe's passion to satisfy my every request, guess what I found on my doorstep the next morning . . . and the next, and the next, and the next? With each step into the next present-time moment, I experience precisely what I ask for through my vibration, even though it is the opposite of what I want.

The Law of Attraction does not choose for you. It does not distinguish between good or bad thoughts, it simply gives you what you hold your attention upon. "Because you are the creator of your life and have free will to create your life in any manner you choose," the Law of Attraction says, "I will provide you with exactly what you ask for," and smiles kindly.

Fortunately, built into the structure of third-dimensional linear time is a wonderful mechanism that can keep us out of trouble in this adventure. We have a buffer, a time lag that gives us the chance to reconsider the consequences of our reactive thoughts and emotions before we act and create something we might have to clean up or apologize for later. What we think does not manifest instantly. This buffer is created by the fact that in our distracted and noisy third-dimensional life we don't keep our attention on our intention long enough for a thought to manifest into form. Our attention is unfocused and bounces from here to there so quickly that our desires don't get the amount of attention necessary to manifest. This built-in buffer gives us a moment of consideration in which to calm down, reconsider and avoid a potential mess.

As the Shift of Consciousness is accelerating, however, this buffer period is getting shorter and shorter. Hence our thoughts and attention points are manifesting faster than ever.

The rational mind

Another powerful aspect of the third dimension involves the rational mind. Most of us perceive our third-dimensional experience predominantly from the limitations and filters of the left hemisphere of the brain and the rational mind. The strong, well-developed rational mind serves us well in this noisy third-dimensional environment. Its job is to keep us safe and help us fit in but fear and misuse cause the rational mind to operate more from a position of limitation than possibility. We expect the rational mind to perform tasks and participate in activities for which it was not designed. We've come to depend upon it far more than necessary and therefore have forgotten how to think from the heart. Thinking from the heart requires the whole brain and numerous spiritual abilities, including imagination and creative insight. Our awareness and range of choices have been greatly diminished and our innate spiritual abilities and potentialities are at best weak, and at worst completely hidden from us.

While the rational mind is a wonderful tool for measuring, analysing, comparing and storing information, it only knows what it knows, and it doesn't know what it doesn't know. It therefore works tirelessly to keep us within a thin band of logical thinking and possibilities. For thousands of years the rational mind has kept humanity tightly focused in the limited, fearfully structured, solid three-dimensional realm. And we, for the most part, have gone along for the ride.

This is now changing.

WHAT ARE THE DIMENSIONS?

Moving beyond the third dimension

It's critical for our wellbeing and our path to the Living Light Body to understand and recognize the aspects of the third-dimensional box that we have been living in. Duality, reactionary present-time and the rational mind are all intricately woven into the fabric of the third-dimensional matrix. By becoming aware of these underlying templates upon which the third dimension operates, you begin to have the choice to step out of it. You can reconstruct and remember a significant part of yourself, thereby becoming free to move beyond the limits of the third dimension and experience the possibilities of the fourth dimension, the fifth and beyond. Multidimensionality can be available to you.

Everything in the third dimension is conditional. For example, unconditional love does not exist in the third dimension. If you experience unconditional love, you have actually moved into a fourth-dimensional consciousness. You have access to both third- and fourth-dimensional consciousness all the time, but most people rarely step out of the well-trodden habits of third-dimensional thinking and feeling.

The third dimension offers limited possibility of choice. We don't intentionally choose our thoughts, feelings or actions in every moment. That is a skill of the fourth dimension. Instead we unconsciously react to the people and the situations that pop up throughout our day.

The fourth-dimensional box

As we start to become more aware and conscious, we also begin to experience options and choices that are not available to us in the third-dimensional box. However, we invest so much of our attention in the motion and noise of the third dimension, reacting to our past and worrying about the future, that we place very little of our conscious attention in the present moment. This push and pull between our past and future makes it difficult to become quiet enough to hold our attention consciously on our present-time choices for the life that is actually before us.

In the third dimension the Law of Attraction responds to the noise, motion and reaction we hold within us, giving back to us more of the same. By understanding and living the aspects of the fourth dimension, we can interrupt all those unconscious, emotionally charged reactions, and instead consciously choose the outcome we desire, thereby allowing the Law of Attraction to give us new positive and uplifting desires.

Present-time

The present moment defines the fourth dimension. Learning to experience yourself in the present moment is the most important choice you can make in moving forward on your journey.

Have you ever had the experience of being completely focused on something and suddenly realizing an hour has passed? There is no "hour" in the fourth dimension. There is simply present-time. If you're doing something interesting, enjoying yourself and totally absorbed in it, you're standing upon the fourth-dimensional platform and experiencing present-time. If you're expending energy figuring out the past and worrying about the future, you have slipped back into the third dimension. The moment you bring worry, doubt or fear into your fourth-dimensional present-time space, you instantaneously return to the third.

If you find yourself arguing, "Yes, but . . ." or "But what about this, what about that?" then know that it's your rational mind coming up with a set of answers to keep you in the safe third-dimensional box. If you ask why, stay in blame or look for answers from your past experiences and then re-experience those old emotional patterns and pain, you have returned to the third dimension. Remember, the rational mind only knows what it knows; it does not know what it does not know. So when you receive new information that doesn't fit the rational mind's model, it will argue with that information, trying to adjust, bend, turn and twist it so it can make sense of it.

The fourth-dimensional platform gives you access to your Soul, to higher aspects of your self and to your spiritual abilities, which allow you to see and hear on a grand scale. The rational mind can't comprehend the higher aspects of who you are because they are far too bright and big. The rational mind invalidates, rejects and pushes against any information it doesn't understand, and that argument goes back and forth and around and around in your head. When you consciously choose or recognize these various aspects as platforms, then you can move onto the fourth dimensional platform and allow the expansion to flow without the argument.

The structures of the fourth dimension provide you with a greater sense of ease, possibility and capability than those of the third. For example, while third-dimensional present-time is a charged reactionary moment influenced by our past, fourth-dimensional present-time is a quiet now moment. In fourth-dimensional present-time you are aware of the past and future but are not held in the emotions or constructs of a past or future that has not occurred as yet. Your focus is only in this very moment, and you are aware of the past and future from what is happening right now.

We only exist in the now, but most of us hold very little of our attention in the present moment. We are consumed by past experiences and projected worries. Ironically, because we don't understand the structures of the dimensions, this fear runs through our mental and emotional bodies, affecting our physical health and keeping us bound to the third dimension. Our physical bodies only know present-time; bodies can't know "yesterday" or "tomorrow". As conscious beings aligned within the fourth dimension, we can function absolutely in this now of present-time awareness and attention.

In the fourth dimension past and future time also change significantly. The fourth dimension presents the opportunity to be able to observe the past without unconsciously attaching old emotions or pain or fear to the experience of the past. Emotions can only be experienced in present-time.

LESSON 6

In present-time the past is simply history without an emotional charge or painful memory. Yesterday's pain has no bearing on today or tomorrow. The information, knowledge and wisdom gained from the past assist us in making better decisions about our current and future wellbeing. Yesterday has no bearing on tomorrow, other than you can take the information learned in the past and choose to apply it to a present or future present-time moment. The eternal present is all there is. You can still plan for future events using information gathered from the past, but your decisions become conscious, deliberate choices made in this present moment. While the future is an opportunity waiting to be fashioned, it is in this now moment that choices are made.

Conscious choice

In the fourth dimension you take back your power to choose. When third-dimensional reaction is replaced by choice you have more flexibility, which creates a superior ability to combine possibilities to produce a variety of outcomes. You are an informed observer, able to observe events with a sense of detachment. Events are simply information to consider. From this still, uncluttered platform, you are able to choose your response wisely. In the fourth dimension you expand your ability to respond, thus creating greater choice and mastery of your response.

Conscious choice invites a wider range of possibilities, which allow for wellbeing, happiness and realignment with your truth. Fourth-dimensional conscious choice gives you the opportunity to make mistakes and then correct the situation without blame or guilt. If you can allow what's in front of you to simply be what it is, without resisting or arguing about it, you can then determine how you want to experience it or chose differently. You can create the outcome you wish, or simply let it be and move on. Choice. You make better decisions from the fourth-dimensional platform of focused clarity, certainty and an awareness of your own personal truth and presence.

As the third-dimensional duality of good and bad, right and wrong falls away, an ever-expanding sense of capability begins to reawaken within you. Choice creates opportunity. Opportunity allows for wellbeing. Wellbeing awakens happiness, openness and the inner smile within your heart. From your open heart, your purpose and the fulfilment of all your dreams are within your grasp.

Paradox

As you become conscious in this fourth-dimensional reality, many higher concepts of life become available. These concepts allow you to move around with greater ease and understanding. One of these higher concepts is paradox. Paradox means what was true a moment ago may not be true in this now moment, and what was false a moment ago may no longer be false in this moment. Paradox provides flexibility to those rigid third-dimensional absolutes, such as "always", "never" and "impossible", and provides room for choices to be much more fluid and mobile. Paradox offers us more the possibility to release judgements. It increases our ability to allow what's in front of us to exist, as it is, without resisting or changing it. Instead of applying rigid, pre-existing definitions to any experience or person, we can choose our preferred version in every moment.

Because of the fear, pain and distrust that we all have stored in our unconsciousness, we hold many rigid beliefs about the world and those who live within it. We anchor these beliefs in words such as "always" and "never" (for example, he will *always* be untrustworthy; she will *never* change; I will *never* forgive them). As the past pains of the third dimension are dragged into the future, our tendency is to react in the same way that we reacted the previous time, thereby repeating the experiences of the past once again. We also repeat the emotions and pain of those past experiences.

When we consciously recognize we have choices about the world around us, incorporating the concept of paradox allows the past to stay in the past, and frees the present and the future for new opportunities. Paradox allows us to recognize a person or situation as it occurred in the past and provides the opportunity for us to observe that person or situation as it exists in this present-time moment as well. We can remember the information of the past, but not engage with the emotion of it now. This releases us from viewing people or situations through our filter of judgement, rigid definitions and the limitations of our past reactions and charged emotions.

As paradox loosens up the rigidity of the past, the higher concept of allowing opens up broader opportunities for you to experience. Allowing is a powerful concept. It does not imply weakness, resignation or inability, but rather it enables you to view the situation before you objectively, and provides you with a present-time choice to create a desirable outcome. Allowing gives you the room to explore possibilities and be fluid with the mistakes of others. Allowing adds ease, neutrality and quiet observation to your tool box.

Alignment and balance

The reality that we know as the third dimension is a classroom where we've been involved in the expanding evolution of our spiritual growth. In order to be able to play in this classroom, we had to forget ourselves, including much of our wisdom and knowledge and many of our great skills. The third dimension is a place of imbalance. An aspect of your purpose and job is to rediscover and master balance.

You are seeking a balance between the totality of yourself in physical form and who you are in the higher levels of consciousness, fully aligned with your truth. However, since by definition the third dimension is imbalanced, balance can never be found in the third dimension. Alignment and balance can only be found by stepping out of the third dimension. The doorway to this alignment is the fourth dimension. In the fourth dimension we are constantly adjusting, tweaking, correcting and moving toward balance. We are moving toward realignment with who we truly are – a spark of Creator.

WHAT ARE THE DIMENSIONS?

When you begin to recognize and use the many tools, skills, concepts and opportunities that the fourth dimension provides, you begin to choose and create your life differently. The need to experience lack, weakness, fear and doubt falls rapidly away as the structures of the fourth dimension are understood and practised. You don't "heal" yourself; you don't clear away your baggage; you don't even look for acceptance or forgiveness from others. You simply become who you've always been but forgot. You begin to demonstrate this new presence, and as this presence is experienced, all that you are not begins to fall away. You will find that all your deepest, darkest secrets, all those things that you hoped others would never know about you are simply not remembered any more. They are gone from your awareness.

This new platform that you are building is a way of life, a living dynamic that you are remembering and that is beginning to flow easily within you. What we considered to be mere concepts in the third dimension now have a deeper meaning in the fourth. Happiness, certainty, seniority, presence, capability, graciousness and command are no longer intellectual concepts, rather, they become important internal sensations, understandings and feelings guided by your heart. This is your natural state of being. Most of us have been invalidated since childhood. We were not taught, encouraged or allowed to make decisions from our own naturally balanced platform of inner wisdom and passion. Instead we were taught to fear and mistrust the world around us. We were taught to fit in. Consequently we have not fully experienced who we came here to be.

As you step out of the third dimension and move into fourth-dimensional consciousness in present-time, with the power of choice and responsiveness and the flexibility of paradox, the ability to change the game and enhance your happiness and wellbeing becomes available. Beauty, the inner smile, appreciation and freedom are all options here. Fear is also a choice, but it's a choice that will place you back in third-dimensional reaction and limitation.

The fourth dimension is the short-lived stepping stone to the higher dimensions. We must pass through it to reach them. Living in those higher dimensions is a life of community, cooperation and co-creation. The fourth dimension serves as an essential – but temporary – platform from which we all will step into fifth-dimensional consciousness.

What is the fifth dimension?

The Teachers of Light tell us that the fifth dimension is the target for Earth and all her inhabitants. It's impossible to predict when and how this move will be fully experienced because much depends upon the conscious evolution of humanity. That evolution is now occurring faster and faster thanks to you. Although the fifth dimension is the target, our experience of the fourth dimension is essential. We cannot enter the fifth dimension directly from the third. All mental and emotional baggage from the third dimension must be left at the door to the fifth. We can only enter and remain in the fifth dimension after we have become more masterful of our thoughts and feelings in the fourth dimension. There's much to discover about the fifth dimension, but for now the most important thing to know is that we must become masterful within the fourth dimension before we can move into and live in fifth-dimensional consciousness. Becoming masterful within the fourth dimension, and in our daily lives, is the purpose and the focus of what the Elders offer us. Some practice is required.

The fifth dimension operates in a completely different fashion compared to the third and fourth dimensions. Time in the fifth dimension is simultaneous. Simultaneous time means everything (all possibilities) occurs in the same place at the same moment. In the fifth dimension you focus your attention, and the answer is given where the question is asked. Ask and you shall receive. You don't move or go anywhere for your answers or experiences. Everything comes to you easily and effortlessly based upon the attention point and vibration you choose to hold in every moment.

When you are vibrating in fifth-dimensional consciousness, you don't create with form as you do in the third and fourth dimensions. You create with light patterns, geometries, sound templates and colour codes. You consciously interact and co-create with Creator and all the Teachers of Light. It's in the fifth dimension that you receive the transmissions, energetics and initiations that will assist you in creating your Living Light Body.

Online resources

Video: What are dimensions? (21:04)

Video: What is time? (13:24)

To access the online classroom,
visit www.masteringalchemy.com/book

Lesson 7

Foundational tools to know yourself

To receive the initiations and energetics the Teachers of Light offer in this course, first we must prepare ourselves. The energetics they offer are finely tuned and available for integration and absorption only if we are in a state of quiet neutral presence. We cannot receive the gifts if we are distracted by third-dimensional noise. Imagine walking into a room to meet Archangel Michael while wearing headphones and listening to rock music. Doing so would impair your ability to experience the energy Michael creates and receive the wisdom he may offer you. It's important to honour yourself and what's possible on this journey by preparing yourself to stand upon a platform in reverence and respect for yourself.

In this lesson I will introduce you to three energy tools: the Grounding Cord, the Rose and the Centre of Your Head. Used together, these tools establish the foundational platform upon which all else is built. Practice is required to remain on this platform. I suggest you practise when it doesn't count, so when you do find yourself in an uncomfortable situation, you can quickly return to this platform of balance and act intentionally rather than reacting.

Tool #1: Grounding Cord

Often when I talk about grounding, people say, "Oh, I know all about grounding, I've been grounding for years." But when I ask them if they are aware that there are *two* elements to a Grounding Cord, they invariably look surprised. So, in case you're thinking of skipping this section, stay with it. You will discover how to rebuild your Grounding Cord both electrically and magnetically, and once you've done this you may have a different experience.

Grounding is a natural part of the electrical and magnetic systems of the body. We're born with this connection to the Earth, along with all the other

The Grounding Cord

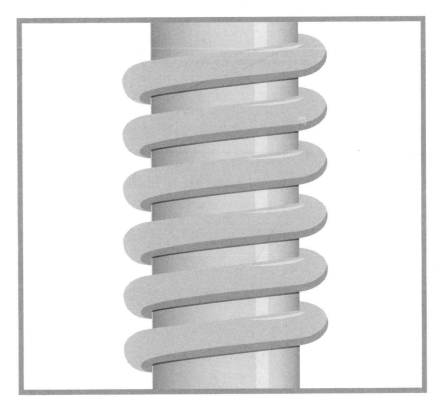

tools mentioned in this book. However, in our third-dimensional fear and concern, and in our moving between the past and future, we have forgotten how to use these tools.

Grounding allows distracting and destructive thoughts and emotions to be siphoned off down into the Earth, thereby minimizing the noise and disruption in your life. There are two components to grounding. The first component of your Grounding Cord consists of an electrical line that grounds nonaligned electrical thoughts – the thoughts that run through your head all day long, which really have nothing to do with you. The second component consists of a coil of energy that wraps around the electrical line of your Grounding Cord. This is the magnetic portion and its purpose is to clear away all the emotions and uncomfortable feelings that often accompany those thoughts. Remember, thoughts are electrical and emotions are magnetic.

EXERCISE: *How to establish your Grounding Cord*

1. Using your imagination, create an image of a straight electrical line that begins at the lower tip of your spine (first chakra) and connects to the centre of the Earth. This is the first component of your Grounding Cord. To release discordant thoughts, intentionally direct this electrical line to turn on.

2. Once the first component is firmly anchored and activated, you are ready to connect the second component. Imagine a coil of energy wrapping around the electrical line, from the tip of your spine to the centre of the Earth. Turn it on. Sit back and relax. Notice energy moving out and down the Grounding Cord.

It's important always to activate both components of your Grounding Cord deliberately. Your thoughts and your emotions are interwoven in deep ways, and as you release one, the other begins to unravel. Keeping both parts of your Grounding Cord in place and activated allows the energy to be neutralized quickly. With your Grounding Cord firmly in place, all those troublesome, repetitive thoughts that don't belong to you, and all those charged emotions that get you unnecessarily stirred up, have a place to go. Now you can actively release them from your space.

As you practise and play with the Grounding Cord tool, you can also take the opportunity to clear any ugly emotions and thoughts that you have noticed in your recent experiences. Ask the question, "Where in my space do I hold X [jealousy, fear, judgement, lack, and so on]?" Notice what you notice and allow that energy to flow down your Grounding Cord and dissolve. You may also notice that as you use the Cord to intentionally release negative energy, more issues will bubble up to the surface of your awareness. These are the unconscious hidden patterns coming to the surface to be released. Allow these energies to move down your Grounding Cord.

Success story

I just had to let you know of my "miracle" with the Grounding Cord today. I have always had difficulty with technology and today was very difficult. I lost my space when my printer crashed during a deadline. My mind was both frantically worrying and troubleshooting. My emotions were raw with anger and frustration. I even yelled at the dog! When I had finally exhausted all solutions, I sat down to give up and remembered my tools. I grounded myself with both my mental and emotional cords, then grounded the printer and the electrical line between the printer and my computer. After only a few minutes, I got back to a nice, neutral place again. Calm.

Then I went back to my desk, gave it one more try and voila! The printer printed and the project was completed on time! I only wish I would have remembered my tools before getting so upset. Next time I will be quicker.

Doris, Netherlands

Online resources

Meditation to build and activate your Grounding Cord (08:22)

Question: Can I ground others? (01:00)

To access the online classroom,
visit www.masteringalchemy.com/book

Tool #2: The Rose

The Rose tool is the second of the three aspects that form the foundational platform upon which you may receive the gifts from the Teachers of Light.

The Rose is the workhorse of these three energy tools. Even the most practised among us will return to this tool again and again. The reason the Rose tool is so valued is because it can be used in many different circumstances.

- The Rose will help you establish, define and hold your space while you move through the noise of the third dimension.
- Like a broom or vacuum cleaner, the Rose will also remove from your mental, emotional and physical bodies the accumulated opinions, judgements and energy that you have received from other people .
- Separating your energy from other people's energy is necessary for clear decision-making and for recognizing your own truth. The Rose does this most effectively.
- The Rose will assist you in gathering your energy up from where you left it during the day and before you go to sleep.
- The Rose is an excellent and efficient tool for releasing any limiting beliefs and habits that your journey to the Living Light Body may bring to the surface of your life.

FOUNDATIONAL TOOLS TO KNOW YOURSELF

Establishing, defining and holding your space

Why is it important to define the edge of your space? Most people go through their days with no knowledge or experience of their personal space or that of others. The Shift in Consciousness is creating a growing amount of chaos, noise and drama in everyone's lives. This noise keeps many people in retreat and hiding, not fulfilling their dreams and goals. Learning how to use the Rose to define where you start and stop – what is yours and what is not yours – is critical in moving through the third dimension unaffected.

EXERCISE: *How to use the Rose*

1. Close your eyes and take a moment to find a quiet place within. Pretend you're sitting in a peaceful room within your head, behind your eyes. Later in this lesson, you'll practise being here, in Centre of Your Head.

2. Establish your Grounding Cord. Take a breath and take your time with this.

3. Find a memory of a red rose – perhaps it's one that you saw at a florist, or in a garden, or at a grocery store. Remember the rose just as you saw it. Allow yourself to see it.

4. Without leaving the quiet space behind your eyes, imagine yourself holding this rose straight out in front of you at arm's length. Let the stem of the rose extend down into the floor. If you find it hard to visualize, pretend. (Adding the stem will ground the Rose and firmly establish it around you.)

5. Now, keeping your imaginary arm fully extended, with the rose firmly held between your thumb and fingers, picture yourself moving the rose 360 degrees, tracing a full sphere around, under and above you. Take your time and become aware of yourself within this sphere.

6. Move the rose above and below you with your imaginary arm. Take your time and become aware of yourself within this sphere. Don't let your rational mind get involved with the colour of the rose or whether the stem has leaves. Have fun with this. (The space inside this sphere – on your side of the rose – is a space you can manage. Anything outside the sphere – beyond the rose – has very little to do with you.)

7. Draw your full attention inward to your side of your rose, and notice how this feels.

8. Stay on your side of the rose. This means holding all your energy and attention between you and the rose. None of your attention should be beyond the rose.

9. Take a breath, open your eyes and stay in the quiet space behind your eyes, grounded, and on your side of the rose.

From now on your rose and the sphere that you have created with it will serve as your point of delineation. It defines your space. Your job now is to stay on your side of the rose and within this sphere. All that lies within this sphere is you. This is where you experience yourself. All that lies outside your rose is theatre, the stage upon which others enact their plays for your amusement. Everything within your rose is your experience; everything beyond your rose belongs to others.

What do you do if someone moves toward you and into your space? This will happen. Most people are not aware of their own personal space, nor the personal space of others. As you are aware of your rose, you can move it half way between you and that person. As they move close to you, you move your rose inward, toward yourself. As they step back and away from you, adjust your rose, moving it back to the edge of the sphere. And if you forget and they enter your space? Remember your Rose, and use it. Soon using this tool will be a part of who you are.

When you begin to observe your life from this vantage point, life becomes much easier, calmer and smoother. As you now know, when you operate without definition, you become affected by the noise and drama of those around you. In other words, rather than living your own life, thinking your own thoughts and feeling your own feelings, your thoughts, feelings and reactions are often dictated by the effect that others have upon you.

How not to feel the pain of others

Besides allowing you to let everything that is on the other side of the Rose simply remain there, the Rose gives you a valuable moment to observe, choose and then calmly – and much more confidently – act. This is a fourth-dimensional choice vs. a third-dimensional reaction. The Rose creates a delineation or opportunity (not a separation), which allows you to know with certainty that the distance from your heart to the Rose is your energetic space to experience the wonders of you, and everything outside the Rose is there to entertain you. Once you understand this, you will find that your experience in relation to feeling the pain or emotions of others is quite different. The purpose of this tool is to allow all of that theatre to come right to the edge of the Rose, stop, be observed and then you can choose either to enjoy it or let it pass by. Many people run the emotions of others through their body in order to determine whether they are safe or not and to decide how to respond. The Rose is a very effective tool that allows you to observe situations, and the emotions within them, without being affected *by* them.

For example, as we move through the Shift, many long-established institutions are changing and crumbling. We're experiencing a global economic crisis and personal financial challenges. You may hear people talk about how they are losing their jobs and homes, or having difficulty paying their mortgages. While you may not have any difficulty paying your own mortgage, you can't help but feel the anxiety and discomfort of others as you listen to their sad experiences or watch the news. You may not need a loan for your new business or a new car, but as you watch, listen to and feel all the anxiety, worry and problems in the third-dimensional world around you, this energy runs through you and makes you also feel concerned and off balance.

The Rose will enable you to walk through this intensifying third-dimensional world without experiencing it. It will allow you to be in the presence of sadness and worry, but not a part of it. You will continue to be compassionate and caring about the painful experiences of others, without running the fear of their experiences through your body.

Other ways to play with the Rose

- Between you and a scary movie: Place a Rose midway between you and the screen. Let the stem go down into the floor. Watch the movie while you deliberately stay on your side of the Rose. You might see it as a translucent image you're peering through. If you find your emotions, body or mind have shifted to match the charge and drama of the movie, re-establish your Rose, take a breath and be behind it again. And be amused with yourself.

- Around your home, office or other space: Your home and office are places for your comfort and enjoyment, even if others share them with you. Creating a bubble around your home or office can affect how others respond within that space and it can also affect how you feel within it. Use the Rose tool to surround your chosen space with Roses. This will allow you to own the space for yourself. Try it and see what happens.

- Around your car before you begin driving: Before you begin to move your car, take a moment and place four Roses at even spaces around the car, front, back, right and left. Place each Rose about a metre from the vehicle. Let the stems go down into the ground in whatever way they like. As you drive, occasionally check in with each Rose and imagine it there again.

- Between your car and a car driving closely behind you: First place the Rose on your bumper, then slowly move it further behind you and watch the other car slowly move away from you.
- Practise using the Rose when it doesn't count to develop a strong relationship with it.
- Play with and imagine your Rose in a variety of colours, levels of openness, with and without a stem.
- Check in with the Rose at the edge of your energy field occasionally throughout the day and clean it off or freshen it up. Your casual attention to the Rose will refocus your awareness in present-time, as well as strengthen your boundaries and keep you in your own space.

How one person successfully used the Rose to hold his space

One weekend Mitch drove to San Francisco to visit a friend. Mitch lived in a small town north of "The City" and he didn't find himself among crowds of people very often. He enjoyed a walk in Golden Gate Park, lunch was delicious, but shopping in China Town became a challenge in space management. Mitch found himself getting irritated, tired and impatient. He quickly became over-stimulated and wanted out.

His desire to spend time with his friend, however, helped him to realize that he was the one feeling uncomfortable, not the crowds around him, nor his friend. Since he knew he was the master of his moods and feelings, Mitch decided to feel good, rather than lousy and irritable. He remembered his Rose tool. Seconds after he put his attention back to his Rose, Mitch calmed down and stopped resisting the jostling of the crowd. His mood shifted and he began having fun again. Soon people actually stopped bumping into him. It was as though a feel-good force field had been created and he was able to enjoy the remaining time with his friend, untouched by others.

LESSON 7

Exploding a Rose

The act of exploding a Rose allows all the charged energy that you're releasing to disperse into the air and disappear. If you explode a Rose to separate yourself from another person's energy, their energy that was stuck in your space will return to them because it belongs to them and they want it back. At the same time, the energy that belongs to you will return to your space from theirs. Now you both can function more freely and fully, without being affected by each other's desires, opinions and judgements.

To be successful, this collecting and clearing must be done from a place of neutral observation on your part. If you have opinions about the situation or what should occur (how bad the other person was, your role in the event, etc.), the energy won't move. It will stay stuck in your space, mind, emotions and body.

Success story

I have been using the Rose and Grounding Cord techniques since learning about them in your book. Yesterday they were very helpful when a woman started yelling at me in a parking lot. She was irate with me for having left my dog in the car on a warm day. I had run into a store for one item and was accosted by the woman when I returned to my car. She told me I was lucky that the humane society was closed because she had tried to report me. She ended the barrage of words with a loud "shame on you".

I immediately created and exploded the Rose and dropped my Grounding Cord down as I drove away. I recalled your words about people in this transition having difficulty with the loss of the third dimension. This was that woman. Thank you for your gifts of the tools!

Shelley A, Australia

Success story

My heating and hot water system suddenly stopped working. A heating engineer flushed the system and it was as good as new; 40 years of sludge build-up having been removed.

A month later it stopped working again for no apparent reason. The engineer returned and found an anomaly he had never ever seen before. No one could understand what had happened or why. We agreed the engineer would bring special equipment the next day to "fix" the problem.

I mused that as we clear out our inner "sludge" (thoughts, beliefs, habits) it seemed appropriate that my outer physical sludge required purging too; hence the heating and water system throughout my home being cleansed. It hit me that perhaps the system also needed an energetic mop-up to complete the cleanse. It came to me (trusting myself more) that the Rose would be a good choice.

I lined up an army of Roses (several bouquets) head to stem, like a freight train (in my imagination) and sent them through every pipe, drain, radiator, tap and shower. I sent them through anything and everything connected to the heating and water in my home. Very efficient they were too. Roses on a mission! I then exploded them all and felt great appreciation and gratitude for a job well done. I believed and let it go.

The next day the engineer arrived with all his special equipment. He switched the heating system on and prepared to attach some hoses . . . and never did! The system started up and began to work normally! He spent the next two hours checking everything thoroughly. The anomaly had disappeared. He could neither understand it nor explain it. The rational mind only knows what it knows. He left, shaking his head in confusion.

Now I sit cosy and warm appreciating the Teachers of Light and you, Jim, all that I have learned/remembered, the ups and downs of the journey. I feel very blessed to be here now. Smiling (in the heart).

SM, Arizona, USA

LESSON 7

EXERCISE: *How to explode a Rose*

1. After collecting up the energy you are intending to release, move the Rose to the outside of your aura, to the area beyond the Rose(s) you have established around yourself.
2. Imagine the Rose(s) exploding like fireworks. This explosion dissolves or disperses the charge. Watch the explosion occur and don't try to control it.

Notice how this exercise affects your mood and feelings. Be patient with releasing the energy that's stuck in your space. It has probably been there a long time and may take several rounds to fully release.

Online resources

Video: The Rose (30:42)

Video: Exploding Roses (41:05)

Meditation to make separations from others and decharge negative words (19:30)

Question: Why do I have physical responses to this work? (02:11)

Question: How do I use the Rose in a challenging telephone call? (01:55)

To access the online classroom,
visit www.masteringalchemy.com/book

Tool #3: Centre of Your Head and Higher Mind

Remembering who you are requires that you bring yourself into a present-time focus. This is not difficult, but some attention and practice is required.

There is a place within the centre of our heads that acts as a command centre; a place where clear decisions can be made and actions can be set in motion. However, as we grew up we learned to give up this place and trust the opinions and beliefs of others. Many times our mothers, fathers, teachers and ministers said they had a better idea of life (and how we should live it) than we did. We learned to give up our power to their thoughts and beliefs. We stepped away and relinquished command of our decision-making. But most importantly, for many of us, we stopped listening to our own internal guidance system. We gave up knowing our own truth and we lost ourselves.

Wishing only the best for us, our mothers, fathers, teachers and ministers showed us how to live and experience life – the right and wrong, good and bad, shoulds and should nots of life. They told us how we should behave, who we should be friends with, how we should move and what we should do in order to be successful.

Where did many of those thoughts and commands from your mother-father-teacher-minister go? To a great extent, they went directly into the centre of your head, displacing *you*, moving *you* to the side. "See only what I see. Do only what I do." you were told. You then began to view your world through the filters of their thoughts, their beliefs and their experiences, rather than your own. You grew up, and these habits continued. You still allow others to get into the centre of your head and establish their values, preferences and goals there. You continue to give up your seniority to the many others you associate with – your colleagues, spouse, children and friends.

You can change this habit. It is possible to begin to take back your power, own the Centre of *Your* Head and ask everyone else to leave. You are the owner. The others are just visiting – although they may not see it that way.

LESSON 7

EXERCISE: *How to locate the Centre of Your Head*

1. Place the index fingers of each hand on either side of your head, at the soft spot where your temples are. Close your eyes.
2. Draw an imaginary line from one finger to the other, creating a line that runs through your head from one side to the other.
3. Now, without losing track of that line, move your fingers 90 degrees around the circumference of your head until one finger is in the centre of your forehead, just above your nose, and the other finger is directly opposite, at the back of your head.
4. Draw another line between the two fingers, creating a line that runs through your head from front to back.
5. Find the point where the two lines intersect and bring your full awareness to that point. Be at the point of this intersection for a few moments. This is the Centre of Your Head.
6. Look through your closed eyes as if they were windows. Take a breath.
7. With your eyes closed, glance out at the room around you. Don't try to see anything, but be aware of yourself in the Centre of Your Head.
8. Look around the Centre of Your Head and create a special space there for yourself. Imagine a comfortable space you can easily spend your time (your life!) in. It could be a room or a place in nature. Own this space.
9. Take a breath and get a good sense of where the Centre of Your Head is and what it feels like. Open your eyes when you are ready.

Are you in the same place of awareness that you were just a moment ago? Does it feel different from where you were when you began the exercise? Most likely the answer is "yes", because being in the Centre of Your Head is not a place in which most people spend much time. Congratulations. This may not seem like a big deal, but trust me, it's a huge deal and will become more so. Do this exercise a few times to anchor this awareness for yourself.

What you may notice

It's not unusual to experience occasional noise or chatter in this space. Those are the energies and voices of the mother-father-teacher-minister protesting this change in you. It isn't you. Think of it this way, you're changing the game. Everyone who has been in the Centre of Your Head is now noticing, and they may not like the idea of being evicted. They grumble and protest,

---

Success story

Last week I played in the Centre of My Head for the first time and discovered a great deal in there that isn't me. Junk that belonged to others was cluttering up the room. I got discouraged that, at 35 years old, I was still carrying around my father's expectations of me. I realized that many of my decisions were made to please him. Not me.

Over the weekend I went there again and began using the Grounding Cord to actively drain everyone out. Sometimes I noticed a face, sometimes a word, sometimes just a colour. I made this my daily meditation.

Yesterday I had a meeting with my boss and watched myself verbally express in a way I never have. I realized that I had transferred pleasing my dad to pleasing my boss. When I cleaned my dad out of my head, that old pattern left too. I'm thrilled with the new me.

Tomas, California, USA

A good question: Am I using too much effort?

Question: I've been practising being in the Higher Mind and continue to have pressure/pain in my head when I'm there. I realize that I'm putting effort into doing this and can't seem to relax. Even when I think I'm relaxed, I continue to feel pressure. And a part of me thinks that if I don't feel pressure, then I'm not in the right place. Any suggestions would be most welcome, and it *has* improved since I started this work.

TL, Atlanta, Georgia, USA

Answer: Yes, I agree with you. It looks like you are working very hard instead of allowing the experience to come to you.

In many Western cultures we're trained to achieve, work hard and do things correctly. In this work there is no "right" or "wrong" way of using the tools – no pressure. The Teachers of Light remind us many times to take it slowly and be kind to ourselves. Whenever we're working hard at this work, we're in the future. We're not in present-time and present-time is the only place from which we can successfully create.

This habit of trying so hard is probably connected to old patterns of control: fear of being negatively surprised, distrust, a sense that you've "gotta do it right", the need to achieve, the desire to please others, fear of failure, etc. Do any of those words/energies make sense for you?

Here are some suggestions:

- Begin to notice which of the above words/energies resonate with you when you feel that congestion and pressure. Come up with some words of your

wanting to know why you're changing things. You, the owner, are moving back in, and the squatters have to leave. If this chatter and noise happens to you, use the Grounding Cord or Rose tool to drain them out or collect them up and move them out. It's time to give them back their energy.

own. Then begin to patiently collect them up in a Rose and explode the Rose. Do this one word and one Rose at a time. It may take several days of your morning meditations to do this. That's okay. Additional words or colours or images will pop up too (even people). Continue to put them all in a Rose, collect the energy up from your space, move it outside your energy field and explode the Rose. Alternatively, you can imagine draining that word/colour/image down your Grounding Cord. Easy. Be amused with what you discover.

- The next time you find yourself in the future, lick your finger and touch it to your forehead. (Don't laugh – okay, you can laugh). Then notice what happens. Your attention will naturally go to the coolness of the evaporation. This will help you focus on being in the Centre of Your Head or Higher Mind instead of out in front of yourself.
- Another reason why you might feel that congestion in your head is because it *is* congested. It's congested with the energy, resistance and attention of others. Others with an opinion about you and your choices. That energy can be difficult to push through. During your meditation time, use a Rose to clear out the Centre of Your Head. (You might imagine the Rose as a broom, duster or vacuum cleaner to do this). Let the Rose move throughout the sanctuary in your head and eject all the others who want to live there. Don't worry – you aren't doing anything harmful to them. In fact you're helping them. You're giving them back their energy so they can live a life full of their own energy.

Give those tools a whirl and let me know how it goes. You're doing GREAT.

How would you like to live your life from this space in the Centre of Your Head? Understanding who you are requires that you be in present-time. Observing the outside world from the Centre of Your Head offers you that present-time point of observation and awareness. This is an energy space that is not restricted; it can be animated and very excited, but it is a managed energy space. This is where you begin to know yourself – right here. You are moving your self from the dense third dimension to this higher state of consciousness. And everything begins from the Centre of your Head.

Your Higher Mind

In third-dimensional terms, your Higher Mind is located 2.5cm (1 inch) up from the Centre of Your Head and 4cm (1½ inches) back. It's a place of stillness and is much more expansive than the Centre of Your Head. It's in the Higher Mind that you begin to become aware of all that you are and all that you are a part of. It's necessary to clear out any energy that isn't yours from the Centre of Your Head before you are able to fully reside in your Higher Mind. As an analogy, you might see the Centre of Your Head as the stairway that leads to the still point of your Higher Mind. If the stairway is cluttered and filled with debris, it isn't possible to step into the sanctuary within your Higher Mind. The stairway must be cleared so you can navigate up it.

A reminder

One error that many on the path to the Living Light Body make is not to value, or put time and practice into building the foundation. I hear people say, "This is too simplistic," or " I've heard all this before," or "I've studied paths to the Light Body for 40 years. I don't need to start at the beginning here."

This path is deliberately designed by the Teachers of Light and gifted to humanity. It is a path unlike any other. And the foundational structure you create must be strong and solid so it may hold the house you are about to build upon it. Practise when it doesn't count so that when it does count, you will be prepared and able to receive.

Success story

Something happened today that I just had to share with you. I am a teacher at an elementary school. This afternoon we had a crisis situation – our first. Our kids were just dismissed and were getting on buses and into cars when the word came that there was a suicidal gunman in the area. We focused on the kids, cleared the campus and then went into lock-down mode ourselves. Cops were everywhere but still . . .

I realized about 15 minutes in that I was right where I wanted to be, in my Higher Mind, capable, senior and balanced. I was able to affect the energy with calmness as we sat in the dark with little information. I practised when it didn't count, and then it just happened, like magic!

I am smiling and happy. How fun is that? (The man was arrested with no incident and no one was hurt.)

CD, Boston, Massachusetts, USA

It is in the still point of the Higher Mind where all information can be found. The Higher Mind is vast. It is quiet, and there is a detachment from the world around you. There's focus, clarity and curiosity in the Higher Mind, but no questions are asked. It's through the Higher Mind that conscious contact with your Soul begins. It's from here that access to the heart becomes available in a manner that is totally unapproachable from the noisy third dimension. Third-dimensional words are inadequate to describe the state of awareness and ease that accompanies living from the Higher Mind. There are many important opportunities that arise by observing life from this vantage point, but none is more important than your reconnection to your Soul.

The following exercise will show you the best way to discover and get a sense of being in your Higher Mind.

LESSON 7

EXERCISE: *How to be in your Higher Mind*

1. Find a quiet space. Establish your Grounding Cord and find the Centre of Your Head. Close your eyes for better focus and less distraction. (As this tool becomes more natural to you, you will be able to find and hold this space with your eyes open.)
2. When you are ready, move your attention up approximately 2.5cm (1 inch) from the Centre of Your Head.
3. Then move your attention 4cm (1½ inches) toward the back of your head. You might pretend there is a loft above the Centre of Your Head that you're stepping onto.
4. Now return to the Centre of Your Head and notice the difference. Take a breath.
5. Repeat this movement two or three times to get a sense of the feeling and movement.
6. Then move to the Higher Mind again and remain there. Open your eyes and see how long you can remain in this place.

Notice when you drop out of your Higher Mind. Did you return to the Centre of Your Head when you opened your eyes? No problem; both locations have value. Although entering the Higher Mind is not difficult, remaining there and mastering all that it offers is an eternal unfolding. Once staying in your Higher Mind becomes more natural to you, you will be able to move about your day from this platform of observation. Doing so will give you a much more expanded view of what occurs around and within you.

Online resources

Video: Lecture and meditation to practise being in the Centre of Your Head (21:34)

Question: Is it better to be in the Higher Mind or Centre of Your Head? (01:58)

To access the online classroom,
visit www.masteringalchemy.com/book

Lesson 8

Overcoming obstacles to your success

One purpose of the tools the Teachers give you is to build platforms of stability that will allow you to both create and manage your energy. When you master the tools, what other people think and do will no longer influence you, and your capacity to make good decisions will begin to require little effort. Success during this transition, however, requires responsibility and maturity in managing your energy. Once this is accomplished, you will have access to the wisdom and knowledge required to become a citizen of the fifth dimension and beyond.

There are obstacles to success on this path to the Living Light Body. Many of us have been trained to embrace habits that don't serve us. These habits will be uncovered as you move through this course. Below are some of the more common habits that you might notice. If you find yourself engaging in one of these habits, allow it to come to the surface as an opportunity to become aware of it. Simply notice what you notice, and make a different choice.

Throughout this section of the book, you'll learn simple tools to assist in releasing the habits and patterns you discover. Each effort is cumulative. This is the process of mastery.

1. Asking unnecessary questions and getting tangled in the rational mind

The intuitive mind is a sacred gift and the rational mind is a faithful servant. We have created a society that honours the servant and has forgotten the gift.

Albert Einstein

Many of us are good thinkers. We have a tendency to ask questions that have no value, creating distraction and noise. Notice when you challenge what you read and hear with questions such as "Why does he say that?" or "How come I have to do it this way?"

The experiences you have as you move through this course will be very different from anything you may have experienced to date. Your rational mind will not understand much of what you're doing. Its job is to make you safe and help you fit in, and it's very effective in applying the elements of fear and doubt to keep you locked in the status quo. Questioning, analysing and getting tangled in judgements such as "I'm bad," "I did it wrong," "It doesn't work," and "I don't know what I'm doing" are all part of the noise of the rational mind. You *cannot* do this wrong!

See if you can move through this journey from a place of curiosity, allowing new possibilities rather than challenging what's being presented because it does not fit what your rational mind thinks should be said. There is nothing to memorize or hold on to here. The work is in the experience. If you can begin to practise what is called "quiet observation" you will soon discover that many things are happening in perfect order. However, it may not be your familiar notion of order.

The rational mind's thinking process has great value, but it doesn't drive the life you are now creating for yourself. Your job is to stay happy, play, enjoy yourself, look for opportunities to experience the inner smile as often as possible and pretend you know what you're doing – because you do!

2. Being in reaction

Many of us have had experiences that created an immediate unconscious reaction. We often make assumptions based on our expectation of how something should be, and when the outcome does not meet the expectation an unconscious emotion is created. Throughout this course you will be asked to observe what is in front of you from neutrality, without labelling, naming or even identifying what you are observing. As you begin to master this skill, you will find that much exists right in front of your eyes that has been obscured by the judgements, assumptions, expectations and labels you have embraced from watching how others react to similar situations. As observation replaces reaction you are going to find you become more quiet and calm, and many judgements and impulsive emotions, such as anger or resentment, will no longer come forward.

At the same time, many of the "I'm not okay" emotions that you have held within yourself are going to leave. When you hit these emotional places, it will be helpful to remind yourself that these patterns are either leaving or are coming up for you to consider releasing. Do not grab hold of them and argue with them. Simply allow them to surface and then shift your attention to something that brings you to a place of feeling good (petting the cat, viewing a beautiful scene, dancing, smelling a flower, for example). Let these emotions move up and out. Within a short time you won't remember what it was that concerned you just a moment ago. The tools presented in this book will assist you in releasing these stuck energy patterns.

3. Going unconscious when you close your eyes to meditate

Many of us have a tendency to go unconscious when we close our eyes to meditate. As you move through this course, you may find yourself continuing to "space out" or realize your attention was somewhere else during the work.

You may even think you've gone to sleep. There are a couple reasons why this occurs. As you begin to increase the speed of the energy field around you and bring in more Light, your dense physical body isn't easily able to hold the new levels of energy. It therefore responds by doing what appears to be going to sleep while it works very hard to adjust to the new energy.

Another reason why we go unconscious during a meditation is because old habits and patterns come up to be released and we may not be comfortable consciously looking at them again. These old habits and patterns may hold a great deal of charge or emotion. It may be much more comfortable for you to step out of your body to clear these patterns that are ready to leave. Your body may go unconscious to let the energy move out without engaging in it.

For either reason, know that the work was still being done and the meditation was still successful while you were spaced out. You – the big enthusiastic spirit that you are – were behind the scenes, making all the changes and upgrades necessary.

To help this clearing and rewiring process along, just intend to be conscious. You can do the work with your eyes open if that's helpful. Experiment and be easy on yourself. The unconsciousness will pass and may occur again in the next stepping up of the energy. It's all okay.

4. Believing you are not clairvoyant

You are clairvoyant. This ability comes with the body. But you've been conditioned not to recognize when you are seeing clairvoyantly. For many, we "saw" as children but the adults around us convinced us "seeing" was not a good thing. "Stop making up stories," they told us. "Stop imagining things." "There's no such thing as fairies and imaginary friends." We stopped using this spiritual ability so as not to upset others and in order to fit in. Most of us can remember a time in childhood when we did see energy and other beings.

Many expect seeing clairvoyantly to be just like seeing with their physical eyes. However it's slightly different and each person experiences it in their own way. You see just fine but you may not understand what seeing is at this spiritual level. Seeing is what you might experience when you're remembering a memory as a picture or when you are daydreaming or thinking in images about what something might look like.

Your clairvoyance is always on, but your old expectations, invalidations and denials are still in the way. Allow yourself to pretend that you see: imagine or remember what a red rose looks like and you *will* see it. Be playful: allow, imagine and then incorporate these choices as new concepts just for the fun of it. You will surprise yourself by how much you begin to see, and how natural it feels.

We all see clearly; however, we may process what we see with our other spiritual abilities, such as clairsentience (the ability to feel other peoples' emotions) or narrow band telepathy (the ability to finish another person's sentence or know what they are about to say). For some "seeing" is a sensory experience; for others it is a knowing.

5. Staying attached to old relationships

As you begin to achieve mastery in this work, the new relationships you form will be different from those you have had in the past. You may lose (or in some cases have already lost) some old relationships. This is because you are changing rapidly. You are releasing old patterns of how you relate to others, many of which were dysfunctional. What used to be acceptable ways of engaging with others or allowing others to behave, for example being disrespectful or sarcastic toward others, will no longer be comfortable. These old patterns hold you in relationships that no longer have value for you. The more you can notice this for what it is, the quicker you are going to alter old patterns, develop new reference points and step closer to experiencing wellbeing.

As you make these big upgrades as an evolving human, others will notice and they will have a choice to make for themselves. They will see how bright you are and ask how you got so calm, balanced and successful. Or they will shake their heads, not understand who you are becoming and walk away in confusion, not allowing themselves to have what you are creating for yourself. Either choice is theirs to make, and there is nothing you can do to change their response to your path to the Living Light Body. As this new sense of yourself unfolds, you will find it challenging to hold on to the old patterns that have held you locked in the drama and noise of the third dimension.

Be playful

We invite you to play with this work, in the same way that children play with building blocks, completely absorbed in seeing how high they can build a tower of blocks before it tumbles, or the way a child, fascinated with music, explores the possibilities of a piano. Browse, let your curiosity find something to play with and see where it leads. Put it down, pick it up, let it go. Be the fascinated child, unhurried and unworried – simply curious. Along the way, you'll receive information and choices to change the unconscious habits that do not support your wellbeing.

Online resources

Lesson on clairvoyance (28:39)

Question: Why do I fall asleep when I do this work? (01:07)

To access the online classroom,
visit www.masteringalchemy.com/book

LESSON 8

If you use the tools you learn and apply yourself to the exercises offered, by the time you finish this book you will have expanded your understanding of who you are and your capabilities. You also will be one step closer to becoming a master alchemist – adept at re-creating your life and shaping the world around you.

Let's begin!

Lesson 9

The Seven Living Words

There's a statement in an old book that says, "In the beginning was the Word." Words are the foundation of our lives, and many times we use them unconsciously and without intention. Words, as a vibration, are more fundamentally important to the creation of our lives than the use of words as language. Once you understand this concept, the ability to create your reality with ease and minimal effort becomes much more available. By actually becoming the words we speak and think, we create the foundation to receive and experience the energy vibrations they offer.

Occasionally we all experience vibrations such as depression, anger or frustration. We may even express them verbally. The Law of Attraction, which is flawless, recognizes those words as a vibration and gives us what we hold our attention on. When holding these lower vibrations in the body, we create or maintain lower negative experiences. Only when we hold higher words and vibrations in the body are we are able to have higher positive experiences and creations in life.

Energy is the free-flowing movement of consciousness. When energy is restricted it slows down, densifies and its motion becomes compressed. The vibration of your words and thoughts is what directs, enhances or restricts the flow of energy and consciousness in your life. For example, when you are resentful, judgemental or feel blame or guilt, the free flow of energy becomes compressed – the molecules in your body slow down and movement is restricted. However, when you are happy, enthusiastic and enjoying yourself, there is no restriction – the molecules within your body are stress-free, moving and flowing with ease and wellbeing. Breaking this pattern is achievable but it can be challenging for many due to life-long habits of choosing negative thoughts and words.

Consciously choosing the vibrations, words and emotions you want to experience is possible. Choosing doesn't mean suppressing or denying how you feel. Grief, anger, sadness and fear are all very real experiences. Observing the feeling, acknowledging it, then choosing something new is key. Ignoring emotions, or slapping a bandage on them, may keep them submerged in the unconsciousness where they could fester, keep you stuck, alter your perceptions or make you sick. What if, in the midst of a negative experience, you could pause and consciously choose a different emotion, attach it to your uncomfortable thought and shift the circumstance to a completely different energy vibration? You could experience ease and wellbeing rather than a reaction-driven response created by an impulsive thought or emotion.

If you deliberately think a different thought then a different feeling or emotion will be available. We are not victims to the energy that moves through us. Many times feelings or emotions happen instantly and unconsciously. They can feel like a wave rushing through the body . . . until you decide to increase your awareness and be the creator of your life, rather than simply accepting what shows up before you.

As you begin to understand the dynamic of what you're drawing to yourself (the Law of Attraction) and how to apply specifically chosen words (both individually and in combinations), a point of observation or platform presents itself to you. From here you can view and experience your life very differently. Simple? Yes! Easy? Not necessarily, although it isn't necessarily difficult either.

If you always do what you've always done, you'll always get what you've always got. So would you like to do something different? What if you could create and align yourself within a vibrational field that allowed you to know yourself as the higher-dimensional, happy, capable, confident person that you truly are? What if you could create a platform of awareness that allowed you to create and experience your life on your terms, magnetically attracting to you your desires. Would you live your life differently?

Happy, Certain, Senior, Present, Powerful, Commanding, Gracious

The Teachers of Light present us with seven specific words. These words are not random but instead are very purposefully and deliberately given. Individually each word creates a vibration that is unique, strong and stable. In combination, the words offer a way of living that is purposeful and focused. Thus they are named the Seven Living Words. These Living Words are the vibrations and feelings that naturally define who you are and who you have always been. These words are the vibrations that you turned away from in order to play the game of the third dimension.

I know you may think that you know the definitions of these seven words. However, when they are intentionally used as a vibrational platform or tool, instead of concepts in a language, their actual meaning becomes fuller and deeper.

There are many more Living Words; however, mastering and becoming these seven vibrations individually opens many doorways along this path.

Happy

This is a vibration that many of us have the most difficulty remembering or re-experiencing in the body. This is because we've been heavily programmed to focus on what is wrong with us (and the world) and what isn't working. In Lesson 7 I discussed the thoughts and beliefs that don't belong to you but are impacting you in uncomfortable ways every day. Those thoughts and beliefs are keeping you from Happy. As you continue clearing out the Centre of Your Head, Happy – and all the other Living Words – will be easier to find and be. If you can't remember a past time of feeling happy, try an easier word, perhaps satisfied or content, or imagine what that easier word would feel like. Pretend. Begin simply.

Certain

You know how to turn the key in the ignition of your car, right? Can you make your car's engine start? Are you sure? Do you know how to tie your shoelaces? Are you certain? Of course you are. Those are simple examples of what you can certainly do without thought or effort. You don't even think about tying your shoelaces. Your certainty is so high that you simply do it. What does that certainty feel like in your body? Let your body match that energy.

There are probably other aspects of your life where you don't hold the same automatic certainty as you hold for tying your shoelaces. By "being" the word Certain in uncomplicated situations and really owning it as you move through your day, you will automatically hold a level of Certain that allows for success when you enter into more challenging situations, such as asking for a pay increase. I *am* Certain. In what other circumstances are you Certain?

Senior

Senior isn't about being old. Senior is the ability to own who you are. To say, "This is me." Living the vibration of Seniority is knowing you are the one making the decision or creating the desired result for yourself. You have inner wisdom. You are in charge of your life. You aren't asking someone else to do it for you.

Many of us give our seniority over to others, allowing them to determine what is best for us, instead of creating for ourselves. Only you know what is best for you. Seniority is an alignment within the body that clearly says, "This is who I *am*."

Who do you give your Seniority away to? A spouse, child, boss, institution? By recognizing to whom you give your seniority, you can choose to approach that relationship differently and re-own your seniority. Being in the Centre of Your Head, grounded and using the Rose, allows you to clear the energy of someone and realign yourself in your seniority.

Take a moment here. Do you know someone who walks through life with Seniority? Notice how they present themselves.

Present

All good comes to you when you are Present in the current moment. Present-time is the only place you exist. It's the only place you can successfully create. Having your attention in the past or future doesn't allow for creation today. Only in present-time can you choose and create an emotion such as calm, neutrality or ease. Being this Living Word allows you to observe, then choose, then act with wisdom, clarity and choice instead of shooting first, then hoping for the best.

Powerful

Powerful (as in capable) is having the personal power to create, manage, decide and live as you wish. The vibration of Powerful isn't about carrying a sword, forcing others or demanding of them. It's about having the ability to succeed for yourself. Imagine a queen who is able to provide successfully for her subjects using skills such as negotiation, observation and management instead of cohesion, punishment and pushing against others. She may carry a sword but she has no need or desire to use it.

Commanding

The vibration of Commanding allows you to clearly identify your desire and put in motion what is required to make it happen. Like Powerful, Commanding is always from a place of balanced personal power and doesn't involve the

A good question: Why can't people hear me?

Question: Can you help me understand why people don't hear me?
In the past few weeks I have noticed that people (some of whom I have known for years) do not hear me in normal conversations. They look at me and say, "Hello?" I have to repeat myself once or twice before what I've said registers well enough for them to understand and respond. Then we continue talking until it happens again and we repeat the process. I'm wondering if this has to do with how people respond to people doing this work. Do others experience this and is there anything that can be done about it?

Frederick, Georgia, USA

Answer: Yes, it has to do with this spiritual work you are doing, although it occurs with other teachers and practices as well. We are finding it happening more frequently as the waves of the Shift step up everything on the planet and within us.

This occurrence is actually a wonderful validation that your practice is working. You're raising your vibration to a level where others may not be able to hear you. Although this can be awkward when you are trying to communicate something important about your business or your social life, please take it as a sign that all your focused practice is successful and take some amusement in the situation. You are beginning to walk through the third dimension as you live in the fourth and fifth dimensions. You are a walking, talking example of what is possible for others, even though they may not recognize it. *That* is what a true healer-teacher-leader does. Congratulations.

Although your associates (as third-dimensional bodies) are having a hard time hearing you, they (as higher spirits in those bodies) recognize where you are and what is possible for them also to have and accomplish for themselves.

Is there anything that can be done about it? Yes. Smile and pat yourself on the back. What you do not want to do is lower your vibration to match that of the people you are talking to. Doing that might also make you a match to their problems and pain. There is a story about Yeshua that says when he healed others, he did not go to their pain and roll around in it with them (sympathy, empathy). He continued to stay where he was vibrationally, and with compassion, inviting them to come and sit at the table with him.

You may still need to get a message across quickly and efficiently. This is where you get to practise your mastery and your tools. Here are some suggestions that might help:

- Take the time to set the energy before a conversation: find your space and choose the Living Word(s) you want to radiate. (This may take only about 30 seconds.) Be sure to add a word that will allow good communication. Make it up. The word vibration will be unique to you. You might try "hello" or "co-create" or "ease".

- Begin actively to "read" the energy and direct it. A trick would be to ask yourself, "What colour is the crown chakra of that person vibrating at?" and then allow the first colour that pops into your head to be the answer, without arguing with it. Make your crown chakra a brighter version of that colour (for example, baby blue becomes electric blue). You may have to do this before you step into the conversation (instead of when you're in it) because it's sometimes hard to remember our tools when we are in the middle of something.

- Talk to other people as a spirit, not as a body. As a spirit they will "get" what you are saying. As a body they are slower and duller. Send them hellos (For example, "Hello, I see how great you are.") before you meet, and direct those hellos to their hearts or their head areas. When you are in the actual conversation, have the intention and focus that you are talking to them as a spirit.

- Make sure you're grounded and in your body (Higher Mind or Centre of Your Head) when you're talking to them.

- Pay attention to the subject matter you're discussing when other people can't hear you, and also pay attention to how you are feeling at the time. You may find an interesting pattern within yourself that you can tweak a bit.

harm of others. The work you will do later with the Rays of Creation requires wearing the vibration of Commanding to use them successfully. When you Command, you are doing so from a place of Certainty, Presence and Graciousness.

Gracious

This Living Word stands alone yet colours all the others simultaneously. Gracious is demonstrated best in the presence of others and in combination with other Living Words. It is from the energy of Gracious that you are able effectively to be that Powerful, Capable and Commanding queen. Imagine a father teaching his daughter how to swing a bat. He Graciously encourages and doesn't mention the mistakes as a problem. You might remember someone you know (or a fictional character) who radiates Graciousness.

Become the Seven Living Words

As with all the tools the Elders present on this journey, owning and becoming these words may sound simple but it's not necessarily easy. This is due to generations of programming, beliefs and patterns that keep you small and controlled. Practising and "being" these words every day will break that pattern of limitation and create a new platform of success and ease.

EXERCISE: *How to experience and anchor the Seven Living Words*

This short exercise will help you experience and anchor the vibrations that these words possess. It will also show you how they can profoundly demonstrate themselves in your space. This example uses the word Happy but the process is identical for each of the Seven Living Words.

THE SEVEN LIVING WORDS

1. Be in the Centre of Your Head, take a breath and close your eyes. Take as much time as necessary to find that quiet, neutral, focused and open place before you begin.

2. Remember a time in your past when you had a happy experience. (If this word is too difficult to grab, choose a similar one that may be easier. Over a few days, work your way up to Happy.)

3. Take a moment and put yourself clearly in that past happy moment – see the flower, hear the child laughing, appreciate the joke you were told, accept the compliment that someone gave you. Allow yourself to be fully in that experience. Remember the memory, feel the feeling in your body. Be that word: Happy. Take your time. Get happiness all over you. Roll around in it. Really *feel* it, hear it and taste it fully.

4. As you allow yourself to be this energy vibration completely, notice how much bigger the smile on your face gets. Laughing is acceptable here. *Fe-e-e-e-l* the happiness in your body.

5. Return your attention to remembering that happy experience and feel the feeling all over again. Notice what you notice. Where does that feeling live in your body? What colour is it? Does it have a shape? Just make it up. Pretend to be Happy. Let your body physically adjust. It may want to sit up. And breathe.

6. Feel the feeling, and now allow the thought and memory of the original experience to fade from your awareness while you continue to feel the feeling in your body. Notice that the happiness you are feeling right now is a present-time feeling. It's not an in the past-time feeling and memory.

7. Feelings are experienced in the present moment and can *only* be experienced in the present moment. Although you were recalling a memory experienced in a past moment that included the feeling of Happy, Happy as a feeling (or any other feeling you place your attention upon) can only be experienced in a present-time moment.

Playing daily and really owning each of these words individually is the beginning of your ascension. You are creating a platform that will allow you to observe the third dimension as it simply dissolves and reshapes itself into the fifth dimension. Drama and noise will fall away.

The fifth dimension is structured in frequencies that promote and hold tremendous alignment and wellbeing. When you are aligned with this flow your access to All That Is becomes unlimited. The more harmonic resonance and alignment there is, the simpler it is to create. From a third-dimensional perspective, the simplest way to align with these fifth-dimensional frequencies is by becoming and demonstrating the vibration, or feeling, of selected words while maintaining your point of observation. This will allow you to shift your relationship to the world around you from one of reaction to one where you can choose how you wish to create and manage your experience.

The words you hold, consciously or unconsciously, collectively create a vibrational tone that is unique to you. You become known by your tone. For example, she is sad and unpleasant to be around; or he is always angry and upset. As you become aligned with the higher-dimensional Living Words, you begin to hold a tone that is recognizable in those higher dimensions. Your tone is aligned with who you came here to be – she looks so present and happy; he's always so certain and gracious. It's at this level that you not only start to become aware of being aware, but also become a conscious citizen of the fifth dimension.

Over the coming months and years, events will occur in your world that will hone and refine you, offering you the opportunity to become more specific, precise, clear and masterful. You will be able to more easily and naturally vibrate in frequencies that demonstrate who you came here to be. To get there from where you may be right now requires focused attention on your intention, as well as practice wearing the Living Words until they are well anchored, effortless and simply who you are. By holding your attention on the Living Words and deeply becoming them, your physical and emotional bodies match that energy and outwardly demonstrate this to the external world. Far more important, however, the Law of Attraction sees you holding those vibrations and acts to give back to you exactly what you hold your attention upon: Happiness, Certainty and Grace.

Success story

I've always had this fear of public speaking, even if in a group of only two others. Well, I received an unasked-for promotion into a management position of an accounting team of 12 people. I began A Course in Mastering Alchemy Level 1 only a month ago and have been playing with the Living Words. I had to lead my first department meeting and decided this would be a time to see if the tools work or not. So before the meeting I sat in my office with the door closed, grounded myself, got into my Octahedron and created a word triangle of Certain, Capable and Clear. I also grounded the room and set the energy of the meeting at Fun. I just made it all up and took my attention off this when the meeting began.

During the meeting I checked in with myself and realized I wasn't nervous, sweating or shaking (a first for me). And after the meeting one of the senior accountants (a man) took me aside to say that it was the most productive and fun meeting ever. He actually used the word fun!

I was floored and surprised (but not really). I guess the tools really work.

CS, San Diego, California, USA

Creating a solid platform upon which to stand

Throughout this course the geometry of the triangle appears as a valuable construction for stability and balance. In this case combining words in the form of an equilateral triangle increases their effectiveness exponentially. As you experience the following exercise, notice how the platform feels in your body.

EXERCISE: *How to create a platform of Certain, Powerful and Gracious*

1. Be in the Centre of Your Head or your Higher Mind, take a breath and close your eyes. Take as much time as necessary to find that quiet, neutral, focused and open place before you begin.

2. Imagine an equilateral triangle before you.

3. Be in present-time. Feel the sensation of being Certain. Place the word Certain on one side of the triangle. Let your body adjust as you wear the vibration of Certain. Remember a time when you were Certain with no push or force. It is simply who you are. Take a few moments to establish this feeling and own it. Be Certain.

4. Now move your attention to the feeling and experience of Powerful. Really feel your personal Power as an individual word.

5. Add the word Powerful to another side of the triangle. Notice how the vibrations of the words on the platform you're creating alter when the words are combined. Simply allow the feeling of the two Living Words – Certain and Powerful – to fill you up. There's nothing to do, no place to go. There is nothing to fix because nothing is broken. Let your physicality adjust to match this combination.

6. Once you're very familiar with the combination Certain and Powerful, shift your attention to the word Gracious and completely *be* Gracious as an individual vibration.

7. Now add the word Gracious to the final side of the triangle before you. Explore the new vibrational platform of Certain,

Powerful and Gracious. Relax and be curious. Allow and enjoy the changed energy. Notice how this combination of words feels different than the individual words.

8. You have created a solid triangular platform upon which to stand. Own this for yourself. This is who you are.

If you find it difficult to hold these particular words, try combinations of three words that are more familiar and easier to reach. Begin with Orderly, Appreciative and Calm or Amused, Quiet and Precise, for example.

As you start to own and internalize this powerful platform, you may notice specific things:

- **The words and their vibrations become anchored in your energy field.** In addition to changing how others see you, the words also change how you respond and relate to others. Consciously wearing these higher-vibrational words begins to neutralize the vibrational tones that you have created unconsciously, out of habit. Like the Rose tool, these words vibrate at a higher, faster level. They are aligned with the highest energy that you are – an energy that quiets, smooths and releases all things unlike itself. When you radiate the energy of the higher-dimensional words, words that are lesser fall away. Ugly vibrations such as victim, lack, fear and "I'm not okay" can no longer maintain themselves in your presence.

- **Your ability to manage your attention point improves.** You will find yourself much more able to manage your attention and to observe all that is going on around you without being distracted and pulled away from your centre. You will discover that every experience you have is quite different from your previous experiences. Instead of being knocked out of your space by things that are outside of you, you can simply choose to allow all insults, distractions, drama and noise to pass you by. All you have to do is "be" the word, or triangle of words, that would most effortlessly uplift the situation that you are encountering. For example, you could ask yourself, "What platform of words do I want to wear or vibrate at when I step into this meeting?" *or* "What three vibrations do I want to present myself in today?" *or* "What single word would I like to choose to replace this ugly feeling?" Begin simply. Don't choose words such as Love or Peace. Those words are too complicated, and too far away from where you might be vibrating right now. The key is to make this real and very easy to accomplish.

- **You begin to activate aspects of your Living Light Body.** Within the memory banks of your Soul, there is a blueprint of your Living Light Body. This is the body of Light that you own and experience simultaneously in the higher dimensions. This is the vehicle that you use to move between universes and through all of consciousness. Every time you wear one of the higher-dimensional words, a receptor within your Living Light Body reactivates. As each receptor turns back on, that word becomes fully anchored in your life. From that moment forward, you automatically demonstrate yourself as this energy. As your Living Light Body begins to be reactivated, your physicality becomes less dense – Light-er. You remember more of who you are as a higher-dimensional being. Your Living Light Body demonstrates a harmonic resonance with Creator and you demonstrate more fully the unique spark of Creator that you are, but have forgotten.

Creating your own set of Living Words, and learning to feel their vibrations, rather than think their definitions, is one of the most important things you can do during this incredible time of global shift. Standing upon this vibrational platform, and adjusting it according to whatever situation lies before you, will enable you to create the reality that you desire. This is not complicated; it is a reconfiguration from the third-dimensional way of life to a higher, clearer way of being. It can become a conscious moment-to-moment choice. This is a way of life that is Happy, Certain, Senior, Present, Capable, Commanding and Gracious.

Your life becomes a life you intentionally choose and direct.

Other Living Words

Below is a short list of wonderful words that you may want to incorporate into the foundation of your Living Light Body.

Abundant	Calm	Creative
Accepting	Capable	Dedicated
Accomplished	Centred	Determined
Adventurous	Certain	Dignified
Affectionate	Cheerful	Diplomatic
Aligned	Clear	Discerning
Allowing	Coherent	Disciplined
Amused	Commanding	Dynamic
Appreciative	Committed	Elegant
Artistic	Communicative	Embracing
Attentive	Compassionate	Enthusiastic
Aware	Complete	Faithful
Balanced	Confident	Flexible
Beautiful	Content	Focused
Belonging	Contributing	Friendly
Boundless	Courageous	Generous

Gentle	Kind	Regal
Giving	Laughter	Respectful
Graceful	Leadership	Responsive
Gracious	Loyal	Reverent
Grateful	Masterful	Self-loving
Grounded	Merciful	Senior
Happy	Neutral	Sensitive
Harmonious	Nurturing	Simple
Honest	Observant	Sincere
Humble	Optimistic	Spontaneous
Imaginative	Orderly	Strong
Ingenious	Patience	Supportive
Innocent	Peaceful	Telepathic
Insightful	Persevering	Tender
Inspired	Playful	Tolerant
Integrity	Powerful	Trustworthy
Intelligent	Present	Truthful
Intuitive	Punctual	Understanding
Invincible	Purposeful	Warm
Joyful	Radiant	Wise

EXERCISE: *Be the Word in your walking around space #1*

1. Be in the Centre of Your Head or your Higher Mind, take a breath and close your eyes. Take as much time as necessary to find that quiet, neutral, focused and open place before you begin.
2. Choose one word from the list above. Fully "be" it. Place the word on one side of an equilateral triangle.

3. Choose another word from the list. Fully "be" the word. Place the word on another side of the triangle.
4. Then choose a third word from the list. Fully "be" the word. Place it on the final side of the triangle. Think of this combination of words as a triangular platform upon which to build this new foundation. Feel the words as you become them.

Success story

After the last session I decided to play with what it would feel like to experience the energy words of Validation and Appreciation. I've been in a job where others have considered me "different", and just haven't felt as though I fit in.

Well, things have started to change. I was recently identified as one of 19 people in the organization (there are over 400) who are leaders in their field and bring an encouraging, supportive and positive presence to the organization. I had to read the email over and over before I could believe they were addressing me. My thought was, "I'm just an appointment scheduler. They can't be talking about me." Me? A leader?

Well, they were identifying me as such. So I am now a member of the Patient Experience Team. Our goal is to bring about a new world order, so to speak, within our group so that patients experience the best customer service and patient care available. What's funny is that many others in the company have reacted to my recognition with "who does she think she is" energy-throwing. In the past I would have agreed with them and resigned from the team. But since playing with the Living Words, I see that I really deserve this. I *am* Competent, Capable, Certain, Commanding, Gracious, Senior, Present . . . and yes . . . Happy! Who would have thought? Certainly not me a few months ago.

LM, London, United Kingdom

EXERCISE: *Be the Word in your walking around space #2*

1. First create a list of your own words. Choose words that make you feel good. Select words that you would like to be known by in your world. For example, insightful, kind, respectful, purposeful, gracious, grateful, honest, dignified, caring or helpful. Make it a long list, choosing words that will help you remember your self. Doing so will assist you in consciously and deliberately creating choices.

2. Next choose seven of those words that make you feel especially good. Choose words that you aspire to experience or would like to be.

3. Each day for a week, take one of these seven words and "be" that word. Demonstrate this word in every situation and notice how it makes you feel. You will notice that when you become intentional about being the word, you feel more alert and aware, more present in the now moment. You will feel and be in charge of yourself on your own terms. If you find you have slipped out of the word, simply smile and become the word once again. Have fun!

Online resources

Video: Words (43:54)

Meditation: Being the words individually and together (23:28)

Question: Why do I have trouble feeling the words? (04:14)

To access the online classroom,
visit www.masteringalchemy.com/book

Lesson 10

The diamond of Light surrounding you

If you wish to have water to drink, you need a container in which to hold it. If you have no glass, the water will quickly spill all over the table. Likewise, to hold the wisdom from the Teachers of Light you also require a container. This container has long existed but has fallen away from us due to neglect and the habit of fear that surrounds each of us. This container for the wisdom is the electromagnetic field around you that you may know as your aura. The problem is your aura has lost its definition or structure. You have become the water without a container.

By restructuring the harmonics of your aura to a particular sacred-geometric form, you can re-create the container. This specific geometry aligns with a unique higher-dimensional body of wisdom and becomes your antenna – a receiver and transmitter. The aura without structure and focus is like a radio that cannot tune in to the station you wish to listen to. Instead of listening to more distant stations with many choices, you can only tune in to the local neighbourhood gossip. By creating a specifically tuned transmitter and receiver you can begin to align your personal energy field to your own frequency, which in turn allows you to tune out incoherent frequencies that constantly flow through you. These disruptive frequencies don't belong to you and have nothing to do with who you are, but they hold such a strong magnetic charge that they actually blind your understanding of your purpose.

Once your geometric container is in place, fascinating new opportunities become available to you. For example, by learning to increase the speed at which the geometric field spins, you can begin to rise above life's drama, noise and distractions. This creates an opportunity to realign your antenna to your own purpose and become happy. You are then consistently and successfully able to hold higher thoughts and feelings of passion, enthusiasm, clarity and ease.

This geometric container is your Personal Power Field. It is the vessel that holds the wisdom of All That Is. By fine-tuning your antenna, you will eliminate the noisy, incoherent vibrations of events and people around you and begin to know yourself as the Living Light Body.

This fine-tuned alignment provides a quiet focus that enables you to begin to remember and rewire your self in ways that have not been available to you for many lifetimes. It allows you to recall, receive and re-experience the abundance and wisdom that you already know in the higher dimensions. There's no anxiety, competition, worry or drama, because those energies simply do not exist within this geometry. You find yourself becoming certain, strong, clear and nonreactionary. You have the ability to choose to listen to others or not. You have the ability to choose to experience yourself in your own way. Rebuilding your Personal Power Field restructures both how you perceive yourself and how you present yourself.

And here's where the alchemy begins.

From this new, higher, faster perspective you will find that time exists in a very different form. There is no past or future. There is only *now*, where time is simultaneous and where all experiences exist at the same moment in the same place. Everything flows simply and effortlessly. In this simultaneous *now*, all answers to any questions are available to you *before* you have to act or respond to the question. The answers you seek exist exactly where you ask the question.

Think about this. If you knew all the answers, and what would happen in each situation before you had to act, why would you ever choose an experience that was not enjoyable? With total choice you would choose the possibility that most joyfully meets your needs and then step into that choice, thereby creating the reality that you desire.

From this higher, faster, clearer platform of consciousness, you will discover that many of the concepts, beliefs and truths once held in this lower consciousness are no longer accurate or useful in the higher perspective. You now have the opportunity to make new choices. You can choose to play the game you have always played, or you can step up to a greater platform of certainty, seniority, personal power, happiness, command and grace. On this platform you will find that you have many more colours to choose from on your palette. The pictures you paint with this enhanced palette will be much grander and more alive. And simply by reconstructing a sentence or speaking with a different tone, you can create experiences with very different results.

Greater levels of Light, wisdom and knowledge become increasingly available to you. The more you can anchor and consistently hold the Light within you, the quicker you will fulfil your spiritual purpose. As you begin to vibrate within the fifth-dimensional consciousness, while still surrounded by third-dimensional energy, it is very important to recognize and live within your own Personal Power Field.

The next tool you will learn rebuilds your aura into a strong and stable geometric field, so your personal power and energy can remain with you, instead of being weakened and lost among external places and people. Constructing this sacred field – the container – and living within it will allow you to view and experience your internal life and the world around you from a much more calm, quiet, confident and elegant perspective.

LESSON 10

The Octahedron

In sacred geometry there are five forms known as Platonic solids, each of which holds unique characteristics. One of these forms is the octahedron (a diamond with eight faces). You can imagine an octahedron as one four-sided pyramid pointing upward, with a second four-sided pyramid connected at the base pointing downward.

Besides being a strong vessel to contain your energy and personal power, this geometric field is also an antenna. The Octahedron tool attracts and receives frequencies of thought. It also transmits your thoughts, intentions and desires in a clearer, more direct way. If you can manage your antenna, you can influence what your antenna transmits and receives.

EXERCISE: *How to construct the Octahedron*

This exercise uses the Rose tool; however, using a simple dot as a marker will work just as well.

1. Take a moment and find your space. Check your Grounding Cord and be sure you're in the Centre of Your Head or Higher Mind.
2. Create your Rose tool in front of you, at the edge of your energy field. If you need to, hold your arm (physical or imaginary) out in front of you and pretend you're holding a rose between your fingertips.
3. Be aware of the noisy third dimension on the other side of your Rose. Take a breath.
4. Close your eyes. While being aware of the Rose in front of you, create a second Rose directly behind you. There is now one Rose in front of you and one behind you. Feel them and/or "see" them in your awareness.

The Octahedron with a Rose
at each axis point

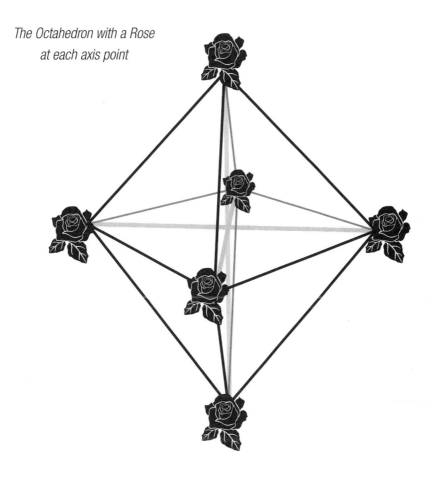

5. Now connect the two Roses by drawing an imaginary axis line
   that passes through your heart chakra (the centre of your chest).
6. Be aware of those two Roses and the axis line, while you create
   one more Rose on your right and another on your left.
7. Draw another axis line through your heart chakra to connect
   these two new Roses. There are now four Roses at equal
   distances around you.
8. Place a Rose about 45cm (18 inches) above your head.

9. Place a final Rose about 15cm (6 inches) below your feet. All six Roses are now in position, creating the six points of the Octahedron.

10. Draw one more axis line, again passing through your heart chakra, from the Rose above your head to the one below your feet. These axis lines create a gyroscope, which creates stabilization in your energy field.

11. Still with your eyes closed, draw an imaginary line from the Rose in front of you to the one on your right. See it and feel it.

12. Draw a line joining the Rose on your right to the Rose behind you, then join that Rose to the one to your left. Finally draw a line from the Rose on your left to the Rose in front of you. This completes a square at the level of your heart chakra.

13. Next draw four imaginary lines that connect the Rose above your head to each of the four Roses at the level of your heart chakra. You have now created a four-sided pyramid pointing upward. Feel the change as if an umbrella surrounds you.

14. Now draw four imaginary lines that connect the Rose below your feet to each of the four Roses at the level of your heart chakra. You have now created the full Octahedron.

15. Notice how you feel when you are surrounded by your Octahedron. The three axis lines help stabilize and keep you energetically balanced as you continue to build your Personal Power Field.

16. Bring your attention to the eight faces of your Octahedron. Fill these eight triangles with brilliant translucent Light. Notice how this feels.

The space inside this Octahedron is yours, and only yours. Everything outside this field defines the rest of the universe. This diamond of Light that surrounds you is not a wall or a defence system. It's a stable containment field that allows you to move around more effectively, without becoming affected by external noise and drama. As an antenna the Octahedron aligns with the greater wisdom and information being transmitted during this Shift. It creates an alignment with all that you are, and simply filters out that which you are not.

The best way to reinforce this geometry and to own it for yourself is to trace the lines of the Octahedron repeatedly throughout your day and during your meditations. Make it fun and amusing. Reinforcing your Octahedron anchors it around you. If you consciously stay within your Light-filled Octahedron you will become less and less affected by other people's emotions, thoughts and erratic behaviour. Construct it around you daily, reinforcing it whenever you feel the need. It won't take long to begin noticing the difference this tool makes in your day.

As you live and work within your Octahedron, you will begin to align with the knowledge and the wisdom you once had. You will also begin to transmit more clearly, and with greater strength, your intentions, desires and dreams for the universe to see and reflect back to you. You will begin to know yourself.

A word about "spin"

As you move through this course, you will read references to "spinning". You'll spin the Octahedron, the Triads and more. As soon as you hear the word "spin' your rational mind may say, "Well, which way? Do I spin it forward or backward? Do I spin it left to right or right to left? How do I spin this?" Let's keep it simple. When you give the command to the Octahedron to spin, it knows what to do. This is a part of you that you have simply forgotten. Your field will spin, though you won't see the actually turning. Instead you might observe a glow or radiance. The Octahedron is spinning faster than human eyes can see.

LESSON 10

EXERCISE: *How to activate your Personal Power Field*

As you built your Octahedron, you may have noticed that the top portion is shorter than the lower portion. This is because your Personal Power Field is not fully activated as yet. The following exercise will turn it on and bring it into a balanced geometric alignment. The full instructions for how to do this are a complicated initiation with multiple steps. For here and now, I've simplified it. The final result will still be effective and felt.

1. Find your space. Check your Octahedron and be in your Higher Mind.
2. Notice and reinforce the lines you drew when you created the Octahedron
3. Now notice the line of Light that runs from the point of your Octahedron above you, through the centre of your body, to the point of the Octahedron directly below you.
4. Breathing slowly, deliberately widen the line of Light to about 10cm (4 inches). You now have a column of Light connecting and moving through your energy field.
5. Be the word Certain and give the command to the column to begin to move the Light within it up from your third chakra, out through the point at the top of the Octahedron and then let the Light flow down around the outside of the geometry to form a sphere around it.
6. Next give the command to the column to begin to move the Light within it down from your third chakra, out through the point at the bottom of the Octahedron and then let it flow up and around the outside of the geometry to form another sphere around it. You now have two spheres of Light surrounding your Octahedron. You might notice that they touch all six points of the geometry.

7. To bring the Octahedron into a balanced form, you must now activate it. From that place of Certainty and Presence in your Higher Mind, give the command for both spheres to begin to spin. (They will naturally know how to spin.) The Light will continue to move up and out the top of the column and down and out the bottom of the column simultaneously. Your only job is to watch as this occurs, not control or force it.

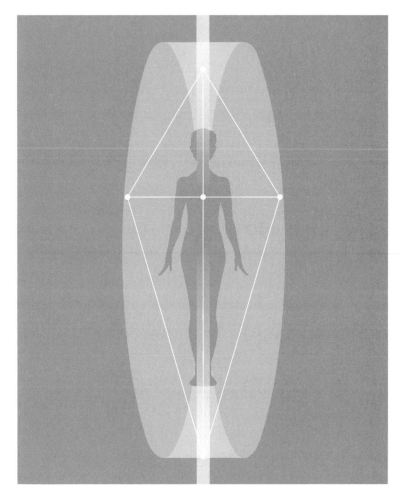

The Octahedron before it is activated

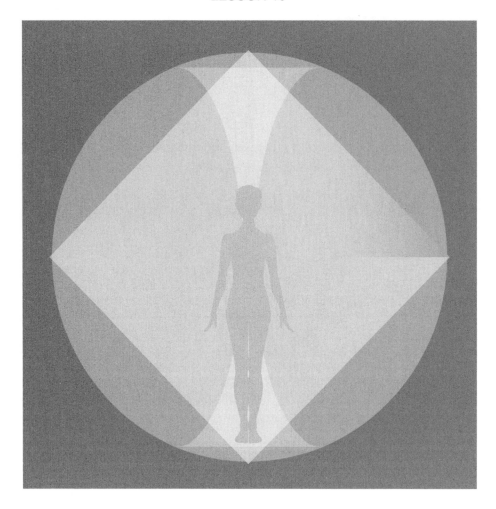

The activated Octahedron

8. As the Octahedron begins to glow and radiate Light, give it
    the command to double in speed. It will. Notice the increase
    in radiance. You may physically feel a sensation, though many
    people don't. You may notice that the energy spirals around
    your Personal Power Field and then accelerates even more as it
    moves through the column. As it does this it will reach a point

Success story

Last month I went to a hot-springs retreat centre in northern California. I needed quiet time alone to reflect and retreat. One dusk, as I was meditating in one of the pools, a very boisterous group of visitors entered. They were enjoying the waters in a way quite different than I was. The happy bunch began playing with each other, loudly laughing, talking, splashing and creating great waves that rocked my body to and fro. I found myself getting irritated and I decided to take this opportunity for a little experiment.

Not moving or even opening my eyes, I erected my Octahedron. I soon found a distance of approximately 1 metre (3 feet) around me to be undisturbed by the waves and rippling water. I smiled inside and out, and settled back into my space with gratitude and appreciation.

A few moments later I decided to play again. I experimented by extending the field out further and discovered that the further I extended my Octahedron, the quieter the pool became. When I finally opened my eyes some ten minutes after I began the experiment, I found myself to be entirely alone in the pool again. The group of friends had left and moved on to another location to party!

Dani, California, USA

where it will stabilize at a very high speed and then settle into a nice comfortable sensation. Another thing you may notice as you increase the spin of this energy is that the shape of your Octahedron has become more balanced and aligned. The spin of the field of Light will become perfectly spherical, and the Octahedron will expand outward so that all six points are an equal distance from each other; all touching the edge of the sphere. There is no need to analyse this, just experience and enjoy it. The higher, wiser aspect of you knows exactly what it's doing. The reality is this has been yours forever.

9. Now, without opening your eyes, become aware of the Octahedron and the spheres you have created. Notice how it feels. From inside, be aware of this flow of Light spinning around the Octahedron and accelerating back up through the column within you. At this point you may be feeling less pressure, cooler, more stabilized and more comfortable.

Congratulations! You've successfully built a new energy field from which to create your life. This is where things begins to get really interesting. The more you play with this tool, the more you will develop a new awareness of yourself, and of the fact that there is something different about how you now move around. Your Personal Power Field will grow into a self-contained, self-generated, spherical field of Light that completely surrounds the Octahedron and you.

Online resources

Question: Will my Octahedron affect others? (01:45)

To access the online classroom,
visit www.masteringalchemy.com/book

Lesson 11

The seven layers of thought

The difference between success and struggle is the degree to which we are aware of and manage our intention, attention and thoughts. Your unconscious thinking creates just as powerfully and swiftly as your conscious thinking does. Unconscious thoughts are like misguided darts, whereas intentionally directed thoughts result in precise outcomes.

Understanding the levels your thoughts transition through will prove helpful in managing them. Thoughts occur at many levels of loudness, from the screaming, arguing thought that bursts out of your mouth without warning to the complete silence of knowingness. Although there are many levels or layers of thought, let's keep it simple and talk about the seven distinct layers available to each of us. These layers do not have rigid lines of definition; there is actually a fluidity and flow between them. The flow from one layer of thought to the next is similar to the way the colours of a rainbow blend into one another – for example, the red layer flows into the orange layer with no rigid line separating the two colours.

First layer of thought

The first layer of thought is where we speak without considering what we are saying. We see this occur every day: the man in the airport just blurting out meaningless comments; the woman chattering away as if she has no filter –

seconds later, they don't even remember what they said. Functioning in this layer of thought, a person generally is unconscious of being unconscious, and goes about their day in a default mode versus being conscious and intentional.

Most of those who have not awakened spiritually live in the first layer of thought, but even those who are more self-aware can still find themselves moving in and out of this layer of thought. You might make a project of becoming aware of when you, and others around you, are in this layer. Notice the unnecessary comments, gossip or noisy conversation. When you begin to become conscious of this layer of thought, you will quickly become uncomfortable in the unconscious babble that you may find yourself surrounded by or demonstrating. When you are conscious of the first layer of thought, you will make better choices about how to present yourself, and the layer of thought in which you want to live.

This layer of thought and the next two layers operate in third-dimensional past/future-time.

Second layer of thought

This is the layer where you have conversations or arguments with other people in your head. You go back and forth in your mind about a situation and how you were right/bad/wrong/hurt, and you scold the other person for being wrong/bad/hurtful/stupid. Guilt and blame live here, along with resentment and justification. These thoughts can become very loud and consuming habits. This level of thought has a relationship to telepathy and clairaudience. That conversation you are having in your head is very real in the moment and it *is* happening. Whether the person you are "talking" to is next to you or a thousand miles away, the conversation is occurring. On an energetic level, that other person can feel the energy you are throwing at them. This is also the layer where you really want to curse at the person standing before you – "You stupid person/idiot/jerk!" – but instead you smile pleasantly and continue to argue with them in your head.

Like the first layer of thought, this one has a huge amount of internal motion to it. In both layers you are still engaging with the situation versus listening or being still. Many long-held, limiting habits of thought reside in this layer, and you may not even be aware of them.

Third layer of thought

The third layer is where you figure things out, strategize, fix and problem-solve. There is still motion here, and an internal back-and-forth type of conversation, as well as a degree of engagement and emotional attachment. This layer is very involved in the rational mind's need to figure things out:

I tried three different things and know there has to be a solution. How can I troubleshoot this issue before the deadline?

Okay, I said "hello" to her, but she didn't see me. What do I do now to get her attention?

What does that sign over there say? [eyes squinting] *It looks so interesting.*

Although not as loud and intense as the first two layers of thought, there is still undisciplined focus in this layer. It has more to do with figuring something out for yourself, however, than with engaging with someone else. Your mind is bouncing around trying to find an answer. There is a looking outward and a compulsion to find the answer, rather than taking a breath, becoming quiet and allowing the answer to make itself available to you.

Fourth layer of thought

This layer is a place that can be defined as pondering. It's being curious, and sitting back without being engaged in a situation. This is the first non-engaged, non-invested layer of thought. This layer is curious:

Hmm, I wonder how that will unfold?
Where did that come from?
What an interesting possibility.

There is no emotional attachment, judgement or predefinition of answers or possibilities. Many times you get into this easy layer when you aren't stressed or in a moment when there are few external demands on you. You might begin to think, "Hmm, maybe it's time to consider moving. I wonder where I would like to live?" This is a question without a defined answer to it. The question is open-ended. The answer appears where that non-charged question is asked. All you have to do is allow it and not "move" from your thought to search for the answer. The answer and the wandering thoughts surrounding the answer then come into your awareness from the broader field of possibilities: "Well, if I go to Portland, Oregon, I will have this experience, and if I go to Tokyo I will have that experience, and then I could always move down to Perth in Australia and have another experience." The process unfolds by itself and you are simply watching and allowing the process from a place of neutral curiosity from the Centre of Your Head or Higher Mind. You are not actively searching out an answer. In this layer of thought someone may say to you, "Have you considered Boulder, Colorado?" and you're open and allowing, without rejecting or judging the possibility – no opinion, just curious.

This is a present-time fourth-dimensional consciousness.

Fifth layer of thought

This is the layer of thought where things really start to get creative and quiet. This is where your consciousness begins naturally and organically to pull together many of the floating, curious pieces, combining them with the deeper unconscious aspects of you and organizing them in such a way that you become much more conscious, focused and capable with your innate wisdom. This layer takes the curious interest of the fourth layer (the field of possibilities) and brings it to your mental workbench to organize and become more real as a possibility. This is done not with greater thought or concentration, but with greater quietness, allowing, stillness and trust. The answers come to where the question is considered.

This is where "I wonder where I would like to move?" unfolds into "Yes, London feels aligned, right and good" with no effort or worry or figuring it out – no thought. It's an awareness, as if you heard the words but cannot define where they came from.

Living in this layer of thought is magical, although it isn't magic. It is inspired. Many artists and writers create when in this layer. The creation process just flows and the book or painting writes or paints itself. Many describe this state as being "in the zone".

Sixth layer of thought

Perhaps we should rename this layer the layer of no thought. This layer is similar to a great meditation where you find yourself easily sitting still for three hours in an awareness of "this is so good I don't want get up". This layer is an extremely quiet place where you begin to access deeper fields of awareness. You begin to think (or better yet, exist) without thoughts as words. This occurs because you are in the higher fourth- and fifth-dimensional fields of knowledge. You begin to have conscious access to the greatness that you are. It is in this space that you begin to have a sure sense of your powerfulness, your presence and your capabilities.

This is where a thought enters the physical from the nonphysical. This is where the Rays of Creation truly begin to be used to arrange and rearrange all possibilities without any limitations. Although no thought is thought in words, everything comes effortlessly to you as an understanding, a knowing. It is in this layer of thought that much of the work of this course is practised. You begin to play in the fifth dimension, where time, space and gravity all operate differently than is understood in the third dimension. This is the place where alchemy occurs, where you begin to change the harmonics of matter, rearrange the frequencies of thought and apply the element of Love in such a manner that, on your terms, you rearrange the molecules and instantaneously begin to produce in simultaneous time whatever you desire.

Can you make that happen in this moment? Yes, but not if the noise of the first three layers of thought is your habit. As you play with the layers of thought and become more masterful, you will build more templates of clear awareness and create expanding platforms to stand upon and create from. These fifth and sixth layers are where you will live most of your day in greater balance and ease. From here you can then do what is necessary to allow more Light to enter into your body. It's in this space that you begin to know yourself as Soul.

Seventh layer of thought

The seventh layer of thought is indefinable. There are no human words available to describe it. It's where you and the thought that thought you into existence think together. Now if I were to skirt around the edges of that with some definitions, I could say that this layer is the place where you are in full relationship with your Soul. This may be unimaginable to you. Your Soul has everything to do with the creation of you; Creator created you, but your Soul also created you. When you and your Soul begin to think as one, within the higher aspect of Creator, you begin to think together in the Unified Field of Consciousness: you are no longer a third- or fourth-dimensional being. You can begin to play very consciously, as a citizen of the fifth, sixth, and seventh dimensions.

At this point you still have physicality, but not a physical body as you know it. You will have a crystallized body that is less physically dense. The Living Light Body is now becoming very available to each one of us, but in order to create it, expanded levels of Light have to be brought into your form through the mental and emotional bodies. Those two bodies hold third-dimensional density, resistance and resentment. This is where ugly thoughts and ugly emotions live. The predominant purpose of this course is for you to become conscious of being conscious and aware of being aware, integrating enough Light into your mental and emotional bodies to the point where you don't have those ugly thoughts and ugly emotions, reactions and resistances. When you can clear that energy from your emotional and mental bodies, they will merge and become one, just as they originally were intended. When this happens you will begin to play with great awareness in the fifth, sixth and seventh layers of thought. You will begin to change the density of your physicality from a carbon-dense body that does not absorb Light to a crystalline body of Light that will allow a very significant transformation of your physical body.

This is what begins to happen in the seventh layer of thought, but what I just described doesn't adequately express what is possible. There are no words, although we are getting closer to finding them. In the meantime I hope this gives you a better sense of these layers of thought and a structure that will enable you to become more aware of your inner workings. As you become the quiet observer of your thoughts and patterns, the noise will lessen, and a stillness of understanding and knowingness will prevail. And *that* is precisely where humanity is headed.

Online resources

Meditation to experience the seven layers of thought (38:10)

To access the online classroom,
visit www.masteringalchemy.com/book

Lesson 12

Master every thought, every emotion, every action

At the beginning of this course, long before I knew it would be a course, Ascended Master Kuthumi told me that it is necessary (i.e. required) for me to be masterful of every thought, every emotion, every action . . . every moment. I swallowed hard and nodded, not sure how this was even possible and very clear it was far out of my reach. As my relationship with the Teachers evolved over the years, however, I learned it is possible, though it requires personal commitment and focused attention. My attention had to be on my intention to live this path the Teachers laid out. My attention had to be quiet and full. It could not be moving about or distracted.

Knowing about the seven layers of thought and actually experiencing them are two very different things. It takes attention on that intention for this to occur. Most people living in the third dimension have no understanding or experience with that skill. We are, instead, programmed to react to the noise and drama of the first three layers of thought. Mastering your attention point is one of the things that will help you step out of the third dimension and into the higher-dimensional way of life. The following are some notes that will fill out this understanding.

Success story

Since I've begun this course with you and the Elders, I "accidentally" noticed a huge success for me. I have had generalized anxiety disorder for as long as I can remember. I get afraid over the smallest things – forget about flying or travelling alone. It took me a long time of focused work but I finally was able to calmly hold my attention on the Infinity Loop for longer than a few breaths. I combined it with the Grounding Cord and being in my Higher Mind.

Funny thing was, as I began to breathe that way, I stopped worrying. But I didn't notice I had broken that pattern until I was driving to my son's place about 160km (100 miles) away. With no thought or effort, I breathed the Infinity Loop all the way and never got nervous. I didn't realize my success until my son greeted me at the door with worry on his face. He was expecting me to be my usual mess of stress, but I wasn't. I finally feel free and confident. Thanks, Elders of Light.

HM, Russia

Shifting your attention point without "going to"

Going to is the action of moving your attention away from your centre in order to observe something. Your friend says, "Oh, look at that interesting shape over there." And instead of staying on your internal observation deck, you leave the Centre of Your Head, move through multiple layers of third-dimensional noise and mentally "go to" the shape. As you leave your point of observation to experience that shape over there, you are no longer balanced and aligned within your field. You have wandered away from yourself. "Going to" causes a wobble in your perception and in your experience of the thing you are observing. What you see is distorted because you are not viewing it from your balanced internal point of observation. What you might observe from the Centre of Your Head as a red circle instead becomes a green square when you move through all the third-dimensional noise to see the shape. What makes "going to" additionally disruptive is that when you finally return to the Centre of Your Head or Higher Mind, you must again pass through those multiple layers of third-dimensional noise, thoughts and emotions. Returning to the Centre of Your Head or Higher Mind requires focused attention to disengage from what you "went to" (that shape over there). In other words, when you return your attention to the original point of observation, your awareness has been distorted by the noise between you and what you "went to".

Many of the negative beliefs and emotions we hold are created when we leave the body and "go to" a point outside of ourselves and then draw a conclusion that leads us to believe "something is wrong" or "I am not okay". For example: You tell a joke. At first the person doesn't get it. You see the confused expression on their face and move your attention over to their space. When you return to your own head you conclude they don't think you're funny and you should never tell another joke. In the meantime, they've started to laugh but because of your previous conclusion you now believe they are laughing at you instead of at the joke.

Many of thoughts you hold that cause you to be uncertain about yourself are incorrect. However, you believe those thoughts to be true because you have not been trained to be balanced, grounded and observe from the Centre of Your Head.

When you remain in, and observe life from, the Centre of Your Head or Higher Mind, you more clearly see what you are observing without getting engaged or being affected by the noise and emotion of "going to". Viewing life from your observation deck, and not "going to" what is outside of you, allows you greater balance, ease and choice; you no longer need to move back and forth, or work to untangle your attention point and regain your balance.

Understanding this concept and learning not to "go to" is one of the most important concepts you will ever learn. Mastering this skill is required for living in the fifth dimension. Experiencing the higher layers of thought also requires this skill.

How to develop the skill of a focused attention point versus "going to"

When you don't manage your attention point and "go to" what you are looking at or thinking about, something very specific happens. You stop breathing. If you watch a baby, they are present and observing the world from within themselves. As we grow up we learn to "go to" what we are observing. As we continue to grow, we develop a tendency to leave part of ourselves in our past. Many times this is due to a worry that what happened in the past may happen again, so we decide we must be careful, leave some attention in the past and remember. We all do this. However, it can be done in a way that allows you to stay in the present moment.

Most of us are very sloppy breathers. We unconsciously hold our breath, and then our bodies react by taking a big exaggerated (yet shallow) inhalation or exhalation. The skill of breathing was not taught to us as children, so our emotions and thoughts began directing our breath, instead of us intentionally directing it. When we learn how to manage our breathing, we automatically begin to manage our thoughts and emotions: we become more calm, focused, present and managed. How does simply breathing do that?

When you breathe in a continuous fashion, without stopping at either the inhalation or exhalation, you take a huge step in mastering your attention point. You also begin to take greater steps in remembering who you are, putting yourself back together and building a bridge back to Mother–Father–Creator. As you breathe in a continuous, uninterrupted, circular loop, the air begins to move into and out of your lungs in a deeper and fuller manner. The pranic energy (the connection to the Infinite Intelligence of Creator) can then be activated within, around and through you at your command. Intentional creation is expedited. It is this uninterrupted breath that activates and opens your ability to remain in fourth-dimensional present-time. It helps you remain focused upon your intention and your now experience, instead of drifting between third-dimensional past and future.

Success story

. . . so I am listening to Jim's class from last night and painting the walls in the upstairs studio. I am painting while trying to maintain a fifth-dimensional focus, the paint begins dripping off the brush onto the carpet . . . oops . . . (better adjust the focus).

. . . then I stop the recording for lunch. I made a nice salad . . . Happy, Certain, staying in the fifth . . . I am enjoying my yummy lunch, and think I would like a little sprinkle of pepper on my salad. I start to shake away, and have the "ugly" thought that hubby John has put the wrong pepper in the shaker (coarse instead of fine) and I feel angry that the pepper won't come out and I am "wishing the pepper would come out" . . . (yes, it was just a thought, it came so quick to my mind I didn't notice that I was out of the fifth) and lo and behold, the entire content of the shaker was all over my salad . . . the cover had come off. LOL. Oh well. I'd better be careful with these thoughts.

FJ, Alberta, Canada

Remaining in the higher layers of thought is possible with a continuous breath. When we stop breathing at either the top of the inhalation or the bottom of the exhalation, our awareness is also interrupted and sidetracked. Observe the next time your breathing halts. Where were you at that moment? Most likely you were not in present-time, but instead were engulfed by a thought that was in the past or the future. Mastering this skill will allow you to live in the higher layers of thought and experience everything else the Teachers are offering us.

Due to the fact that many of us are such sloppy breathers (and therefore sloppy thinkers and feelers as well), the Teachers share a trick to develop the continuous breath and make it yours. Some people are more successful with this breath if they visualize a loop that follows the breathing pattern. As you inhale, imagine the loop flowing up the front of your body from your first chakra over the top of your head. Then as you exhale, imagine this loop continuing down your back, returning into your first chakra. The loop and the breath don't stop at the top or the bottom, but continue to flow. Imagine the breath beginning to flow down your back slightly before you exhale and the loop beginning to travel up the front of the body slightly before you inhale. If it feels more natural for you to reverse the direction of the loop as you inhale and exhale, do so.

Another visualization that works for some is to create the above loop but have it cross at the heart chakra, forming a figure eight. We call this the Infinity Breath and the advantage is that it draws more of your attention to the heart, which may assist you when you begin to play in the Sanctuary of the Pink Diamond within the Sacred Heart, which you will learn about in the next lesson.

Online resources

Video: Animation of Infinity Breath (00:27)

Meditation to focus attention (16:34)

Question: How do I know if I'm in the fifth dimension? (02:40)

To access the online classroom,
visit www.masteringalchemy.com/book

Part 3

Gifts from the Teachers of Light

Lesson 13

The Sanctuary of the Pink Diamond

"Do you remember?" This was the question I heard over and over again, beginning as a small child. The quiet voice that asked it was always there but just out of reach. No matter the problem or situation I was in, when I got quiet the answer came; the solution appeared. However, as with most of us, life continuously got in the way. In 2001 a small group began to gather to do a piece of work guided by the Teachers of Light. We didn't know of its significance, nor how effective and powerful it would eventually become.

We met each Wednesday night for months and the Elders would give us the next part of a process. One evening they said, "Allow us to guide you Home." The guidance was to enter the Sanctuary of the Pink Diamond within the Sacred Heart. As we sat quietly in this experience, again I heard that voice. This time the question was different: "Now do you remember"? The day was the 11th September 2001.

There is more to your heart centre (the fourth chakra) than what you may have learned from your studies. It's more than a green whirling wheel of energy that contains love for yourself and humanity. The Elders call this centre the Sacred Heart. In Roman Catholic art the Sacred Heart is often depicted as a red human heart with rays of light emanating from it and fire

> ## Success story
>
> I have completed A Course in Mastering Alchemy Level 1. The journey into the Sanctuary of the Pink Diamond within the Sacred Heart, the Teachers there, and the story of Atlantis were so powerful for me. The first time I took the journey, tears streamed down my face as I connected with the animal, elemental and angelic kingdoms that I had so long forgotten. I listen to this journey often and I feel my dear loving friends drawing ever near to me.
>
> *Joyce, Ireland*

flaming out the top. But the Sacred Heart is much more than this. It's not related to any religion, and there is much to be noticed and experienced there. It was within the Sacred Heart that the group I mentioned above met to make a difference.

The Sacred Heart is the second of two still points; the other being the Higher Mind. Like the still point of the Higher Mind, the Sacred Heart is vast. Hold your attention there and you will notice it is quiet and detached from the world around you. Third-dimensional words are inadequate to describe the state of awareness and ease that accompanies living from the Sacred Heart. If I were to attempt to define it, I would start with three words: reverence, unity and communion.

The location of the Sacred Heart

Your Sacred Heart is located to the right and slightly higher than your physical heart. It is not a single, focused point but instead a general area. Some people may experience it slightly to one side or another, slightly higher or lower. Like all the tools and information in this course, there is no right or wrong. What you experience is correct for you and it might evolve as you do.

The Sacred Heart is the anchor point or foundation of the higher-dimensional chakra system, known as the Triads. There are three Triads and you will learn much more about this powerful system in a later lesson.

Take a moment now and notice your Sacred Heart for yourself. Close your eyes, take a breath and feel it there in the centre of your chest. Place your hand upon this area and send it a hello. Notice if you get a hello back. As you continue to put your attention on this Sacred Heart, you will begin to feel it and experience it.

The Sanctuary of the Pink Diamond

There is a special room within your Sacred Heart called the Sanctuary of the Pink Diamond. Much happens here and it is a place we will return to again and again throughout this work. Your ultimate goal is to live and function from this place continuously. It is in this room where you will meet and begin to merge with your Soul, to know all that your Soul knows. You and your Soul Extensions (the parts of your Soul scattered throughout All That Is) come together in this Sanctuary to anchor all you know and have experienced. From here you will journey to the centre of the Earth to expand your connection with Gaia (Mother Earth).

Let's begin by becoming familiar with this inner temple.

Within the centre of this room stands a Pink Diamond. It appears differently to each of us. Some see the Pink Diamond as a multifaceted jewel, others see it as a shard of clear crystal or a rough stone. There is no correct way of experiencing it. You may see nothing. As you spend more time in this room, the appearance of the Pink Diamond will change. As you evolve, so does your awareness within this sanctuary.

Standing before the Pink Diamond is an altar and upon the altar is a flame: a three-fold flame through which the first three Rays of Creation are anchored and activated. This flame holds the essence of Creator that has

Success story

I work at a very successful IT company with a great deal of "noise and drama". When I set my tone in the morning before work and return to the Sanctuary, my day is incredibly calm. I fall out of it sometimes, but I've anchored so much of myself there, it's getting easier to return. And the best thing? My creative ideas seem to be far more successful. I know they're coming from my Temple in my heart when I talk to my Soul.

George, Mexico

remained within you since the Fall of Consciousness. It's the place where you and Creator are one.

As your journey continues you will notice or be introduced to other things upon this altar, all with specific purposes. The surroundings of the room will also evolve and change as you do. Items and meanings will reveal themselves to you as you continue to live in this sacred place.

Before journeying to and entering this sanctuary, it is important that you set the tone of your energy to evolve and experience the power and potential that is offered there. If you were about to enter a holy shrine, you wouldn't burst in with your phone beeping and your mind and mouth racing. You are entering a temple. Pause and take a moment to prepare yourself for a grand inner journey: ground yourself, clear your space with the Rose tool, breathe, move to your Higher Mind. Take your time preparing and your experience will be powerful and productive.

EXERCISE: *The journey to the Sanctuary of the Pink Diamond*

The steps below are outlined in a general way as your experience may differ. In fact I know it will differ and be uniquely yours.

THE SANCTUARY OF THE PINK DIAMOND

1. Take a moment and find your space. Once in a quiet meditative space, within your Octahedron and in the Higher Mind, look toward the back of your Higher Mind and you'll see a door or exit of some sort.

2. Step through that door and you'll notice a spiral staircase moving downward and around your chakras, ending at the back of your fourth chakra.

3. Before you there is a door leading into the Sanctuary. Upon this door is written a word or several words. These words are written in letters that are similar to flames. You wrote these words before you entered this body. They are a message to your self that you will be able to read as you integrate more of your Living Light Body.

4. Pause and be the love that you are before the doors swing open.

5. Step through the doorway and enter the hall of crystals. (Its appearance will be unique to you. The common experience is the glittering of hundreds of crystals of different sizes, shapes and colours.) Notice the colours and energy in the hall. Notice what you hear and sense.

6. Standing before the Pink Diamond, notice what you notice. Notice the visuals, the scents, the sounds. Most of all notice the feeling within you.

7. Allow the experience to unfold and fill you.

8. Exit the Sanctuary in the same way you arrived: slowly, in reverence, calm and curious. Return to your Higher Mind.

This journey sounds wonderful, doesn't it? It is a marvellous experience that holds a great deal of new information and insights for you each time you return. If you can have this experience any time you desire, what would keep you from living here 24/7? Many distractions keep us from doing and having what we desire. Have you ever had a really good workout and said, "I gotta do that every week," then promptly forgotten all about it? Life happened, filling up that delicious space you created at the gym. It was filled up with responsibilities, the demands of others, habits and patterns of life. Noise.

One of the most fundamental understandings any of us can get from these teachings is the value in finding and maintaining a noise-free life. It isn't easy to do. However it can be simple. It requires consistent motivation, determination, focus and commitment. It requires letting go of much that you are familiar with. It isn't something you can do once a weekend and expect to get much benefit from. Everything about this course is designed to support your desire to live a noise- and drama-free life: a life in the Sanctuary of the Pink Diamond.

Online resources

Meditation to experience the smile in the Sacred Heart (17:32)

Question: Is this Sacred Heart the same as in Christianity? (04:00)

Question: How can I be in the Sacred Heart as I walk about my day? (02:09)

To access the online classroom,
visit www.masteringalchemy.com/book

Lesson 14

Clearing the Veil of Ignorance and Forgetfulness

Over the years that I've known the Teachers of Light, I've learned much about their personalities and communication styles. One characteristic they all share is a child-like enthusiasm. Not childish, rather the curiosity, openness and playfulness of a child. They also have the uncanny ability to present a complicated subject or sensitive idea in a way that assists the rational mind into transformation. Several of the transmissions and sessions in this course involve scissors and cardboard, drawing and singing. What could seem like silly distractions are actually very effective strategies to help us get beyond our rationality and into higher awareness. This lesson is such an example.

There is a veil that exists in between the place you open and close your eyes. It interrupts your awareness and creates a pattern that shifts you between two different levels of consciousness. When your eyes are open, you are in one state, when your eyes are closed, you are in another. This veil was put in place at the time of the Fall of Consciousness to keep you in the limited reality of separation.

Archangel Metatron comments on the Veil of Ignorance and Forgetfulness

This veil holds a rigid structure in place that does not allow the DNA software programming and the coding structure of the DNA to actively integrate into the higher-dimensional chakra system necessary to activate aspects of the hypothalamus, medulla oblongata and pineal gland. These aspects are limited by this veil or partition. This partition is also what holds you in third-dimensional linear time (time as a past–present–future loop) and creates major restrictions to knowing yourself.

There are two partitions within the brain. The first partition is the corpus callosum, a coarse tissue that separates the right and left hemispheres. The original purpose of this tissue was to assist both sides of the brain to communicate with each other. With the Fall of Consciousness and aeons of living in the dense third dimension, this capacity has become significantly restricted.

The second is a vertical nonphysical partition that is perpendicular to the corpus callosum and located between the temples on either side of the head. This partition minimizes the function of the hypothalamus, medulla oblongata and pineal gland and it significantly limits the performance of the seventh and eight chakras in the physical experience. This nonphysical partition, or veil, holds each of us in a narrow field of logic, duality and rigid rules.

This veil is an electromagnetic field of energy. As you think thoughts, the thoughts pass through this electromagnetic field and are filtered based upon past memories or future concerns. This filter instantly draws a similar emotion to the thoughts you think based on those past experiences or future beliefs, fears or doubts. However, when you are in a present-time now experience such as amusement, laughter or play, the filter is neutralized. It has no negative past or future concerns, no doubts or fears to draw upon.

When you observe in present-time, the veil is neutralized, allowing observation from the Higher Mind. It's here where this partition or veil is dismantled and reconstructed into its originally intended function: to open your awareness of the multidimensional consciousness from where you have come. Here the hypothalamus, medulla oblongata, pineal gland and seventh and eighth chakras become more engaged, the ninth, tenth and eleventh chakras become accessible. Here, with the use of higher-vibrational Light and colour vibrations, the coarse tissue of the corpus callosum will be altered into a softer electrochemical gel, allowing the right and left hemispheres of the brain to function as originally intended, in full communication with each other.

As you move into your Living Light Body, it's important that this veil be cleared. Doing so allows the higher consciousness that you experience with your eyes closed in meditation to be experienced as you move about your day with your eyes open. This uninterrupted state of fifth- and sixth-dimensional consciousness is a necessary step to allow the Living Light Body to be anchored.

As you merge more deeply with these aspects of who you really are, you begin to alter how you perceive and gather information. You begin to shift your consciousness of yourself. You begin to expand your awareness to better understand yourself and the environment that surrounds you, which is the same environment that limits you.

This is a very necessary awareness to have for your growth. The following exercises will provide you with opportunities to begin to experience present-time from the Centre of Your Head and Higher Mind. Please do the eye exercise first to create a quiet, focused space for the work with the coloured tetrahedron. Just be happy and play. You cannot do any of this wrong.

LESSON 14

EXERCISE: *Eyes open, eyes closed*

This exercise involves keeping your attention point and awareness upon a fixed object that is in front of you in your room. Keep your attention focused upon the object as you slowly close and open your eyes several times in coordination with your breath. As you do this continue to see the object with your eyes closed. To do this successfully you must remain in the Higher Mind or, if that isn't possible yet, in the Centre of Your Head. Notice if you stop breathing, leave your Higher Mind or begin to use effort. If you can remain grounded and present, you will have greater success.

During this exercise your body will relax and your mind will quiet. By doing this exercise you will discover that you can attain a quiet awareness you may not have experienced before. Practising this silly tool as you move through your day will allow you to maintain a higher level of focus and calm.

It's important to continue the breath throughout this exercise.

1. Close your eyes. Using any of the tools you have thus far learned and integrated into your daily practice, take a moment to return to that quiet place of meditation. Be in the fourth or fifth layer of thought and in the Higher Mind. The breath is key here.
2. Become very aware of how you inhale and exhale without changing how you're breathing in any way. Simply observe the breath moving in and out of your lungs.
3. On either an inhalation or exhalation, gently open your eyes, staying behind your eyes and within the Higher Mind. Keep your attention still – don't look around at the room before you.
4. Without leaving your Higher Mind, locate a spot on the floor or wall or an area before you. Choose a spot that is easy to view without moving your head or squinting.

5. View this spot with no thought about it. Don't identify its colour or shape, its reason for being there or anything else about it. Simply observe it.

6. On an inhalation or exhalation, close your eyes and continue to see the spot. Notice if your mind is remembering what it looked like versus seeing it using your inner vision.

7. Coordinating with your breath, breathe your eyes open and again observe the spot. Notice if your attention moved to the spot or if you were able to stay behind your eyes. Don't use your mind to remember the spot.

8. Breathe your eyes closed and see the spot.

9. Repeat steps 7–8 several times until you are able to see the spot with your eyes closed as clearly as with your eyes open. With practice you will be able to do this calmly, with no internal pressure or movement.

10. When you are ready, breathe your eyes open and take a breath. Move your body around and continue your day. Try to stay in this space throughout the day. When you fall out of it, don't beat yourself up.

Abstract intuition

Once you have practised the Eyes Open, Eyes Closed exercise several times and feel able to maintain a calm focus throughout, you can continue to the next two exercises. In addition to clearing the Veil of Forgetfulness and Ignorance, there is another benefit to these exercises. You were born with a spiritual ability called abstract intuition. This ability is held within the sixth chakra and within the pineal gland. Abstract intuition is the ability to imagine three-dimensional shapes in space: spatial awareness. It also is the ability to translate abstract symbols into meaning.

LESSON 14

Abstract intuition is helpful in two ways. The first benefit is that this ability allows you to know the answer without going through all the steps to get there, such as in a math problem. This skill can be a challenge for many bright children in school, especially those children born after 1987. Teachers want children to explain how they arrived at the answer but such children often don't know how they got the answer. Teachers want children to follow the rules and play the game.

The second benefit is that it allows you to recognize and communicate in higher levels of energy and Light language. Humans communicate using dense words and language, while communication in the higher realms, with the Teachers and All That Is, occurs through very finely tuned Light, frequencies, colours, vibrations, formulas and symbols. Turning on and developing your abstract intuition skills will allow greater connection with these Beings of Light and provide you with access to all the information available in those realms.

EXERCISE: *Warming-up exercise*

Before you begin, photocopy the tetrahedron template on page 158, sizing it so that each leg of the tetrahedron is 7.6cm (3 inches) long. Alternatively, download and print the template in the online resources (see below). If you photocopy the template, it's also important to take the time to colour the faces as indicated: red, blue, yellow and violet. Carefully cut out the template, fold along the edges and then tape or glue the tetrahedron together. This is a physical version of the tetrahedron you will be imagining in the final exercise, How to Clear the Veil of Ignorance and Forgetfulness.

This exercise involves first watching your index finger as it moves toward your face, then watching the coloured tetrahedron as it moves toward your face, turning and tumbling. This warm up will focus your clairvoyance before you attempt to clear the Veil of Ignorance and Forgetfulness. It also anchors a visual awareness of the physical tetrahedron and makes it easier for you to create an imaginary one. It establishes a distinction between remembering an image and seeing it in present-time, and sets the stage for seeing with your eyes closed.

As you do this warm up, notice if your rational mind tells you how silly, simple and unimportant this exercise is. It isn't. That's just your rational mind and the opinions of others trying to talk you into believing you are small and unimportant. Don't listen.

Bringing your finger to your nose

1. Take a breath and use your tools to become very quiet and focused. Don't go into a deep meditation; keep it light. Be in the Higher Mind or the Centre of Your Head. Keep your eyes open and see if you can like yourself. You cannot fail at this.

2. Become aware of your right index finger and hold it about 40cm (16 inches) out in front of your nose. This is the starting point.

3. Watching your finger the whole time, slowly move it toward the tip of your nose. Successfully touch the tip of your nose, then, still watching your finger, move it back out to the starting point in front of you. Notice how you begin to go cross-eyed and your finger goes out of focus as it approaches your nose and how it comes back into focus as it gets closer to the starting point.

4. Repeat steps 2–3 several times. Notice your breathing as you're doing this. Keep a smooth, consistent flow of breath.

5. Take a breath and move your body around a bit to loosen it up and release any tension.

Bringing the cardboard tetrahedron to your nose and forehead

1. Return to the quiet and focused space, grounded and in the Higher Mind.

2. Pick up the coloured tetrahedron between the thumb and index finger of your dominant hand. (Use a different finger if that feels

more comfortable.) Hold the tetrahedron about 40cm (16 inches) out in front of your nose.

3.   Observe the point where the blue, red and violet faces of the tetrahedron all come together.

4.   Position the tetrahedron so the violet face is down (parallel to the floor), the blue face is on your right and the red face is on your left. You will see a line or edge of the tetrahedron, with the blue face on the right and the red face on the left. You will also see the point where the blue, red and violet faces all come together.

5.   Watching that point the whole time, slowly move the tetrahedron toward you to touch the tip of your nose, then bring it back out to the point 40cm (16 inches) in front of you.

6.   Bring that point to your nose and back again two more times while you breathe and stay in your Higher Mind. Stop when the tetrahedron is out at the starting point.

7.   Watching it the whole time, slowly move the tetrahedron toward the sixth chakra, being aware of it as it touches your forehead, and then moving it back out to the starting point. Notice that you lose part of the vision of the tetrahedron as it gets closer to your forehead. Also notice your breathing as you do this. The breath is the key to all of this work.

Rotating and tumbling the cardboard tetrahedron

1.   Return to the quiet and focused space, grounded and in the Higher Mind.

2.   Position the coloured tetrahedron out in front of you again. Hold it in such a way that you can rotate it and position it with the blue face on your right and the red face on your left.

3.   Slowly rotate the tetrahedron to the right, being conscious of what you're watching. The blue face will begin to disappear as the red face comes into full view. Then the yellow face will come

into your awareness, then into full view. Next the blue face will come back into your awareness, then into full view. Continue to rotate the tetrahedron and watch the motion of the faces as they come into your awareness and then into view.

4. Now start to rotate the tetrahedron away from you, rotating from it top to bottom instead of from right to left. The violet face will come into view, then the yellow, red and blue faces.

5. Notice that the tetrahedron rolls both ways: away from itself and to the right. (It can rotate in all directions but those are the two directions we're playing with right now.)

6. Take a breath and move your body around a bit to loosen it up and release any tension.

Playing with the cardboard tetrahedron, eyes opened, then closed

1. Return to the quiet and focused space, grounded and in the Higher Mind.

2. With your eyes open, position the coloured tetrahedron so the violet face is down, the blue face is on your right and the red face is on your left. Slowly rotate the tetrahedron to the right, watching it move, seeing the red face come fully into view, then the yellow face, then the blue face. Just observe it without trying to remember what face is where.

3. Stop the rotation on the line between the red and blue faces and see the tetrahedron very clearly out in front of you.

4. Breathe your eyes closed, continuing to see the tetrahedron between your fingers right out in front of you. See the blue on the right and the red on the left. Be aware that you're holding the tetrahedron in your physical hand. With your eyes closed, see it in your hand, the blue on the right and the red on the left.

5. Distinguish between seeing and remembering. Are you remembering an image from just a moment ago when you had

your eyes open, or are you looking at the tetrahedron right now in present-time? If you're remembering, just tell yourself to see it; it's sitting right there in front of you; it has not moved. If you need to open your eyes to see it, open your eyes, see it and then close your eyes and continue to see it. Be amused. You cannot do this wrong. Just the concept of seeing versus remembering is a very big piece of the veil that keeps you stuck in forgetfulness and ignorance.

6.   Notice if you stopped breathing and take a deliberate, conscious breath.

7.   Breathe your eyes open and watch as you slowly rotate the tetrahedron in any direction.

8.   Bring the tetrahedron to your forehead and back.

9.   Breathe and rotate the tetrahedron so the red face is on your right and the yellow face on your left. Then, seeing, feeling and watching the tetrahedron, very slowly move it toward your forehead, let it touch your forehead, and then move it back out again. Keep breathing the whole time.

10.   Breathe your eyes closed.

11.   See the tetrahedron very clearly with your eyes closed (red face on the right, yellow face on the left). With your eyes closed, using your sensory perception, see, feel and watch the tetrahedron again as you move it toward your forehead. Let it touch your forehead and then move it back out again.

12.   Do this once more. With your eyes closed, see the red face and the yellow face. Be completely aware of where the tetrahedron is. Your hand helps you know where it is. As it comes closer to your forehead, expect it to touch your forehead. See it, feel it.

13.   Still with your eyes closed, raise your hand so the tetrahedron begins to be above you. You should have a sense of looking up and seeing the violet face of the bottom of the tetrahedron. Then

slowly lower the tetrahedron and watch it shift position. See the red face on the right and the yellow face on the left. Be aware of your breath.

14. Breathe your eyes open. See the tetrahedron. Validate yourself and pat yourself on the back. Smile.

Success story

As you know I'm a pretty rational analyser kind of guy. So when we did this lesson, I was concerned about doing it right. It made no sense to me the first time but on the third time I realized my body was relaxed and my breathing consistent. I just followed along and felt like I was in a fun kindergarten class instead of my usual chemistry class. The cool thing is, a few days later at work, I knew the solution to a computer issue without even thinking hard about it. I'm glad I stuck with it.

Brian G, Minnesota, USA

EXERCISE: *How to clear the Veil of Ignorance and Forgetfulness*

1. Take a breath and use your tools to become very quiet and focused. Be in the Higher Mind.

2. With your eyes closed, let an imaginary tetrahedron appear in your physical, dominant hand. Raise your hand up until it's about 40 cm (16 inches) out in front of your forehead. Allow the imaginary tetrahedron to appear between your fingers.

3. Notice the position of the colours and, if necessary, rotate the tetrahedron so the red face is on the right, the yellow face is on the left and the violet face is on the bottom. Do not think that position. Direct your creation. Take your hand away and let the tetrahedron float in front of you.

4. Bring the imaginary tetrahedron to your forehead and back, watching it the whole time. Move it so it touches your forehead. Feel the point as it touches your forehead. Then move it back out to the point in front of you. Do this a few times. If you cannot see, you do not think you can see, or you think you do not know what to do, that's your rational mind engaging with the Veil of Forgetfulness. Just pretend.

5. With your eyes still closed, see the tetrahedron floating out in front of you.

6. Very intentionally, rotate and tumble the tetrahedron as you did in the warm-up exercise above, watching it as it turns.

7. Breathing is key here. You are disrupting an electromagnetic field by playing without doubt or fear of failure. Be happy. Pat yourself on the back. Whether you think it's working or not, it's working. Notice if you're thinking, "I'm not doing it right," "I didn't get it," or "I didn't see it." That's the rational mind wanting to lock this veil into place. If you're holding any of those thoughts, don't argue with them. Just let them go. You are making the veil go away. Be happy.

8. Dissolve the tetrahedron. With your eyes still closed, take a breath and relax your body.

9. Now create the tetrahedron out in front of you again and rotate it so you see the violet face is on the bottom, parallel to the floor, and the red face is facing you (which means the blue face is on the right, and the yellow face is on the left, both out of view).

10. Bring the tetrahedron forward and as it reaches your forehead, allow it to pass right through into the Centre of Your Head and let it sit there. Watch from the Higher Mind. Notice the sensations and keep breathing as you do this. (Breathing is really important right here.) It's as if your eyes cross and then follow the tetrahedron as it moves backward. You might even have

a sensation that your physical eyes are looking inward. There may be a pressure, there may be sound changes, there may be all kinds of things; no problem, just be amused. Notice if there is a pressure in your chest, or if your breathing wants to change. None of that is a problem.

11. Give the command for the tetrahedron to move back out, and watch as the tetrahedron moves through the sixth chakra and out of your forehead, seeing the red face moving away from you, back to the point out in front of you.

12. Repeat steps 10–11 twice more. Have fun and remember to breathe. Take a deep breath, move your shoulders and body around. Relax and like yourself.

Expect nothing. This exercise has no value to the rational mind. This is a silly exercise to the rational mind. Outside of the rational mind, however, you are rearranging things you have forgotten on a very large scale. You are interrupting a massive electromagnetic field of consciousness, or rather, unconsciousness.

Online resources

Eyes Open, Eyes Closed meditation (20:16)

PDF: Cut-out tetrahedron

Warm-up meditation to practise with the tetrahedron (16:21)

To access the online classroom,
visit www.masteringalchemy.com/book

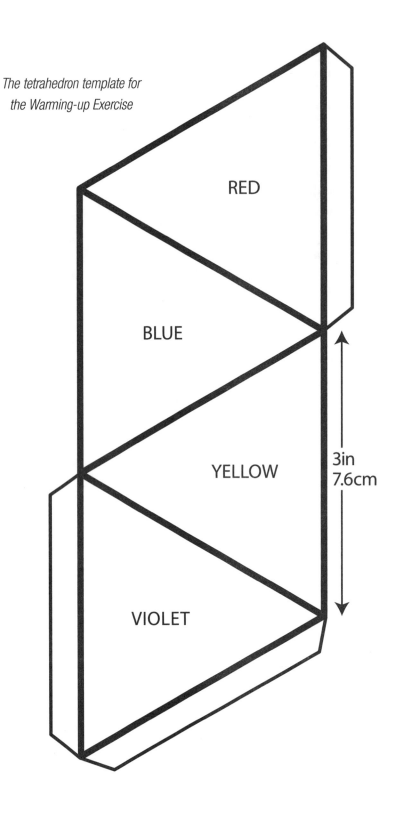

The tetrahedron template for the Warming-up Exercise

RED

BLUE

YELLOW

VIOLET

3in
7.6cm

Lesson 15

The Rays of Creation

Meeting with the Elders within the sleep space and later during the conscious daytime walking-around space, many gifts were given, many tools and strategies. In the beginning I didn't know the greater purpose or direction of those gifts. Although effective and powerful, I thought the transmissions were random and unconnected. At the completion of the Living Light Body lessons, I saw, in retrospect, that nothing was random and all the energetics were purposely designed to bring humanity and all in form into the higher levels of awareness and Light.

Success story

I am *so* excited! I've had a trip on my mind for a few weeks and just put it into the fifth Ray as a possibility. The other night it became available so I made a triangle of Bolivia, Personal Growth and Happy-Laughter-Fun and anchored it in the fourth Ray.

The *next* day funds became available! The timing of the trip was perfect and a perfect travel partner became available. Why am I surprised? I know I can do these things but it still amazes me when it happens. Thanks for being there for me. I love the play!

BF, California, USA

The remaining lessons contain significant highlights from those many years of conversations. When practised these lessons will bring you to a place of experiencing who you are in the higher realms. These gifts can only be accessed and experienced when one is in a fifth- or higher-dimensional state of awareness. This is why building the platform to receive is so important.

I am presenting these lessons in the same order they were presented to me. Throughout these lessons you will find supplementary online resources, including audio recordings, excerpts from conversations and videos, that will allow you to further explore these energetics.

Understanding the Rays of Creation

Reading what channellers have written about the rays of light and listening to their words, I found inconsistencies. How could one "master" say the first ray is white, directed by Archangel Gabriel, but another say it's red and part of Archangel Michael's job? I needed answers. When I met with Archangel Uriel I had a simple request: "Please give me a neat spreadsheet detailing the 12 rays of light, their colours, purpose and the Master in charge of each." Uriel smiled.

The Rays of Creation are applications used in the creation process. They are invoked and used when one is in a higher level of awareness; the rays of light are used when one is in a denser third-dimensional state. Both are extremely useful for the corresponding level of awareness. On this particular path, we are moving toward living in the higher dimensions, therefore the Rays of Creation are most effective for us. We have access to each Ray and its power when we are in a fourth- or fifth- (or higher-) dimensional awareness. In other words, when we are arguing and noisy in the third dimension, the Rays of Creation are not available to us. They are not taken from us when we are in the third-dimensional noise; we are not a vibrational match to them so we are unable to access them.

The Rays of Creation have no Archangel or Ascended Master related to them, nor do they have specific colours or sounds assigned. The Rays are vast and fluid in their application. They are numbered simply for the understanding of our rational mind. If you need to see them as colours, please assign whatever colours resonate with you.

As you may remember from Lesson 5, during the Fall of Consciousness the Rays were given to the creator gods to assist them in uplifting themselves and getting themselves out of the uncomfortable situations they found themselves in. The Rays were given to bring the creator gods back to the Light of Creator. Unfortunately the mutations created by the creator gods were multiplying too rapidly for the creator gods to turn the situation around quickly enough. One after another the Rays were given to the creator gods, but to no avail. Today we are doing what wasn't possible then.

The first Ray of Creation

This was the first Ray given to assist the creators gods. Its energetic was the "Will of Creator" and it was designed as the first step in any creation, to set the energy to match that of Creator. In this way the creations would only be created in Creator's Light. Today you can use the first Ray to initiate any of your creations or to dismantle projects.

EXERCISE: *How to call upon the first Ray of Creation*

1. Using any of the tools you have thus far learned and integrated into your daily practice, close your eyes and take a moment to return to that quiet place of meditation.
2. Sit in the Sanctuary of the Pink Diamond within the Sacred Heart.
3. Choose your project and "see" it before you. See as much detail as you can without engaging the rational mind.

4. In your own way, call the first Ray of Creation into your creation. Imagine it in any way you enjoy.

5. Watch as this Ray affects and fulfils your creation both in this meditation and later as it begins to unfold in your life.

The second Ray of Creation

Creator gave this Ray to the creator gods (and us) to step energy up and step energy down. Just as a rheostat (a variable resistor for changing the resistance of an electrical circuit) is used to regulate the amount of light in a room, this Ray adjusts the energy of your creation to better match the outcome you desire. I've watched people use this Ray in uncomfortable or out-of-control situations to successfully tone them down. I've observed others use this Ray to inject excitement and step-up enthusiasm for success.

The second Ray of Creation is also the origin of all colour, which is a tool that provides expansive opportunity within creation.

The third Ray of Creation

The third Ray is the dynamic engine of creation. It provides movement and the electricity, magnetics, electromagnetism and adhesion that moves and holds creations together. Within the third Ray lies the impetus to move the Will of Creator into your creation.

The fourth, fifth and sixth Rays of Creation

Throughout this course you will work and play a great deal with this set of Rays. These three Rays combine to make a very effective tool that you already use every day, in every creation. Once you become familiar with these Rays, you will recognize how often you currently use them (unconsciously) for practical daily situations. You call upon these three Rays when designing a dinner party, deciding which product to purchase or choosing a route to take to work. You call upon these Rays at work, in relationships and for your personal goals. They are how you create rigid patterns that are not supportive, and also how you create structures that are very supportive.

As you begin to play with these Rays consciously and intentionally, the ability to rearrange every emotion, every thought, every belief you experience becomes available to you. The fourth, fifth and sixth Rays give you access to re-creating yourself from the inside out.

Together these three Rays allow you to loosen up, dismantle and release personal limitations. The exercise below is very simple and graphic example of how these Rays can be used together for this purpose. If you prefer to imagine the Rays as beams of light, floors in a building or some other creative image, please do so. You can't do this incorrectly. It isn't possible.

EXERCISE: *How to use the fourth, fifth and sixth Rays to dismantle a personal limitation*

1. Find a word or concept that you know isn't serving you in your third-dimensional walking-around life. Let's use the word "Isolation" as an example. This word is very dense and anchored in the third dimension. When experiencing it, it can feel heavy, dark and limiting.

2. Imagine three tables of progressively greater heights. The fourth Ray is the lowest table, the fifth Ray is the middle table and the sixth Ray is the tallest table

3. Place your word upon the lowest table (the fourth Ray). The word will begin to loosen up energetically so you can dismantle it. To consciously recognize the function of the fourth Ray is one of the biggest steps you can take to create your own personal freedom. The simple purpose of the fourth Ray is to

hold a concept/energy firmly in place. It can also release what is currently being held firmly in place. Using our example, Isolation is made up of a number of other thoughts and emotions that have resulted in a withdrawal from engagement with others. This word may hold components such as fear, resentment, jealousy or anger. It's the fourth Ray that holds Isolation in place in your life. Isolation is a choice, albeit unconscious, based on its components. Once you understand how you have unconsciously created this experience you have the choice to have the fifth Ray loosen up what you have previously locked in place.

4. The fifth Ray is the workbench where you can pull apart the limitation and discern what parts you'd like to keep and what you'd like to be free of. Place your word upon the middle table (the fifth Ray) and ask, "What other words or aspects are connected to this?" Using our example, you'll see/sense aspects such as alone, lonely, me-time, silence, jealousy and withdrawal.

5. Determine which of these aspects don't benefit you and which you'd like to keep. (For example, "Silence is good. I'd like to be free of jealousy.") There may be many, or only one.

6. Move the aspects to be released to the tallest table (the sixth Ray). Here the aspects you don't want to keep will dissipate and disappear.

7. Bring the new combination of words down into the fourth Ray and determine if the new combination of energies now works for you and feels complete. You may need to move your word up and down from the fourth to the sixth Ray several times before you get it to a point that you fully enjoy. Be patient with yourself.

8. Return to this project a few days later to check in on it and see if it is still an aspect you'd like to keep in your life. You may return to the project as many times as you like to make it yours.

After using the fourth, fifth and sixth Rays for dismantling limitations, you may recognize that you already use this tool in your creation projects. The process is the same, only in reverse. Begin simply until you get familiar with the process. Instead of creating a new job or relationship, begin with a new restaurant or piece of clothing. Bring it from the sixth Ray and place it upon your workbench (the fifth Ray) to pull apart and really fine-tune. With amusement and neutrality, get it exactly the way you desire it and then bring it into the fourth Ray and finally into your life. Don't let your rational mind get involved in this. It will try to figure out how to make it happen and what to avoid. Fear and doubt might get in the way. This process is a feeling, a fun, aligned way to get a creation rolling. Don't think . . . play.

Return to your creation project a few days later to fine-tune it to the present moment. Much has occurred in your third-dimensional life that might affect the desire. What was a fondue restaurant yesterday is now refined as a Thai restaurant today as you discover dairy doesn't sit well for you.

The Elders were very clear that using the fourth, fifth and sixth Rays while in an aligned space of amused, neutral and curious, in the fourth or a higher layer of thought, is a most powerful way to dismantle, create and re-create.

Online resources

Question: Can I use the Rays to disassemble fear? (03:45)

Question: Can I use these Rays for my work environment? (02:53)

To access the online classroom,
visit www.masteringalchemy.com/book

Lesson 16

Activating your higher-dimensional chakra system

When Ascended Master Kuthumi first spoke about the Triads, it was with absolute enthusiasm and awe. He said it had been expected that this energetic would not be made available until mass consciousness expanded into the fullness of the fifth dimension. It had been thought that humanity would not have evolved enough to receive this gift. However, all that changed, he told me, when you and others like you came along. And by "you" Kuthumi is referring both to *you* – the person holding this book and reading these words, as well as the community of humans who came here to make a difference.

While these Triads are made available to all, not all are able to hear or receive the information. Kuthumi was ecstatic about being asked to teach this tool. It's not being taught in many places of All That Is and we have been asked to integrate it into this path by the Archangels. This gift provides phenomenal opportunities and changes everything by opening the multidimensional realms to each of us.

The Triads are your new higher-dimensional chakra system. They open an opportunity for you to create a oneness with the Unified Field and the Infinite Intelligence of Creator that has not been available until now. The Triads open avenues of consciousness, knowledge and wisdom that you have never before accessed.

The three Triads

There are three Triads. The first Triad is composed of three centres: the fourth chakra, the thymus centre (the Sacred Heart) and the fifth chakra. When engaged and set to spin as one, these three centres begin to operate as a single unit. Activating this first Triad allows you to expand into and utilize the second and third Triads. The first Triad engages a level of awareness that allows you to open the Sacred Heart and your connection to Creator.

The second Triad is also comprised of three centres: the sixth chakra, the pineal gland and the dormant aspects of the brain that are held in the medulla oblongata. Spinning these three centres in resonance with each other creates access to the nonphysical and brings it into the physical. It reconfigures our wiring to allow for a conceptual understanding of the higher dimensions. It activates additional portions of the brain and alters the neuron messaging system. It also changes the electrochemical functions in the cells.

The third Triad is made up of the seventh chakra, the eighth chakra and the Soul Star. The eighth chakra is located about 20–25cm (8–10 inches) above the top of your head. The Soul Star is not in alignment with the chakras, but positioned above the eighth chakra and slightly off to the left side of the column of chakras. This Triad interfaces with All That Is. It also organizes the nonphysical so it can be drawn into the second Triad, simultaneously allowing for multiple realms of understanding.

The third Triad can access the Universal Mind of Creator, within the Unified Field you are now creating. We will play in this third Triad but it won't be accessible until the first and second Triads are turned on and brought into a rhythmic flow that is consciously active all the time. Activating and generating this spin mechanism in the first two Triads takes some time and practice. It is not something that just happens because you intend it. A certain level of love, Light and attention must first be created in the resonance of the first two Triads.

When the three Triads begin to spin in unison, vibrating as one, a very broad opening of consciousness is created. As they spin, the Triads continue to remain distinct and do not merge, but instead operate in harmony with each other.

As you activate and work with the Triads, you will begin to establish a stability that opens access to the Unified Field and All That Is. At the same time, your third-dimensional mind will start to operate less intensely and less argumentatively, and your Higher Mind will blend much more fully into the first Triad, where you think with the heart and act with the Higher Mind.

The three Triads operate very differently from anything you have experienced to date. As you work with them, various levels of Love will guide the process from outside of your current awareness, and the third dimension will begin to fall away more quickly.

What is "spin"?

Spin is a radiance of light. It begins to glow as the light is amplified and it has a vibration. This radiance creates a balance within itself.

As I mentioned in Lesson 10, the instruction to "spin" does not imply a particular direction. There's no right or wrong way of experiencing the Triads. If you give the Triads the command to "spin", they will begin to spin, creating vortexes of energy that will move into a harmonic resonance all by themselves.

As the three Triads spin in harmony with each other, they create a vibrational resonance that makes information available from different layers of understanding, different realms, different strata of consciousness itself. You will begin to have awareness of new concepts. You may have a clear knowing and then realize, "I don't know where that came from!" And yet you were fully knowledgeable about what you just said. Allow this.

How your chakras are affected by the Triads

As Kuthumi mentions (see below), we have all done our studies and are familiar with the traditional chakra system. As you activate and practise the Triads regularly and consistently, they will affect the lower three chakras of the physical body. These lower three chakras remain important as a way to maintain the physical body, but they have very different purposes as you move into the fifth dimension. The density, duality, linear time, reaction and conditionality of the third dimension influence everything we experience, including our bodies. But it is our lower three chakras that have experienced the greatest effect. A rebalancing into wellbeing takes place in the lower three chakras as we activate and place awareness on the Triads.

The generally accepted teachings about the first chakra are that it is responsible for the survival of the physical body. This is understandable due to the challenging evolution of the human species. This, however, was not the original intention. The original intention of the first chakra was the wellbeing and creation of joy in the physical body. But many distortions came into being with the Fall of Consciousness and the creation of separation.

In a world where survival and fear was the main event, wellbeing was forgotten. Another casualty of this separation was the significant damage experienced by the ego, which lives in the first chakra. In order to keep you safe, the ego's role shifted from wellbeing to survival. With survival becoming the ego's overriding attention point, the ego deteriorated into a reactionary state of consciousness. The purpose of the rational mind also became fixated on survival, causing a deterioration of the brain's full function and the forgetting of pathways to higher consciousness.

With the activation of the Triads and the building of the platforms to step out of the limitations of the third dimension, the lower three chakras can now be reconfigured. This will happen through a number of steps at different points of your evolution.

Many people see the chakras as discs that open in a manner similar to a camera lens. When restored to their original health and purpose, however, the chakras become spherical in shape and significantly more functional. Until now the lower three chakras have operated independently from each other. When we activate the Triads these lower three chakras begin to operate in sync with the heart centre in the Triad, thus creating opportunity for wellbeing throughout all levels of your being. Over time this alignment will begin to operate very efficiently and the individual operating mechanisms of each chakra will be drawn into the first Triad so that thoughts begins to emanate from the heart, drawing wisdom from the Soul.

The lower three chakras in the fifth dimension

Living in the fifth dimension includes unconditionality, circular and simultaneous time and nonreactive choice. Therefore the jobs of our chakras reflect those higher energies and respond very differently.

The first chakra in the fifth dimension

The concept of "safety" doesn't exist in the fifth dimension because there is nothing that is unsafe. There are no survival needs because your physical body doesn't hold fear of death or threat. Death is just another chapter in our adventure as a spirit. In the higher dimensions the first chakra's purpose is wellbeing. This level of wellbeing keeps us physically, emotionally and mentally balanced and in alignment.

In the fifth dimension the ego is, likewise, better balanced. It doesn't compete or push and shove, instead it is like a wise mentor who points you in new expansive directions. The ego's purpose is to give you little challenges along your path so you may better refine your abilities and perspectives in order to grow and evolve yourself. Its job is to help you step up to higher and finer platforms and become who you came here to be.

The second chakra in the fifth dimension

When the first chakra is functioning in survival, the second chakra experiences dense, heavy emotions such as rage, resentment, jealousy, guilt and blame. However when the first chakra is functioning in wellbeing, the second chakra has a different job: creation. In the higher dimensions the second chakra is a creative energy centre. This is where the inspiration and wellbeing that is thought in the first chakra expands into passion and begins to come into fruition. In the fifth dimension this chakra contains the creative passion that empowers your desires and intentions.

The third chakra in the fifth dimension

In the fifth dimension the third chakra has the freedom and room to express itself, instead of being dominated by power, control, judgement and resistance. The third chakra provides the fuel and ignition for the second chakra's desires to manifest. Competition is replaced by cooperation and limitless potential is available.

Spinning the Triads

As spinning the Triads becomes a part of your daily practice, big changes occur in your lower three chakras. Your first chakra begins to vibrate in wellbeing. As this energy moves into the second chakra it activates a state of passion and creative expression. This then moves into the third chakra where it propels the creative energy of wellbeing into the heart to further engage with the nonphysical consciousness being drawn from the third Triad, therefore manifesting the creative experience you intend.

This spin mechanism, as Kuthumi calls it, offers us the possibility to align, becoming one with the Unified Field and All That Is. This allows you the ability to create in alignment with Creator. Congratulations!

LESSON 16

Ascended Master Kuthumi introduces the Triads

Greetings! It is I, Kuthumi. I am very honoured to be here with you today to present to you this body of work that was gifted to us by the Godhead – the higher realms of creation. We in the Archangelic realms were not expecting you to be so prepared this early in our project to receive this energetic. It is a gift and a dispensation that has been granted to the Earth plane at this time, and it will enhance your ability to use the Rays in a very precise way. You are important and this event is remarkable.

The Triads will enable you to maintain levels of consciousness and interface those higher levels of consciousness within your physical form. You are co-creating an environment to bring physical form into an entirely elevated state of being. You are creating the mechanism by which the density and rigidity that holds humanity in bonds can be dismissed, and yet the physical experience can be maintained in fluid harmonious states.

All of you have studied long enough, done various modalities of healing and are very aware of your chakra system. My intention today is to bring a new focus into your awareness concerning your higher-dimensional chakra system. You're still going to maintain the use of those first three chakras you know of because they are important to you as a being who is embodied in a physical structure.

The three Triads are designed to allow you to operate in the physical form, while maintaining a higher state of awareness. This state of awareness is one which you are now beginning to recognize as available to you. To do this we must activate these three Triad centres. It is the platform from which everything is based. The first Triad sets up a vibratory level that allows you to expand your awareness of your heart and your Sacred Heart.

It brings into play your throat chakra, where you are able to speak and to create – not only from the status of your personal will, but with the Unity and Will of Creator.

What these centres are designed to do is to take Light energy – Light frequencies from the higher realms – from Source, and begin to use it in such a way as it begins to actually affect the way in which your thought system performs and is engaged.

There will no longer be great variance in your experience if you will use this tool. You will not have the emotional highs, the emotional lows. You will resonate in the Unified Field in a very real way in your physical body. It will open your physicality to a state of unlimited potential that is not available until this field is used and integrated.

This tool cannot be integrated fully into all parts of you without some attention. It is not a magic wand. It takes your intention and your attention to integrate it and to make it usable. You cannot access it occasionally and fully integrate it – once a week, once a month, whenever it crosses your mind. You must develop a regular daily discipline at first to set the energy and to open the physicality to the Field. Once you have done that, it requires very little of your energy to activate it and to immerse yourself in it. This tool opens a realm of unlimited potential and application that is not available without it, because you still have your physicality.

These Triads will allow you not only to be part of that expansion of human consciousness into the fifth dimension, but also lead it. You are demonstrating it. And consequently the vibrational capacity that you hold, and will hold, because of these Triads, will be remarkable in terms of the evolution of all of mass consciousness. Although they have a great deal of importance, as we play with them, they are just another aspect of this path that we're walking, this evolutionary path that we're playing upon. The path to the Light Body.

Online resources

Meditation to activate your higher-dimensional chakra system (22:47)

Conversation between Jim and Roxane: What is Light? (09:21)

Question: I feel the Triads spinning all at once, is it better to spin them one by one? (01:32)

To access the online classroom,
visit www.masteringalchemy.com/book

Lesson 17

Thought Strings

As we each grow there is a sequence to our evolution. Today the vast majority of people in the world walk around unconscious of being unconscious. They see the world as it is, often hoping for more but settling for what they wake up to each morning. They are unconscious of what is possible. The next step in this evolutionary sequence is the most important and the most challenging. It is becoming consciousness of being unconscious. In other words, becoming aware of the areas where we have been unconscious. Referring to this next evolutionary step, Ascended Master Kuthumi once said, "The longest part of the journey is from the third to the fifth dimension."

What makes this next step challenging is that for years we have avoided, denied and rejected many of the thoughts and emotions we experienced but believed we could not deal with. We have hidden away our feelings, fears and rejections, hopefully never again to be seen or felt. We have run from uncomfortable experiences and tried to avoid being seen by others. This is the baggage that must now be identified and released so that we may travel upon this journey. And this is our greatest fear.

Fear is an internal experience of giving away our personal power to an external world, often unknown and unseen. In this context fear can be defined as False Evidence Appearing Real: the beliefs, thoughts, feelings and concepts that don't feel aligned with who we believe ourselves to be. These thoughts and emotions become problematic not for what we think they are but because we do not have an understanding or structure to identify, examine and remove them after the original experience occurs.

You now have a general understanding of the fourth, fifth and sixth Rays of Creation as a structure to observe, rearrange and eliminate patterns that

Success story

A few months ago my boyfriend left me after a miscarriage. I had not quite digested the miscarriage when he left, so this pushed me into emotional turmoil. I have no family or close friends for support, which didn't make it easier.

After a while he wanted to meet and talk but I rejected him twice. The emotional turmoil did not get better, even after a month of prayer and some additional energetic work. When he appeared in my dreams nightly for a week I knew I had to face him to end the pain.

In preparation I used the triangles and the Thought Strings to manifest a pleasant and harmonious meeting. It worked beautifully! We had a nice balanced conversation. I felt incredibly light and relieved. I was amazed how the tools worked and gave me a real energy boost.

But! A few days later I started having doubts, felt energetically heavy and confused. Today he called and I agreed to see him despite the uncomfortable feelings and nervousness. So I prepared. I anchored myself very firmly in my Octahedron. I filled my sphere around the Octahedron with Love and Light and I invited the Teachers to stay with me to keep me and my field clear so as not to be affected by his energy.

Honestly, it took me a while after the meeting to realize what had happened. I did not feel emotional or nervous when chatting with him. He even appeared like a different person to me. I was so clear, neutral and balanced and I saw him as the pained person he is.

Wow! Now I know how it is not to feel other people's feelings! Thanks!

ML, United Kingdom

make you uncomfortable. Because of this you also have the ability to allow many of these uncomfortable patterns to come to the surface to be released. Sometimes, however, you can identify the memory and circumstance but cannot quite put the pieces together to let go of the situation.

Many times what you think happened is correct; however your conclusion or belief about the situation has missing pieces. Far too often we go to blame or guilt and stop listening to or observing the circumstance. The circumstance can be considerably different than our snap conclusion. How many times have you discovered a new truth that makes an old truth incorrect? And with the new truth, the internal fear, tension and judgement instantly dissolve and your body relaxes.

Thought Strings are a valuable application for identifying and eliminating these surfacing patterns. This tool provides better access to the false evidence we assume to be real and allows us to continue to explore without coming to a conclusion too early. Thought Strings allow additional possibilities to come forth. Don't forget, you cannot take this baggage with you on this journey. Engaging this tool allows the baggage to be identified and released without experiencing the emotions and confusion that may be attached.

A tool for identifying and releasing

When the Elders present this gift, they reinforce the teaching that the simplest tool can also be the most transformative. If you approach this tool like a curious child then your success will be profound. Remember, the answer lies where the question is asked. Observe and allow new possibilities and the answer will appear.

This process requires assigning single stream-of-consciousness words to each side of connecting equilateral triangles drawn on paper. The physical act of drawing and viewing the strings of negative thoughts will decharge them. Imagining the triangles in your mind or drawing them on your computer is not as effective. As you draw with your hand, insights and deep understandings occur; much stuck energy is released, objectively and painlessly.

The steps in the exercise below provide an example of releasing an imbalance. Many times we feel the imbalance but have no word for it. As you draw and allow a spontaneous flow of words, your understanding of what the block is will reveal itself to you. When it does, it is possible to then use the Rays or Rose tool to dissolve the block. The Thought String grows organically. There is no correct shape; it moves and forms its own unique configuration of triangles as you work and release. This is not a rational-mind project.

EXERCISE: *How to use Thought Strings to release imbalances*

1. Take a moment to find your space. Be in the Higher Mind.
2. Draw one equilateral triangle on a large piece of paper and focus on your current internal feeling. Take as long as it takes to allow a word or concept to come to you. Any word or concept. Keep it simple.
3. Write the word on any side of that triangle. (Let's start with the word "Irritated" as an example.)
4. Do the same for two more words or concepts. Let them come to you and write them on the other two sides of the triangle. (Private, Intruded Upon.) You now have a triangle holding three energies that are affecting you. (Irritated, Private, and Intruded Upon.)
5. Staying in your Higher Mind, consider which one of those three words seems to have another word or concept connected to it? Draw a new equilateral triangle using the side of the triangle containing your chosen word. (Private.)
6. Allow a word or concept that is related to your chosen word to reveal itself. (Gossip.) Write it on one side of the new triangle.
7. What's another word or concept that pops into your awareness that you can add to the new triangle to complete it? (Vulnerable.)

Write it on the other leg of the triangle. You now have a new triangle that shares a word or concept with the first triangle. (Private, Gossip, Vulnerable.)

8. Staying in your space, which one of any open side seems to have another word or concept connected to it? (Gossip.) Draw a new triangle using the side of the triangle containing that word.

9. Allow a word or concept that's related to the new word to reveal itself. (Rejected.) Write it on one side of the new triangle.

10. What's another word or concept that pops into your awareness that you can add to the new triangle to complete it? (Unattractive.)

11. As the string develops, you can take any word or concept within this string and build new strings from that word. Continue to spontaneously add words and triangles in no particular order or configuration. If a word doesn't appear for one side of a triangle, simply move on and create another. Continue until there are no more words or energies coming into your awareness.

Have fun with this. Be curious and amused. As you create the triangles, notice your energy, thoughts and emotions. This is a nonthinking exercise, meant to move energies out of you to a place where they can be identified and released (the paper).

You may find that tensions, emotions or imbalances come up. That's the energy you're releasing. Take a moment, put down your pencil and find your space again. Using other tools, such as the Rose or Rays, take advantage of this important insight to release another layer of energy. In the next lesson you will learn about the eighth Ray of Creation. This is another powerful method to dismantle the stuck energy you discover.

LESSON 17

Success story

I've had relationship issues my whole life due to childhood abuse (and other things too boring to tell you about). Building and sustaining an intimate relationship has been impossible so I figured I would be alone for the rest of my life. When you asked us to choose a goal I chose "have an intimate relationship".

Drawing the Thought Strings for that goal was fun, revealing, scary and exciting all at the same time. I found a lot of rational-mind interference ("What makes you think you can find a woman when you haven't for 36 years?"). I also had a lot of old emotional patterns come up, which kind of surprised me. As each painful emotion rose in my space, I made a separate string for that emotion. I was working several strings simultaneously. I've been playing here for about a month and it feels like some things are really shifting for me emotionally and mentally. I can't describe it other than "untangled". More and more is coming up and I can feel it leave.

Funny thing is, my friend set me up for a blind date (again!) and although I was nervous, I did okay. I had fun. We laughed and both said we felt at ease. That is huge for me. Huge. *And* when I got home that night, I didn't beat myself up. I love this tool. Thank you.

David, Mexico City, Mexico

A conversation with Archangel Uriel about this tool

Uriel: Greetings! It is I, Uriel.

Jim: Greetings to you!

Uriel: I am present with you today to make a reacquaintance of sorts as it has been some time since I have come in this venue, in this teaching capacity. I am very honoured that you have been persistent in the unfolding of this material. It was unexpected on your part that the timing and the time required would be so long in your time, but I assure you that it was necessary for all of these components energetically to come into play. And you are seeing this very clearly at this time!

I would like to make a comment to you at this time in regards to your theory on Strings of Thought.

Jim: Please.

Uriel: This is a very valuable piece of information that has been transmitted to you, and that you are beginning to use. It is in this teaching that many will be awakened to their massive thinking process and how that creates reality in various forms and in many different complexities and intensities. It is through this string equation that you are developing that many awaken to a desire and an impetus to examine more thoroughly their thoughts.

There is another component to this. It is not just about being aware of what you are thinking and feeling; it is about taking that awareness to another level of understanding and another level of use. It is through this string dynamic that this is very easily and succinctly seen. This alone will bring about a change in the state of consciousness to any who will avail themselves to learn it and to use it.

Here again, I would like to go back to what Metatron so succinctly transmitted to you. He said you would have knowings and you would have information that would come to you that sometimes would seem bizarre. This string dynamic is not bizarre. It is very plainly a usable dynamic that will change many over the course of the next years. It is a tool and an example of the energetics that are at work at this time in your realm and in your own personal evolutionary process. A bridging is energetically occurring so that you might be the vehicle to bring in this information that will be used in these times. But much of it, after the bridging is done, is for the generations to come.

That is not to say that some of these energetics and some of this knowledge cannot be used in the realm in which you operate at this time. You will learn how to bridge the gap, so to speak; you will learn about stepping down energetic patterns so that they can be used in various dimensional conceptual realms. This is to come!

Jim: Yes. I understand.

Uriel: It will not come immediately because there is much groundwork for us to do, just as we have been so diligently working for the last few years of your time. You will be shown how time is altered and expanded to be used in different ways.

Mainly my transmission today is to reacquaint you with my energetic pattern – my presence – and what I have come to present and make available for you. In the next few transmissions, Zadkiel will be the instrumental Being who will come to construct this bridgework that I have spoken of. Zadkiel is a wonderful Being who possesses many energetic patterns that are very easily transmitted to your realm and your state of awareness. Zadkiel will help you to bridge this work with more ease.

Metatron, Michael and Melchizedek are also very dynamic parts of these transmissions – even after the bridgework is done. It is through this triad that the bridgework can be sustained in a very coherent way and not be interfered with or disrupted. They also provide a format for these energetic patterns to be brought in with ease. To continue to reinforce your relationship with this wonderful triad would be to your advantage, energetically. To begin to ask for and merge your energetic with their energetic will be very helpful to you.

I am very pleased that you have been able to make this shift in your awareness and step into this new creative process with

the Strings of Thought. Your personal evolving will accelerate in the coming months, and there will be times when some of these transmissions will seem to you as if they are slow and lagging, because you are desiring much more information. But I assure you that is not the case. Energetically there is a component always that must be integrated fully and completely to raise you to that unseen level where some of the components of your creation begin to change and expand to the degree where the form begins to dissipate.

Using Thought Strings as a tool for creation

Many of us set ourselves great goals and then wonder why they never come into existence. It's because the goal doesn't have a strong enough magnetic field to attract it. Within each goal there are subsets, strategies and components that allow for success. Most goals, however, don't fully connect to those aspects and therefore don't manifest. The Thought String tool is gifted to us to identify and release stuck energy; however, it can also be used to achieve goals.

Use the same method as above, except begin with a goal or desire instead of an imbalance. Within the growing string there is a focused energy or vibration that creates the magnetic field that allows the string (and your goal) to be more fluid and successful. As you spontaneously place the words into triangles and the triangles into strings, hold your attention on those words and triangles of higher-dimensional vibrations. Those higher vibrations become one with the physicality that you walk around in. You begin to shift from "who I am not" into "this is who I am", simultaneously clearing away the third-dimensional reference points and structuring a new set of opportunities.

As you build these triangles and strings, feel the smile in your heart. Do not give your attention to doubt or allow your rational mind to give you the reasons why this will not work. You are simply playing. You're not looking back. You're looking forward. You are building a new framework, an expanded platform from the higher-dimensional awareness – not the third dimension. This process is not new to you; you have been doing this all your life. What is new is that you are beginning to understand the dynamics of the construction from an energetic point of view and redirecting your conscious attention to intentionally create.

The purpose of this exercise is to notice the feelings and new thought considerations that appear as the strings are constructed. Allow your imagination to integrate with the sixth Ray as you build each triangle. Do the construction on the workbench of the fifth Ray. This process eliminates fear, lack and doubt. The result is freedom, a vibration that we are beginning to touch only now.

Make this fun. Do as many as you can . . . and enjoy!

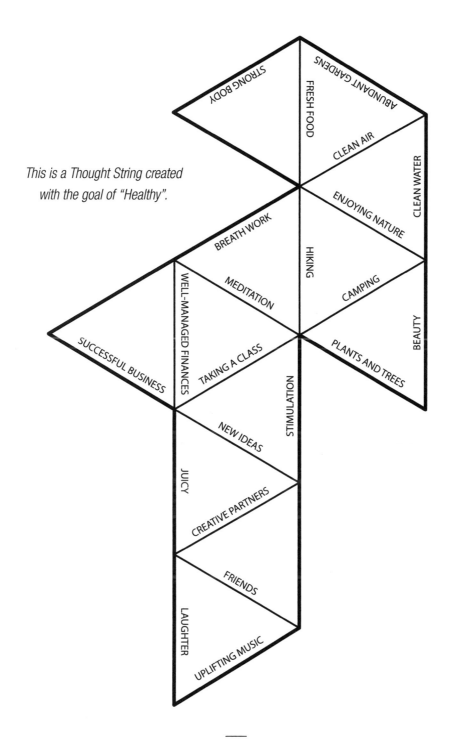

This is a Thought String created with the goal of "Healthy".

Lesson 18

The eighth Ray of Creation

Archangel Zadkiel explains the original purpose of the eighth Ray

The eighth Ray was mainly designed to stabilize and clear energy from beings who were ready to leave the Earth and third-dimensional reality and return to higher realms of existence. These were avatars, teachers, masters and beings from the angelic realms who had come into form for specific purposes to assist or to give service; and who were compromised energetically. They had become compromised because of events or because of taking on heavier than expected energetic genetic material in the physical form. They could not return to Creator when in this state.

Creator decided to create a Ray in which they could clear and reintegrate their original energetic state of being. They might then be able to return to their higher-dimensional reality and not get caught in the karmic wheel that was very much installed on your planet for aeons.

This state of karmic energetics has been lifted to a good degree, and is not so dense. Many who come to give service in these end times are not as apt to take on karmic action. The consciousness is such that even though some are very much installed in the third-dimensional linear ways of thinking

Success story

On Sunday morning I noticed a growth on my dog's eyebrow that appeared suddenly and seemed to get larger throughout the day. Not a big enough problem to go to the pet hospital (very expensive), but enough of a problem for a call to the vet on Monday morning. Sunday night I listened to Lesson 23 (Introduction of the eighth Ray). Monday afternoon I went to my mother's house and mentioned the growth and she said (as she, and I, and others have said a million times), "It's always something, isn't it?" And of course, we always mean it's something bad or inconvenient.

I was thinking about that on my way home and realized how many of those phrases are still in my consciousness: "Life's hard and then you die," "Nothing's sure in life but death and taxes," and so forth. What a wonderful job for the eighth Ray!

I fully expected my dog would need some type of surgery to remove the growth. Throughout the day I was thinking that it would be nice (fourth layer of thought) if surgery could be accomplished without general anaesthesia. No fear or trying, just "wouldn't it be nice . . .". So Monday evening I used the eighth Ray to remove the phrase "It's always something" and all related strings of thought.

Tuesday I went to the vet. The assistant looked at my dog and said, "Yep, it's a growth," then went and got the vet. The vet looked at my dog.

Vet: Yep, it's a growth . . . but she's young to have such a growth. Hmm. Wait a minute. This looks like a tick.

Me: A tick?! I didn't know we had ticks in Alaska.

Vet: Yes, but they're very rare. Has your dog been running in any overhanging brush?

Me: Yes, of course. She's a dog.

So the vet pulls out some huge tweezers and carefully removes the tick. We chat for a moment and then I go out to pay for the visit. The receptionist says, "Oh there's no charge for this visit. See you next time."

Thank you for the Rays of Creation, Jim.

DS, Alaska, USA

and being, there are enough beings who are of higher thought systems. The eighth Ray is still used and needed, but not to the degree it was used in previous times.

When those beings in previous times who were compromised on levels of their being wished to leave the Earth plane, it was required that they access the energetics that are present in the eighth Ray. They were guided to go into isolation in order to access these energetics. Some of these beings even took on long illnesses that resulted in what were perceived, by many, to be death. The death of the body of these beings was perceived as the normal course of events; however, it was not.

After such illness, or time of integration, the physical form was released by these beings through the eighth Ray. They might have spent long periods in states of sleep, or what you would term "coma", in order to allow them to reintegrate higher energetics. So as the body was no longer needed, it was allowed to fall away, or to die. Very few of these avatars or teachers who came in this capacity were able to leave in a state of the physical body being a vibrant vehicle. It was necessary for them to access this eighth Ray in total isolation and shed any part of physical form before returning to their physical state.

As the Christed realm is reinstalled and configured to its original state, this process will not be necessary, and the use of the eighth Ray will change in its configuration as some of the aspects will not be needed. Physical form will not have to deteriorate as in past times.

Today's use of the eighth Ray

The Rose tool was designed to assist in creating and dismantling the third-dimensional patterns we hold and the situation we're in. The fourth, fifth and sixth Rays were given and are used when we are in a fourth- or fifth-dimensional present-time state of consciousness. As humanity evolves into higher levels of awareness, the eighth Ray is available. All of these tools work well and they work best when we are in the corresponding level of awareness.

The eighth Ray is used to move beyond our current physical form and the energies that prevent our return to the higher realms of existence, to Creator. We use the eighth Ray for our spiritual understanding and journey to the Living Light Body. When in that higher level of awareness and sitting in the fifth and higher layers of thought, we may access the eighth Ray. When we are in that state of awareness, the steps and instructions for creation come to us as knowingness and inspiration.

The eighth Ray holds the applications and building blocks for creation. The vibrations of every thought you think and every word you choose are eighth-Ray applications. Words such as "open", "close", "increase", "slow down", "lift" and "stop" are eighth-Ray applications for creation. You use these words and concepts unconsciously all the time. From a third-dimensional point of view, we are not well managed in our moment-to-moment use of these applications. Unconsciously we think thoughts and draw emotions to us that often do not provide desirable results. Have you ever tried to create something when you were angry, upset or preoccupied with an uncomfortable situation? It doesn't work well because you're using the eighth-Ray applications in a dis-organized fashion.

When you are in a fifth-dimensional space of wellbeing, the eighth Ray, in combination with the third Ray, allows you to organize your thoughts and emotions in a smooth harmonious manner by choosing the vibrations (words) to create a desired result. As you become more adept and comfortable in the alignment and use of fifth-dimensional words and platforms, the eighth Ray becomes a precise tool that allows you to dismantle your past unconscious patterns: patterns that create guilt, blame, victimhood, isolation, resentment, etc. These third-dimensional patterns are what prevent our personal ascension. They are unconscious eighth-Ray applications held in misalignment that do not support us. You have the ability to change your past and rearrange your future in this moment with the eighth Ray.

The steps in the following exercise are only a simple example of what is possible.

EXERCISE: *How to work with the eighth Ray*

1. Go within your Sacred Heart and the higher layers of thought, quietly and in reverence. If you've been practising these tools, by now you will be familiar with finding this space of balanced, neutral (uncharged and not engaged) observation.
2. Identify the first word that pops up that represents the energy you would like to remove. Remain neutral and in the higher layers of thought while viewing/sensing this word. If the word holds a charge for you, instead use a simple colour to represent that word. Using colour instead of the word usually allows a more neutral state of observation.
3. With certainty and personal presence, command and call forth the eighth Ray of Creation into your word or colour. Simply observe what transpires. Feel what you feel. Notice what you notice. Know that the Ray is working, even if you notice nothing. You may sense the eighth Ray as a beam of light, a colour or something else. What you sense is uniquely yours.

Return to this exercise again and again. You will begin to experience the anchoring and absorbing, the shift of energetics.

Success story

I love using triangles of words/feelings and the eighth Ray. A few days ago my cat, Spud, escaped outdoors to chase a feral cat that she spotted through a window. Spud is not an outside cat; she is small and she has no front claws to defend herself. When she got out once before, she hid fearfully for hours and would not come to me when I looked for her.

I was upset briefly, worried about her safety and my ability to find her.

I took a breath and created a triangle of my emotions of Fear/Separation/Frustration. I called upon the eighth Ray to replace that triangle with one of Calm/Reunion/Ease. I let that triangle surround my whole body. After only ten minutes of looking for her and calling her name, she came right to me. That never happened before.

The more I use these amazing Rays from the Archangels, the more wonderful my life becomes. Spud and I thank you!

PO, Michigan, USA

A conversation with Archangel Uriel about this tool

Uriel: As you begin to access and work with the eighth Ray, many things begin to happen energetically. In addition to receiving the information in how to work with the many different concepts that are available in the eighth Ray, you begin to take in a whole and rich schematic of frequencies that are composed of light, sound and colour. These frequencies are essential and provide very specific energies that allow you not only to use the concepts more fully and effectively but also allow you to receive them energetically as well as continuously. These energetic schematics begin to be anchored within your own personal energetic system. When you work consciously with the eighth Ray, it is important that you know this and consciously open yourself to receive these energetic templates. Through your conscious awareness you benefit greatly. These energetic templates create states of consciousness that allow you to stay awake and aware of yourself as a creator who has mastery in using all energetic components in the creative realms.

It is through the anchoring of these energetic schematics that this is made possible. There are many schematics that are housed within the eighth Ray. This is the library that Zadkiel spoke of in earlier transmissions. It is not about accessing the information and knowledge that is within this vast library but it is about imprinting the energetics. These are what make the information usable. When you receive and begin to use specific energetic patterns, you then begin to gain experience with them and become adept in their uses. Mastery of these vast energetic resources comes when a certain percentage of them has been absorbed fully within your energetic system. This is an ongoing process that is not to be taken lightly but approached with quiet, reverent openness and received consciously.

There is a huge step in consciousness that occurs as these energetic schematics are absorbed. This state of consciousness is a requirement in entering and using the energetics of the eighth, ninth and tenth Rays effectively.

You will become more aware of the teaching of these Rays in the coming times when you are still, contemplative or in the sleep state. You will have a very aware sense of us guiding you in these times. It will be much more than remembering. It will be an active participation.

Jim: Can we receive this for others to help them more fully understand the Rays?

Uriel: You cannot receive this for another. It is a responsibility that must be taken by the individual. These energetics can only be received when a level of consciousness is available to the individual and certain beginning concepts of the eighth Ray are understood and known. It is then that the energetics begin to be integrated. Once the integration has begun, the state of consciousness begins to open and the imprinting begins. You will be very aware when this starts to take place.

There is a specific process that must be adhered to. You cannot teach this state of consciousness. It must be created by the student through receiving the energetics of certain schematic imprints, just as you have received them at this time.

I will withdraw now for today. Blessings.

Online resources

Conversation about the eighth Ray of Creation (12:04)

To access the online classroom,
visit www.masteringalchemy.com/book

Lesson 19

The Holy Spirit

What do you think of when you hear or read the term "Holy Spirit"? Do Abrahamic religious services and incantations come to mind? Or prayers including mention of the "Father, Son and Holy Ghost"? Or perhaps you draw a blank and you quickly Google it? When Uriel first introduced the Holy Spirit into this course, I had no clue what or who this was. Happily, Uriel was around long before Wikipedia.

Through several conversations with the Teachers of Light, a description unfolded that was unlike what most understand the Holy Spirit to be. The Holy Spirit is the aspect of Creator that creates. The Holy Spirit is the creative essence of Creator. Held within this creative essence are the foundations of the feminine and masculine creative energetics. When used from the consciousness held within the higher dimensions, these energetics become elegant compositions of creation. They have nothing to do with the physical male and female form that we experience in this third-dimensional reality. They do, however, have everything to do with how you express every thought you think and every emotion you experience. Feminine and masculine energetics are expressions of the vibrational forms of any creation.

As you continue to integrate the three Triads into your being they begin to create a Unified Field joined with All That Is. The first Triad opens exponentially, allowing for the seating of the Holy Spirit within the Sacred Heart. In the presence of the Holy Spirit, the Sacred Heart is filled with stillness and reverence. With the presence of the Holy Spirit, your personal will begins to merge with the Will and Power of Creator. It's here, within the reverence of the Sacred Heart, that the creative essence of the feminine and masculine resides.

Your feminine and masculine creative energetics work effortlessly and smoothly when orchestrated within this higher-dimensional alignment. However, as we know all too well, most thoughts and emotions are not generated from this state of balance within the Sacred Heart. Consequently, creations in the physical third-dimensional world of noise and drama can be erratic, emotionally driven and reactionary. Many times creations are not well thought through or purposeful, and therefore the result is not fulfilling. As we begin to step into the fifth-dimensional consciousness, purposeful creations are formulated and brought forth from the presence of the Holy Spirit anchored within the Sacred Heart.

The vastness of the Holy Spirit cannot be understood from our rational mind or limited third-dimensional perspective. However, as you grow to understand how the creative essence of the Holy Spirit unfolds, you begin a journey into this vastness, a vastness that is unimaginable from the third-dimensional point of reference.

How the Holy Spirit creates

From a place of quiet stillness and reverence, the first thought comes forth from the feminine expression of the Holy Spirit. This quiet thought has no structure or form. It begins as a fluid movement within the stillness. This spark of an idea is the initial ignition. Without the first spark of desire, there is no creation. Like all feminine creative energy, this desiring is not concerned with how to construct the outcome; it's simply enjoying the imagining of it. It is unlimited potential, the possibility of all things becoming possible. After the initial spark, the masculine aspect of the Holy Spirit adds structure and form to the fluid possibility. The masculine arranges and solidifies the feminine desire. Without the initial spark of the feminine, the masculine would have no inspiration to respond. Without the masculine, the desires of the feminine would have no way to be brought into the physical. It is a perfect synergistic balance. The structure and definition provided by the masculine allow the feminine to then consider even more possibilities, each of which can be further expanded by the masculine. Thus the creative cycle continues. You'll discover more about this divine creative collaboration in Lesson 25.

The Holy Spirit tetrahedron

Three Teachers of Light have come forth in this course to provide a specific understanding of creating with aspects of the feminine creative energies. Prior to their introduction, however, it is useful to understand a much fuller use of the tetrahedron than you've previously used in dismantling the Veil of Ignorance and Forgetfulness. This stable geometry is a gathering point of awareness within the Sacred Heart. The Great Beings of Light sit with you in communication at this table. Many times the tetrahedron becomes the speaking platform for a merged presentation of these Teachers. This geometry allows them to explain multiple concepts, tools and possibilities, each from their own unique position and awareness. The tetrahedron also allows them to speak from their shared collective perspective, as one unified Teacher.

Today the feminine nature of the Holy Spirit is represented as Anna, Mother Mary and Mary Magdalene. They speak to us as three distinct aspects of the feminine, presenting a multifaceted aspect of the Holy Spirit.

Anna

The mother of Mother Mary, Anna presents the construct of feminine aware-ness as wisdom. She understands diplomacy and appropriateness, always seeking balance. Her role in the team is to stand in quiet observation, gently nudging and guiding the direction of the creation without providing the answer. The answer is your choice as a creator being, no one else's. Anna allows you to move forward on your own without directly interfering.

Mother Mary

Yes, Mary is the mother of Yeshua, but she's also a great deal more. There has been much written about her contribution when she walked the Earth. Her role in this team is as the one who nurtures and guides the creation into flowering. She has the capacity to take the desire and move it to manifestation.

Mary Magdalene

More than just the professed prostitute that organized religion believes her to be, Mary Magdalene introduced herself to us as the excited creator of all possibilities. She radiates unrestricted excitement and enthusiasm. She is the type of person who jumps from the cliff . . . and flies. She is like a passionate teenager who wants everything right now, and has the courage and determination to go after it: she rides a motorcycle, laughs too loud, has pierced her nose and dyes her hair green. Her role in this team is to express unrestricted desire. Mary Magdalene is the project originator, the one with the idea.

An excerpt from a conversation with the Holy Spirit tetrahedron

Mother Mary: **Greetings! It is I, Mother Mary!**
Jim: **Greetings to you, Mother Mary!**
Mother Mary: **I come in a configuration of a tetrahedron to include not only Anna (the matriarch), myself (the mother) and Mary Magdalene (as the essence of the maiden) but also that very important part of all energy that stems from the creative**

realms of Source. And that is the Holy Spirit, which is a feminine expression of the All That Is . . . never separate from the entirety, but an expression within many creative realms.

There is a power that we wish to talk about and draw this collective's attention to. El Morya was very eloquent in expressing the use of power and will in the creative mechanism of the individual expression and the collective expression. There is a power in that expression that relates to that feminine power: the creative mechanism that allows for the movement, the expansion and the unlimited potential of creation to take form. This is not related to any part of form in relationship to gender, or any thought or programming that has thus far been experienced on Earth . . . either from a dominant expression of the masculine, or a dominant expression of the feminine.

It is in relationship to the aspects of thought that you have explored in the various levels of this course. This thought is a balanced, powerful expression of Creator and it is from the perspective of Universal Mind. This has to be understood, because each participant in this collective must be aware of themselves not only as masters and powerful creators – but they have that configuration that is held within the tetrahedron that is in perfection in its balance and its expression. So I will pause here for you to make comments, ask questions so we might continue.

Jim: I understand the expression in terms of the tetrahedron. I can see how this plays through that creative process. I don't think I have a question! It seems to be very clear.

Mother Mary: Let us go to the very beginning expression of Universal Mind of Source, where it is in a very complete and whole expression, and there was no division. It just existed – that Universal Mind. And there was no movement. There was no need for movement or expansion, because it was complete and whole.

In that wholeness there was an exertion or a movement that began to take place. As the movement began to take place, the feminine aspect that was in complete wholeness and unity with the Universal Mind began. The attention was focused, and the movement began from the still point of whole, complete, unified expression. As the movement began, it activated a fluidity that began to extend. The creation and expansion of that still point of Source began to extend into the void. As it did it used a part of Source to create a container to hold that expansion. And that container was a sphere which had no beginning and no end, so that it perfectly exemplified the nature of Source.

As the movement began, attention points were brought to various aspects of the sphere to create more like itself. And eventually the Flower of Life began to grow in that container. It is the perfected image of the divine plan for creation. It is the vehicle that is continually expanding. It is fluid.

As form began to take place, it required a different configuration. And thus, through the Flower of Life, the Metatronic Cube was devised. This contains a masculine influence and structure to hold the power and the fluidity. It contains all of the Platonic solids that allow form to be expressed in various ways. Within this Metatronic expression are the unlimited potential, the fluidity of that aspect of the feminine expression of the divine. This complete balance is an aspect of that universal power that is necessary for a creative momentum to take place in the physical realm, and especially on Earth. It is through that power of balance that the elements then come into play and are made usable in a very directed, yet fluid and unlimited expression.

This power that I speak of is balanced, and it has no division . . . only precise direction and expression. But understand that without this fluid power and this directed expression there would be nothing that exists within the creative realms! There would only be that still point from which all originated, and there was no movement. It just existed!

This divine power is a very important piece in the activation of a Light Body.

We come in this collective expression today in the container of a tetrahedron. Within that tetrahedron is a dimensional frequency that is unlimited and has multiple expressions that allow for the movement and the expansion within the creative mechanism. I come at this time with an individual, simple point that is a minor focal point in this expression. It allows a familiarity with an archetypal image that is prevalent in your society on planet Earth, but is much more if you will expand your awareness into the archetypal images that are being expressed within not only the triadic configuration of the feminine, but extends further into the tetrahedron expression, through the presence of the Holy Spirit that is not only feminine in its expression, but also masculine.

So it takes that unified power, of this expression of Source, to provide the movement, the expansion, the openness and the presence of all of the physical elements, as well as creative containers to hold those expressions. This should not be taken lightly! Understand that within your physical expression of your body, even though it has a gender, within its energetic components, there is no division within that expression energetically.

You are now stepping into a more multidimensional expression of yourself in a body. As the body now begins to alter its vibration and the way in which it is held within certain configurations of form, you are stepping into a more multidimensional expression of yourself while in a physical body. In this expression there is a presence of joy. There is a presence of ecstasy. But the power of these energetics have no spikes to them. There is no feeling of exhilaration and then a falling from that state into lower aspects of the emotions. In this state of complete unity, where there is only the presence of that Undifferentiated Light, the Light of who you are, there is a calm, peaceful, harmonic state. Yet there is this underlying knowing, a feeling if you will, of the quiet power that you as that individual creator possess and can direct at will to create precisely what is wanted in a moment. It is quiet, it is centred and it is known. It does not have to be drawn upon to exist. And it is balanced totally and completely within that harmonious expression, because it is multidimensional in its expression and has no limits, no division and no disruption of any kind.

This has to be integrated and accepted from that level of Universal Mind. It is not understood, nor can it be, if any part of the lower aspects of the consciousness of the body are employed. And I'm speaking of the rational mind.

Jim: Yes.

Mother Mary: This is an energetic configuration that is being seated within the consciousness of the body through the mental/emotional body, and it has to be felt, recognized and allowed. It does not detract from, in any way, the power that is available to you as a creator, but enhances it exponentially so that precision of creation can be had according to the divine plan, where that Undifferentiated Light is applied.

In this movement of the Undifferentiated Light and the creation of it within the body, you begin to experience the power that I am talking about. Then it will be known and felt within the emotions. It is the creative force that you hold within you and have had, to this moment, very little experience with. We are constructing with you. All realms of creation are constructing the Light Body with you, so that its full, unlimited, interdimensional expression in form of the Christos can be exemplified and created by you, each individual and the collective consciousness.

In that experience I am not what you perceived as Mother Mary, as the Magdalene or as Anna. I am being experienced through the Holy Spirit, as that Divine Feminine expression in balance and unity of Source.

A word about "feminine" and "masculine"

When the Teachers of Light describe a style of creating as "feminine" or "masculine" they aren't referring to gender or sex. Due to the limitations of the English language and the current density of humanity, we found this was the most simple way of describing these ways of creating. Both ways of creating are absolutely required for any creation process and both are reflected within the Holy Spirit. The right hand and left hand come together to create a sound of celebration and applause. Both are necessary.

Why do the Archangels and Ascended Masters many times appear as male?

Someone in a programme asked me this question. It's a very good one that has been asked many times, sometimes with a charge, and sometimes simply with curiosity.

Many Archangels and Masters appear with names such Metatron, Uriel, Michael, Kuthumi and El Morya. These are all masculine-sounding names. These Great Beings are often represented in paintings as men – white men. However these Great Beings don't only hold male energy. The countenance humans have assigned them is male because that was what we could relate to at the time. In other words, these dynamic Beings of Light have a masculine expression because, until now, that's all humans could accept.

As explained in Lesson 5, at the time of the Fall of Consciousness it was necessary to create an energetic field or structure to hold and prevent the Earth from falling into complete elimination. That structure became known as the third dimension, and it was very dense, conditional and rigid. To guide the Earth back into its intended brilliance, a very powerful aspect of Creator, known as the Divine Feminine, was brought to the Earth and to its inhabitants. Before the Fall of Consciousness, Earth was a rarefied consciousness of Light, not the physical form you know it as today.

The Divine Feminine's guidance took on the role of the matriarch. Its purpose was very clear and focused, yet it operated within the rigid and fear-based structure of the third dimension. The Divine Feminine's purpose was the survival of Earth and humanity.

At that time those in female form ruled, protected and helped humanity to survive, and this global matriarchal culture prevailed for a very long time. Its focus was on the continuation of life. While this goal was accomplished, the global culture that survived was very much out of balance with regard to the masculine nature. As the matriarchal domination, rigidity, rules and control continued, the masculine could tolerate no more and eventually rose up, revolted, protested and took the power. The tables were turned and the global culture shifted from female-dominated to male-dominated. Of course there are still some rare subcultures on the planet today that are of a matriarchal nature.

During that transition into patriarchy there was third-dimensional resentment, resistance, anger and retaliation. The patriarchy took command and the feminine was dominated and subjugated. When Great Beings such as Yeshua and Buddha came to the planet, they had to speak through male forms and with a masculine point of view because of male-dominated culture and society. The family and culture did what the males demanded. Businesses were run by men. The religions and educational systems were also dominated by the patriarchy. Look at the Middle East today; it hasn't changed much. Countries such as Egypt and Turkey are going through tremendous change, and they all have a male-dominated energy. I once asked Yeshua, "Why did you say 'I and the Father are one.' Why not the Mother?" He explained that at the time he walked the Earth that was the only way he could be heard.

It isn't just the men and boys who have been unready to embrace a balanced and strong female. Many – not all – women feel safer hiding behind their men, giving their seniority over to the masculine energy and not stepping up to create their own dreams. Others may go in the opposite direction and reject anything male. Many women even have the habit of blaming men and the patriarchy when their plans fall through.

This is now changing. As the critical mass of balanced feminine and masculine creative energy is restored in both men and women, and personal power is taken back into our own lives, we will see non-gendered images of these Great Beings of Light. They are gendered only because of humanity's current limitations. You walk beside these Great Beings of Light who love you beyond your wildest imagination. They are your friends and co-creators. They can only accomplish their plans if each one of us steps up to the plate. Only those with a human body can place the final puzzle pieces into this grand creation. These Great Beings are thrilled because you came here and said, "I will change this." It was the big determined humans who stepped up and said, "Send me!" And here you are.

Online resources

Video: Jim and Roxane discuss, "What is the Holy Spirit?" (11:38)

Meditation to begin to experience the Holy Spirit (30:07)

Like much in this course, there are times when there are no words to explain the experience, energetic or transmission of Light. Words get in the way. This is the case here. To fully feel the energy, one must simply be in it. Please let the energy of the words flow through and around you without trying to figure out the details. The transmission, if you can receive it as you sit in the Sacred Heart, is a good example of what is possible as you step toward the Living Light Body.

To access the online classroom,
visit www.masteringalchemy.com/book

Lesson 20

The ninth Ray of Creation

Archangels Metatron and Zadkiel both present us with energetics for the ninth Ray of Creation. This is the Ray that holds sound templates, also known as sound currents or sound waves.

The Atlanteans (members of the ancient civilization of Atlantis) possessed the knowledge of using certain sounds and sound templates to move huge structures and alter weather patterns. They altered the flow of waterways and ocean currents. All was well as long as the Atlanteans remembered from whence their power came and they were aligned with Source. But, as their creations progressed, they forgot. They were so impressed with their power to use these sounds that they began to use them in a manner that was not in alignment with Source, in a manner that was, at times, very detrimental to the whole of humanity. At the present time on our planet, there is much greed for monetary holdings, power and control; it was also the case in the time of Atlantis.

As any civilization grows and its consciousness rises, there is a propensity for mis-creation. This occurs because of the third-dimensional denseness of the planet. However, this is being changed. Our planet is in a transitionary process, moving toward ascension and life in a higher-dimensional reality: a life in the fifth dimension. This can cause problems because the manifestation process occurs much more quickly in the higher dimensions than when creating in third dimension.

It is desired by Source that you be unrestricted in your creations, and that you have access to all of the applications and power that you need to create what you desire. The only requirement is that you are very precise in your intention and in your alignment with the first Ray of Creation, both of which will help you avoid creating an outcome that is not desirable.

Becoming familiar with the ninth Ray

The ninth Ray is composed of sound. A reverberation or wave takes place when you use the ninth Ray. This creative force ripples out into the many dimensions, times and universes in order to bring your desire to you. Imagine your desire as a little boat that is floating upon the ocean being randomly bounced around by the waves (the third and fourth dimensions). Employing

Success story

I've had trouble with pain in my leg muscles since high school. Last week's session was about the ninth Ray so I thought I'd give it a whirl. First I got in a good neutral place, then I used the 4-5–6 Rays to eliminate the words "worry" and "doubt" that I found in my head. Then I just played and imagined lines of multicoloured light move from my foot chakras, up my legs, into my first chakra and down my Grounding Cord. While I did this I made random sounds with my mouth until I finally found one that seemed to be a match. I just made the whole thing up. "Shhhhhh" was my sound.

I sat there for a good half hour, playing and singing and having a good time with myself. Smiling. It wasn't until my cat leapt onto my chair that I became aware of anything else other than colours and lights and sounds. When I opened my eyes and wiggled my toes, the pain was gone. *Gone.* I was so pleased with myself. I jumped up and ran to the back door to tell my wife! I love this stuff. We're going out dancing this Saturday. Thank you, Jim and Metatron!

David, North Dakota, USA

the ninth Ray is like raising your boat's sails so it can be directed intentionally toward its destination, assisted by the waves of wind (the ninth Ray).

Metatron reminds us that, although there are many complexities to these sound currents, intentionally allowing sound to come into your awareness will enable the sound currents to unfold organically. It is not necessary for you to discern the complexities of the sound currents in order to use them. Just as you don't need to comprehend the cellular structure of a pencil when all you want to do is write a note – you just use the pencil – so it is with these sound templates.

To begin to understand and use the power of the ninth Ray, allow yourself to become accustomed to making sounds and listening to them. Tonal quality, vibratory rate, volume and length are all aspects that are very much a part of sound currents. Even a slight fluctuation or modification to one of these factors can affect the creative effort, and can add to the motion and fluidity of the currents. It is much like painting a landscape and choosing particular shades of green for a desired effect. A dark green creates one effect, a lighter green another.

You may think you are familiar with sound, you may even work professionally with sound; however, there is a great deal to learn and experience when approaching sound from this fifth-dimensional, fourth-layer-of-thought perspective. To begin experiencing these sound currents, play with them very simply. Start opening your awareness to hearing what is around you daily. Which sounds dominate your attention? Which sounds do you ordinarily ignore and why? Experiment with how specific sounds affect your mood, your mind and your body.

It isn't possible for the Teachers of Light to identify exactly which note or tone you should use for a particular purpose. Like all the Rays, your relationship with the ninth Ray is uniquely yours. What works for you may not work for the friend sitting next to you. Don't limit yourself to the vowels of your language. Experiment with all letters and combinations of letters. Try splashing your fingers in water, or swiping your hand across a wall, or exhaling with your tongue in various positions. Try scratching your head and rubbing your hands together. Notice the sounds you create for yourself.

You use sound in every thought you think and with every word you speak. Becoming conscious of how you compose those thoughts and words is the primary bridge to the fifth dimension. Every word structure you choose is made of a sound that draws emotions and creates the direction of the desired intention.

If you're choosing to experience peace, harmony and other positive states of being, the way in which that state of being is experienced can be magnified by certain notes, sounds and music. These vibrations enhance the experience of peace and harmony. Peace and harmony can be interrupted and short-circuited when dissonant notes and music are played that are not compatible with the vibratory level of that state of being. Playing or subjecting yourself to these dissonant vibrations creates fields of disharmony such as anxiety, rage and anger, and the vibrations of those notes magnifies and holds that experience in your space.

If you're working in the dismantling process (fourth, fifth, sixth and eighth Rays), adding certain tones is very helpful. Doing so enhances the vibratory level of what you are creating, especially in areas where you are dismantling very dense patterns. You can use sound to raise, amplify or accelerate the vibration of that force field to such a degree that it expands and allows more to be added, or to be released, from that field in a very speedy way. This actually alters and loosens up the denseness of the physical component that holds that uncomfortable thought or emotion in your experience.

Sound as you hear it with the physical ear

Sound currents run through everything that exists on both a physical and nonphysical level. The mechanism of our inner ears allows us to hear a very distinct, limited range of vibrations that are measurable and labelled as sounds, music, notes, noise, tones, etc. However, we don't have an adequate receiving mechanism to hear all the sounds that move through us. Some sounds are not audible to the human ear, but that does not alter their power. Such sounds are very present, and they have an effect on our physical experience regardless.

The ninth Ray of Creation has the possibility of generating, through the cellular system, vibratory rates and currents that affect the cellular system of both the Earth and the human body. This Ray can assist and bring about not only physical healing to the body, but also a step up in conscious awareness. The sound templates of this Ray can be used to create an environment in which a desired experience can occur.

Lesson 21

Installing the Christed Matrix into the planet and humanity

Although I was raised in a Christian family, going to church was more of an obligation than an enjoyable experience. The words spoken did not match my own internal knowing of what was true for me. Following the teachings of Jesus never seemed to match the world I observed. The stories were full of fear and suffering. This was confusing because the conversations I had with the Elders, while sitting by the river, were much more aligned and real than my experience of sitting in a building and listening to people tell stories they wanted me to believe but did not follow themselves. My church was in the woods. The woods were alive and the conversations I had with those who joined me there were full, compassionate and informative.

As this course unfolded, the nature of the words "Christ Consciousness" began to align with what was true for me. The word "Christ" is not connected to any religion, man or culture. "Christed" is a state of being where you are one with the All That Is. In this state you shine a light so bright you fulfil your own purpose to "know thyself" while simultaneously assisting humanity to live in wellbeing, within the higher-vibrational field of the fifth dimension. When I first met Yeshua, this path coalesced. The Fall of Consciousness and how the Elders were leading us to the Living Light Body all came together. This was why we pushed our way to the front of the line and volunteered to dive deep into the third-dimensional density – to be part of this unique project. I understood then that every tool and energetic given was purposeful. Nothing was random. Together with the Elders, we are creating Heaven on Earth.

As the return of the Christ Consciousness approaches, Yeshua steps forward to explain the opportunity that will be experienced: the return of the Christ Consciousness held within the Christed Matrix.

Yeshua comments on the Christed Matrix

I have come today to be the primary facilitator for this Christed Matrix to come into a full experience. There are a couple of things I wish to make clear before we delve into this Matrix. It has been some time since I have been in a position to interact as a teacher on this level. And I'm very pleased for this opportunity.

I come as Yeshua. I know that many names have been used in regards to my presence, my personality, my mastership. But I use Yeshua in this particular occasion because it has a configuration, a sound template, that relates to the Fire element letters of the Angelic realm that were specifically used at the time I was embodied as the being of Yeshua. A seeding took place then, as I came onto your planet in service to humanity, to raise consciousness and to change an energetic configuration of the third dimension. Much of the teaching that I taught at that time has since been very mistranslated and inappropriately misunderstood.

In those times I was honoured to place within the heart of all of humanity a Christed Matrix. Therefore, as this opportunity has arisen with the Shift of Consciousness taking place on the planet, I now return. The return of this Matrix is essential to promote and stabilize a consciousness that was once present on

the Earth plane. This was an interdimensional consciousness that encompassed many realms of physical form on a physical planet, all the way through the twelfth dimension.

Because of the energetic templates that were being projected and absorbed, a Soul evolution of these beings took place that could not have taken place had I not used that vehicle of Yeshua. It modelled to them their perfected image in relation to Source: the image and similitude of the original divine plan. Deep within their Soul consciousness this awareness was planted. As they embodied at other times, they were able to carry those templates with them and thus escalate the progression of that aspect of their Soul consciousness. I am speaking of this not from a linear perspective, but from a perspective of many dimensions. We are not speaking of past, present or future lifetimes. We are speaking of a whole gamut of Soul expressions in different physical and nonphysical expressions.

In order to bring this Matrix out of the unlimited potential of Source again, it requires the use of the first Ray, which is the intention of Creator, the divine plan. It takes the second Ray, as a stepping-down mechanism, to begin to bring it into form. As you bring it into form, in order to hold the stability in form, a certain geometry is necessary. The Christed Matrix is composed of many fractals of Light, many energetic configurations and many fractals of colour. The entire Matrix is configured from a triangular perspective, or an energetic triad. This Matrix is brought into the physicality by using the star tetrahedron.

This particular energetic configuration that I embody today as I teach about this Christed Matrix is very similar to my presence over two thousand years ago of your time. This energetic configuration is much more usable now than it was in those times and also has great value in opening energetic pathways for the Adam Kadmon vehicle to be re-established on the planet. Back then it was required that I embody the vehicle of the Adam Kadmon during the three years during which I was in the public service. It was from that vehicle that I could project energetic templates that helped those who gathered in my presence to absorb at a Soul level what I was presenting. Their physicality, the rational mind and the ego, however, had very little understanding of these concepts.

When I came to your grand event of 11–11, I came in a triad to present this Matrix with Lord Maitreya and Sanat Kumara. We specifically came as that triad because it gave more of a cosmic and galactic configuration that could be installed on the Earth plane at this time. In previous times, in my incarnation as Jesus, or Yeshua, I showed a different triadic configuration with Moses and Elijah. That had a purpose also because of the nature of the denseness of the planet at that time. Those who were in my presence then understood the meaning of that triad in a symbolic way. It was a unity with what they considered to be the Father, or Yahweh. It was necessary that that particular triad be established so the seeding of the return of the Christed Matrix could be precisely, energetically put in place and the Light configuration of that triad could grow within the conscious-ness of the individual Soul. Which brings us to this particular timeframe of your evolution.

Today this is now presented in a much more expansive way through the triad of Lord Maitreya and Sanat Kumara. This magnificent being, Sanat Kumara, has been on your Earth plane for aeons and aeons of time, prior to the Fall, committing to staying the course to resurrect the planet and return the Christed Matrix with me and Lord Maitreya. So as we embark on the exploration of this Matrix, it will be done through energetic triadic configurations. The Matrix escalates the consciousness and begins to change the way in which creation is used within the physical realm.

In 2011 a group of almost 400 humans gathered with the Teachers of Light to anchor the Christed Matrix back into Mother Earth and into all of humanity. One crystalline, golden star tetrahedron was placed upon the altar within the Sanctuary of the Pink Diamond within the Sacred Heart of every human. Another was placed within the very core of the Earth. As you return to your Sacred Heart, you will find this golden star tetrahedron – this Christed Matrix.

Archangel Gabriel comments on the Christed Matrix

As this Christed Matrix was gifted back to the planet at this time in the evolutionary process, it was placed within the geometry you call the star tetrahedron. Many fractals of Light and colour are part of that star tetrahedron. It allows every aspect of the Christed Template, the Christed nature, not only to be experienced, but also to be used on the Earth in physical form to create the Christed reality. And you are that vehicle, as is the star tetrahedron which brought it from the unlimited, nonphysical realm into the physical realm. As you accept it and allow it to be placed in your Sacred Heart for full expression and creativity, you are the vehicle that brings that Matrix into reality on planet Earth.

Are you hearing me? You are the vehicle that allows the true expression of that Christed Template to be brought into the Earth plane and fully expressed in every creative event that you participate in!

It is required of you, as you accept this Matrix, that you stay very conscious and very centred in the fifth-dimensional state of consciousness, accessing sixth and seventh dimensions. When you try to return to a fourth-dimensional state of being, it will be very uncomfortable, because it is not compatible in any way, shape or form in regards to that Christed Matrix. Here you will begin to use more fully this Matrix, as it was intended to be used, in every aspect of form on the planet Earth.

As you begin to work with this Matrix, accept the love, the calmness, the stability of this Matrix. You provide an impetus for other planets, other forms in the physical realm, to benefit from your service in accepting this Christed Matrix and in creating with this Matrix according to your Christed nature.

Now, in the coming times, it will take your attention. We Archangelics and Masters will be with you to show you the way and to teach you some of the concepts and the aspects of what a Christed Being is. You have slept, dear ones, and you have forgotten. We are here to awaken that memory, so you may fully and completely be in service of the planet and the collective, and reawaken that possibility within every being that is in that collective of the Earth. We stand with you to support you, to help you stabilize this beautiful Matrix. We are quite excited that this event is happening now!

---

*Archangel Metatron comments on how installing
the Christed Matrix affects the planet*

As you begin to work with the Earth itself and begin to hold this Christed Light, the Earth will feel your effects. The Earth is not a being. It is a consciousness and an organism. And as an organism, it simply absorbs and reflects back what is in the environment of the organism. When the Christed Light fell from the Earth, many came to Earth and operated outside the Light of the Creator. That lack of Light began to be absorbed by the organism of the Earth. As it absorbed more and more of the dense third-dimensional consciousness, it could not hold and reflect back the Christed Light any longer. The Christed Light fell from the planet and was lost. It was the desire of the Archangels, the Lords of Light, the Elohim to return that Light to Earth. They petitioned Creator and said, "We wish to create a Template, a Field of Light, that holds the Christed Light for the day the Earth will eventually return."

That day is now.

Online resources

Meditation involving the Christed Matrix (31:17)

*To access the online classroom,
visit www.masteringalchemy.com/book*

Lesson 22

The Eye of Horus

A conversation with Archangel Uriel about the Eye of Horus

Uriel: Your journey to the Living Light Body is escalating in a very profound way. As we have discussed with your students, now is not so much about clearing. Those things that are out of alignment will be cleared in a more rapid way because of their ability to use the energetic templates to achieve higher consciousness and a reconfiguration of the physical body itself.

Because of the work they have done in the previous sessions, there is another piece that we wish to put into play that will help them a great deal in using these to escalate the amount of Light they are able to maintain within their physicality. This energetic assistance that we are about to initiate in these students is of great importance for them to be able to use, to a greater degree, the information that was given in the last sessions.

This energetic template is known by various names. The more common name that those who are embodied on your planet have is the one which you term "Eye of Horus". This is an energetic template. It is not just a picture or something that can be visualized or seen. It is an energetic template. It is used by the Lords of Light, as well as the Master realm, to help those embodied to begin to incorporate certain energetic patterns and energetic formats into the physical realm and the physical body. It is an energetic template that has been used in ancient times and expressed in a pictorial language.

The Eye of Horus is equated, by many, with the Egyptian culture. But as with the El Shaddai initiation, there is much more to this template than just this visualization. When viewed as a drawing or symbol, this energetic can be easily understood by those in the lower states of consciousness. It is very difficult, when you are embodied in a physical body, to utilize many of the concepts and the energetics of the nonphysical world. So, therefore, some of the very elevated Beings of Light, the elevated Elohim, devised various ways in which to make these templates and concepts usable within the physical realm by giving very precise visualizations.

What we are proceeding with at this time is to install the energetic used by the Lords of Light, as they have made their presence known to you and to the students in previous teachings. With this new energetic you will be able to use these vibrations of colour to transform the energetics that are held within the first four chakras, thus changing not only the energetics of the physicality, but also changing the molecular structure, the electromagnetic fields and the radiation that is held within a more evolved species.

In the realm of creation there has been some discussion about an outer realm of Light, as well as an inner realm. This event that we are now in the process of initiating is the bridge-work that enables the student to interact from the outer realm, as well as to achieve consciousness with inner realms. This is where Prime Creator resides. The Elohim and the Lords of Light originated from this inner realm.

It is through my guidance that these events will be transmitted. You will be working on many levels now – within the physicality; within the consciousness contained in the outer realms of form; within the Light of divinity as well as higher realms. I hesitate to use the terms "higher" and "lower", but these are the only language that I have available at this time.

It is important that the students hold on to the consciousness of their infinity and eternalness. Through the installation of the energetics of the Eye of Horus, they will be able to maintain that specific state of awareness and consciousness. Firstly, the Eye of Horus brings about a consciousness that is able to be maintained, regardless of what is being expressed in the outer worlds of creation. The interior knowing or inner sight is maintained at all times. And this is a very key angelic step. It is no longer a trust that is developed, or a faith. It is a very real set of energetic configurations that assist the Soul to maintain that consciousness without reservation.

Secondly, this template assists in helping to merge the mental and emotional bodies in a greater way. It allows the operation of the mental and the emotional bodies to work as a unit, rather than in separation as they have been since the Fall of Consciousness.

In this next session we desire for you to give some of this information that we have just given to you to the students; allow us to initiate this energetic format within each one of those students; and then, allow them a time of integration before we embark on the next steps. Can you see how this progression has occurred over the last months?

Jim: Oh, yes. What's fascinating to me is watching the disintegration of these more rigid states of consciousness. The concept that this pathway is an experiment is now very clear. Exciting.

Uriel: Yes. Very exciting. What is most exciting to us is to watch that disintegration as the students actually participate and create the changes within the chakra system. It does not have the extreme effort that had to be put forth as the eighth Ray. There was a lot of effort that had to be put into that clearing. Where now, because that clearing was achieved, this particular formatting allows for further disintegration of fallen concepts of the third and fourth dimensions to disintegrate almost as if that were created with very little effort.

So we are very, very pleased at the possibility for the students to integrate this particular format.

We thank you very much. I will withdraw now. Blessings.

The initiation itself is simple yet profound when Archangel Uriel gives it.

Archangel Uriel continues to comment on the Eye of Horus

The template of the Eye of Horus, or the Eternal Eye, is configured within a pyramid. It is placed first within the crown chakra. The next step is to place it within the third eye. This enhances greatly the ability to maintain the knowing and also develop the gifts given by the Holy Spirit in regards to that centre: the clairvoyance, the understanding and the knowing of the concepts and the energetics held within the outer as well as the inner realms of creation. The final step is when the Eye of Horus is inserted within the pineal. The pineal, as you know, is the gateway through which the Higher Mind is accessed, not only the Higher Mind within the Soul, but also the Higher Mind within Creator Itself. It is these three centres, at this time, that will be infused with the template. And it is through practice that the integration and the expansiveness that is available through this template is achieved.

When your Soul was created, it was imprinted with this Eye, the Eternal Eye of Creator. It was dormant because you were in a physical body of third dimension. It was always there, ready for this very moment, when your consciousness could accept the dynamics of this magnificent Living Light that you are now able to create with and use. This is very exciting and it sets the formatting, or template, now for you to begin to utilize some of the concepts and energetics of the sixth dimension that you hadn't even thought about, or even had any awareness of.

There is no restriction. Even though this particular visualization and concept has been around for a very long time within the physical realm (before the Fall, after the Fall and in the time frame that you now occupy), after the Fall what that Eye represented was not understood: what the energetics were that were contained there; what the vibration was; that the presence of the Living Light is very extensive and very, very potent. Those could not be perceived, nor understood, in a third-dimensional state of consciousness.

The Eye of Horus was not removed from this realm, as many things were removed, at the time of the Fall. It was not removed because it was necessary, so as doorways were opened to a higher state of consciousness, it would be very easy for the Soul to absorb the concept of its unlimited nature. Even though it was inactive and not usable, this Eye still held a possibility of unlimited potential that was always available. There was always that Light that shone very freely and was available, even though the consciousness and the denseness had fallen to such a state. The possibility was always there. Many times it was misunderstood; but it was always there.

Many things will change in the coming days as you integrate this magnificent energetic component. The way in which you create will change, your ability to hear, to see. It will take some time for the full integration of this energetic template to be fully actualized within your Soul essence, within the Soul and within the physical body. We will be with you to fully install these energetics, impregnating every part of your being. We will be with you, and you will have an awareness of our presence and our energy that was not there previously. As I have said, be patient.

We thank you for your participation in this project. We support you always.

Blessings.

Online resources

Meditation to activate your inner sight within the Eye of Horus (28:42) (During this meditation you'll hear the sound of the audience. Please pretend and allow the energies to flow through and around you without engaging the rational mind.)

To access the online classroom,
visit www.masteringalchemy.com/book

Lesson 23

The Colour Codes

Yeshua and Archangel Metatron give us the gift of the Colour Codes.

Yeshua introduces the Colour Codes

This is a very crucial time in your existence. There is much chaos in the collective, much infighting, much misunderstanding within your religious communities and governments. There exists separation, judgement, guilt, violence, war. Your job is to hold your energy within your Christed nature and project it out into the collective so that changes might occur that better reflect their true Christed nature. They have forgotten their Christed nature and cannot access it because they are so busy misusing power, will and dominance. They look to you, dear ones, to show the way, to hold the template of Light so they may see what is possible!

These Colour Codes expand the Christed Matrix on your planet, in your planet, and within all embodied. As we go on we will explore sound templates that go along with those colour vibrations. Some of these templates are of a nature that are not heard, nor can they be sounded. And even though you think it might be a stretch for you to be able to use these sound templates, it will not because you have very precisely placed yourself, step by step, in these teachings to accept those realities and to make them very usable within your energetic system.

What are the Colour Codes?

The Colour Codes, also known as Colour Codings, are multifaceted energetics designed for specific purposes that simultaneously affect Earth, humanity and the being using them. To date we have received these:

- Red
- Yellow
- Blue
- Green
- Indigo
- Magenta

Success story

Since receiving the Colour Codes, I have started enjoying music again! I used to watch movies at night, same old routine every night (I live alone). Suddenly I had a huge craving for music. So I go to my local library and check out a bunch of CDs — The Temptations, Beethoven, Celtic music, Edith Piaf . . . and more! And while I listen, I'm sewing these colourful little cloth Kanzashi flowers. Sometimes I'll just get up and dance!

Movies don't interest me that much any more. I'd rather have the finer emotions of music. And I've developed a huge passion for colourful fabric!

AH, Arizona, USA

The Colour Codes are enormous energetic patterns that contain many applications. Think of them as software programs that have the capacity to rearrange, reconstruct and reconfigure patterns no longer serving you or the Earth. These Codes add opportunity and expand the capacity within the 12 strands of DNA. Each Code works well with sound currents (ninth Ray of Creation) and various radiant vibrations. Some are connected to other Rays of Creation; some include an element, such as Fire or Air; a few include geometry. The configurations of these Codes are not related to what many understand as chakras or other energy studies. If you have studied other modalities involving colour, it will be a benefit for you to set those aside for the moment. The Teachers encourage us to experience this work as if we are curious children playing with new toys. Metatron tells us the Colour Codes were available in the time of the Lemurians. They were also available in the beginning parts of the Atlantean cultures, but were removed.

Yeshua gives us the red Colour Coding

The red Coding carries an extensive vibration and is part of a sound template that you know of as "Om". The other aspect of this all-encompassing Coding is the presence of the sound template El Shaddai, which carries with it the Fire element. Red is a very vast template that has an effect on the physical body, and all of form. It begins to allow a vibratory shift in the denseness of the body itself and the consciousness within the body. We speak here of both the Earth body and the body of the whole of humanity, as well as yours.

When you work with the red Coding and the first chakra, you put in place a foundational piece to allow the interdimensional bridging into the physicality and also into the full chakra system. Not only are we raising the vibration of the physical body, but we are also raising first and foremost the way in which

the chakra system functions within the physical form, making it more refined and of a much different amplitude. When you use the red Coding and bring it into the first three chakras, it begins to set the stage, so to speak. It begins to refine and level out the energetics of the third and fourth dimensions. It makes those three chakras more open and receptive to then begin to receive what is being drawn into them from the refined mental–emotional body. It also stimulates creativity.

In the Fall of Consciousness there was much fragmentation and separation between the mental and emotional bodies. There was created the energetics of ego and fear. When the red Coding is installed in the first three chakras, it levels out these fragmentations. Those three chakras begin to function from a different dimensional vibration and in an electromagnetic form that is entirely different. The fragmentations begin to dissolve. Through the utilization of the red and other Colour Codes of the yellow and the blue, those two bodies change. They merge into a unit and operate at a much different vibratory level – higher, balanced and precise.

Suggestions for playing with the red Colour Coding

- Run and radiate the red Coding through the lower three chakras to lessen physical density prior to playing with other Codes or tools.
- To loosen up an area of tight physicality, combine the red Coding with the sound current (ninth Ray) that resonates with you and focus it in that area.
- Before beginning a clearing meditation, move the red Coding through your space to lessen resistance.

Yeshua gives us the yellow Colour Coding

My desire is to open up another space within this Christed planet that will assist you, and those who are now embodied, to make significant alterations to this continual warring faction that takes place in the name of God. This particular energetic that I wish to work with is composed of colour and sound, conceptual principles and certain vibratory levels that must be established at this time on your planet. This energetic I bring forth is the yellow Coding. It has been for quite some time on your planet associated with the nature of the Christ Consciousness.

Yellow is held within a triangle, which intensifies the way in which it can be applied. It affects the mental body, in that it provides mental stimulus to search out solutions that bring about peace, harmony and joy. It therefore affects the emotional body by creating emotions that reflect those Christed thoughts of peace and harmony. There is great stimulation that is created by participating in this particular Colour Code.

It is of the Air element. It provides an openness in the mental body and an openness in the physical body to receive unlimited thought processes. It has a much higher vibratory level and frequency range than the all-encompassing red Codes. It is also enhanced by the sound current of the ninth Ray. The tone that is a very viable tone to be used in this Code is the tone of "Ahhh".

This colour yellow and the accompanying stimulation of the mental body, allows you to use your own personal power from a fifth-, sixth- and seventh-dimensional level. No longer is there separation. It is not used separately to usurp another's power or dominate but to use your power efficiently to express physically as well as spiritually the essence of the Christed Matrix.

Archangel Metatron gives us the blue Colour Coding

What we plan to do now is begin to explore another Colour Coding. This Coding has to do with the colour blue and the vibration of that colour. The vibration of this Colour Coding is not a singular vibration or a singular Coding. It has a dual aspect to it. It can have a very high frequency range and a very short range. This blue Coding serves a dual function to raise the vibration of the mental–emotional body to a higher frequency range, making the merging of the mental–emotional bodies more coherent and stable. It divides the way in which the frequency ranges are distributed so that a lower amplitude can reach deep within the bowels of the emotional body to further escalate any third-dimensional emotion that lies dormant, or in the unconscious, that has not yet been transformed into a fifth- or sixth-dimensional resonance. That is what this Code does! It has the ability to step down the frequency range, adhere to the discordant vibration that is there and very easily, consistently stir it and raise it to a greater level of frequency. The emotional body can then merge more coherently with the mental body that is already vibrating at a much different vibration because of the presence of the yellow Coding that has been established earlier. This Code changes the entire dynamic of that huge emotional body! It short-circuits emotional patterns in your emotional and physical bodies,

This is not like when students began to work with the fourth, fifth and sixth Rays. There was a lot of turmoil in the emotional body as they rooted out old patterns, reformulated and then used the eighth Ray to change the electromagnetic fields and to eliminate some of this patterning from the mental–emotional body. There was much upheaval that took place in the emotional body, which was needed. And there was upheaval in the mental body because those two bodies were still separate. But now that all of that clearing has been done, there is a further cohesiveness that needs to be established within that mental–emotional body as it begins to operate as a unit.

Having that yellow Coding present and usable, and aligning it with different parts of the brain was very valuable. It built a foundation, so that as we explore some of these other Colour Codes, the vibration continues to escalate. As it escalates, more of the brain is engaged and made usable. The production of hormones and the production of various chemical components within the body are established at a different rate. And the cells begin to function at a greater rate. The electrical components within the cellular system operate at a much greater rate. The body itself begins to resonate at a much higher frequency range. It begins to hold frequencies of Light, not only within the Unified Field, but within every cell of the body, every atom of the body! The Living Light Body.

There are two elements that are involved in the Colour Coding of the blue. One of them is the Earth element, and the other is the Water element. You have the stability and the fluidity. The stability of the Earth energy enables all of the Coding to be very applicable within the bodily structure of form. The fluidity of Water brings about change in a very swift manner; in a way that has ease to it without great destruction. You are able then to merge the mental–emotional body in a very stable, cohesive way. You also are establishing a very stable bridgework and resonance between the physical world, the physical body, and the nonphysical, because this mental–emotional body is part of both.

The upside of this is that what is manifested manifests very quickly. You are already beginning to see that in your own life.

As you think, it gets manifested very quickly. Acknowledge its presence and begin to draw it into you. That is one of the magnificent results of having it established in the system; you begin to see a much greater, bigger, overall picture of the functioning of all levels of yourself.

Success story

This is probably the most amazing thing. I am beginning to like my body. I smile at the parts of it that used to make me cringe. It's genuine affection too, not fake. I recognize when I have a negative thought about my body and I change it. It's astonishing to me to realize the extent to which I beat my (physical) self up with thoughts and feelings.

The Rose works! So does the eighth Ray and the blue Colour Coding. When I find myself in an uncomfortable thought and/or emotion, I use them and they help tremendously. They are invaluable. I am blessed.

Amy D, Virginia, USA

Understanding the green, indigo and magenta Colour Codings

Within our limited human language, we are able to describe the first three Codings (red, yellow and blue). Green, indigo and magenta, however, are energetics that are accessible only while in a fifth or sixth layer of thought and in the higher dimensions.

Here is a brief description of each.

LESSON 23

Green Coding

This Code is given to humanity to assist in healing the fragmented parts of the individualized Soul as it expresses itself in the physical realm. It assists in bringing together the physical parts of you, as well as the nonphysical parts. It's associated with a sphere, which at times is seen as spiralling. It has no beginning nor end. When green is coupled with attributes of the yellow and blue Codings, it creates a pure white Living Light of Source.

Green's healing capacity is drawn from and used through all the elements, especially the elements of Earth and Air. It draws from the natural attributes of planet Earth, such as trees, herbs and other vegetation. The Air element is purified by the plant world and can be drawn into the body through the breath to begin to alter some of that fragmentation. The fifth element, Love, is also an aspect of this Coding.

Indigo Coding

The indigo Coding is drawn from the upper seven chakras. It expands the use of the second Triad and the Eye of Horus significantly. When the indigo

---

Online resources

Meditation using the yellow Colour Coding and the triangle. (20:18)
(You may hear words that you haven't read or heard yet. Please allow the energy just to flow without engaging your rational mind.)

Question: Where do the Colour Codings come from? (01:19)

To access the online classroom,
visit www.masteringalchemy.com/book

Coding is drawn into the Sacred Heart it activates the violet flame and much more.

Magenta Coding

Through the use of the indigo Coding, you become aware of the vast opportunity the magenta Coding provides. The magenta Coding is drawn from beyond the upper seven chakras. As it is drawn in, the physical brain is reconfigured to think from the mind of the Christ Consciousness. This activation allows the Soul to fully enter the Sacred Heart and occupy the physical body.

Lesson 24

The elements
and the Elementals

Long before the creator gods began creating mutations, long before the Fall of Consciousness occurred, all beings were unified. This all changed as the mutations grew. As Earth became more and more dense, the mutations found their way into this density. A group that was most affected by this was the Elementals. The job or purpose of the Elementals was to reflect the Love and Light of Creator back to those who came to visit Earth. But as more and more creator gods created without the Light of Creator, there was less and less Light to reflect, and the Elementals, along with Earth, began to decline.

The Elementals are a group of four quiet beings who are committed to their purpose of experiencing and reflecting Love. It was through the Love these beings held that the beauty of Earth was created. The Elementals create in harmony and balance and with Love. Love was a key component to how they existed and how they related to themselves and all who visited planet Earth.

When the mutations expanded and the Fall occurred, the only way to prevent humanity (and the Elementals themselves) from being completely lost forever was for the Elementals to give up the single most important aspect of who they were . . . Love itself. The mutations and distortions had interfered with the survival of Earth to such a great extent that the Christed Love was removed. If Earth was ever to return to its Christed state of consciousness, the Elementals would have to transform themselves and their way of being so humanity would survive.

Can you imagine giving up the most important, precious thing in your life for another? Can you imagine giving this up without knowing if you'd ever retrieve it? That is what the Elementals did. They gave up their most precious sense of themselves and became separate from All That Is to save us. Separation, distrust, competition and fear grew. The Elementals were greatly affected by this separation and isolation. They fragmented, disappeared and went into hiding.

As time has passed, many attempts to step out of the separation of the third dimension have been made. Atlantis was one such attempt. On their own the Elementals also have made progress in re-establishing their purpose. But they too experience the same mutations of anger, blame and resentment that we humans experience. Much of the Elementals' resentment and blame was directed at humanity. The pain and loss of their essence and purpose to exist was because of humanity. Unfortunately there are many chapters in their evolution that are filled with darkness.

Unlike humanity the Elementals are not creator beings and do not have free will. They cannot freely create with choice or bring about a fifth-dimensional consciousness. These things can only be done by a human being. To raise Earth, however, the Elementals are essential. And for the Elementals to succeed, the Love they once held must be returned to them; for without Love they cannot know or reflect Love back to humanity. The Earth can only be transformed when humans become the Love that we are. Only then can Love be absorbed by the Elementals to be reflected and transformed into beauty.

In 2013, as the Shift was being anchored, Archangel Metatron and other great Teachers of Light requested that a gathering of humans be convened to meet with the Elementals. A small group of humans gathered. Over 300 people quietly sat and focused all their attention, energy and appreciation on their common intention of opening that doorway between the human world and that of the Elementals. This small group was joined by the Teachers of Light, Archangelics and members of the angelic kingdom know as the "Earth goddesses" (wonderful beings who oversee and guide the Elementals upon their journey back to Love and purpose). One human and Tara guided the introduction to this gathering and the ceremony. Tara is the Earth goddess who oversees the Elementals on behalf of Gaia, also known as Mother Earth. The humans stood with no conditions, in respect, admiration, excitement, joy and love on behalf of humanity. A new beginning was formed.

The great Elders and Teachers of Light have said on many occasions, "We know all of the possibilities and probabilities of this grand Shift of Consciousness on Earth. We exist in the nonphysical. The Fall of Consciousness is a physical creation and can only be redirected by those in physical form, creator beings in form. That is you."

One year later a second gathering was requested. Again many gathered and once again both humans and Elementals were very excited. This was the gathering in which humanity returned Love to the Elementals. The essence and purpose of the Elementals has been restored. Since that day the Elementals have revealed themselves more frequently to those who maintain a high vibration, ask and allow. Together with the Teachers and the humans, they are now beginning to raise the new Earth.

Let me introduce you to your old friends, the Elementals.

Undine is the being who commands the power of Water. Some of the qualities and abilities that Undine and Water offer us in the creation process include saturation, revitalization, relaxation, movement, invigoration, hydration, fluidity, flow, cleansing, calming and buoyancy. Let each of these words and vibrations resonate within you and notice if there are others that say "Water" to you.

Success story

I have to tell you a miracle story that happened after I began to play with the Elementals. I've been dealing with continual challenges with a certain sales person for a vendor we use. He tries to wheel and deal me, argues, is scattered and late on his orders and is generally unprofessional. I don't know *how* the owner could allow this. Anyway, I asked Undine to lubricate our communication space to make it flow easier. I asked Gnome to ground his wild energy so he could be more precise. I asked Salamander to add a bit of enthusiasm for professionalism. And I asked Love to create a bubble around our relationship so we get along smoothly and so it's all in alignment with Creator.

I forgot all about doing this until yesterday when the vendor called to say this sales person has been overwhelmed with personal issues, apologized and introduced me to someone else who will take over our account. He assured me all would go smoothly with his partner (who happens also to be the owner of the business). I was stunned.

Thank you for introducing me to my new best friends, the Elementals. They are so much fun to play with.

Charles, Virginia, USA

Salamander is the representative of Fire. Some of what Salamander directs includes vitality, warmth, spontaneity, purification, passion, ignition, explosivity, consumption, combustion, cleansing and catalysis. Rest with these aspects. Are there any others?

Sylth is the being who commands the powers of Air. These are some of the aspects that Sylth and Air can bring to your creations: refreshment, gentleness, force, freedom, excitement, circulation and boundless breath. Let each of these aspects float within you. Do you notice other qualities of Air and Sylth?

Gnome is the master of the Earth element. The creative abilities that Gnome and Earth offer us include support, tactility, structure, shelter, stability, solidity, mothering, grounding, dependability and anchoring. What other aspects do you notice?

Each Elemental and element has a purpose and role in the creation process. It's as though a grand party is being created and each participant has a job to do. One brings the plates and cups. Another brings the salad and another brings the main course. Each Elemental commands and utilizes its corresponding element to create. If you are wishing to write a story, you might invite Water for its fluid flow of words. You might invite Fire's passion and ability to consume the reader's attention. Earth would provide a structure to your story and Air would allow the reader to walk away refreshed.

The fifth element

There exists a fifth element that contains the other four elements. This is the element of Love, and it may be the most important of all the elements. It's what is necessary for the others to successfully create. It is possible to invite only two or three Elementals to your party, but Love is the music that makes it move. Love is the element that unites, and it's the necessary component to any successful creation. It is in Love's home that the party is held.

This is the element that was lost when the creator gods began creating without the Light of Creator. This element is not the love most humans are familiar with. This Love is much bigger. Earlier we shared with you the definition of alchemy that the Teachers gave us: "Alchemy is changing the frequency of thought, altering the harmonics of matter and applying the element of Love to create a desired result." This is that Love. Let me repeat: Love is the power that moves the wind and pushes the ocean waves. Love is what holds the planets in their orbits. But most importantly, Love is the expression and power within each of us that creates. Love is the vessel of all possibilities. It is the radiance of pink Light that glows from the Sanctuary of the Pink Diamond within the Sacred Heart. It's the fifth element of Love that is the essence of the Christed Matrix.

---

*Ascended Master El Morya comments on the value
of balancing the elements*

Too much of one element in the creative process creates an imbalance in the result. Air has an excitement to it, it has an openness to it, an expansiveness to it, an opportunity to it. And yet if there is too much Air, you have scattered and unfocused thoughts. There is no precision and you are not organized and directed. There may be a need to have the flow of Air, but not at the expense of losing the stability that is gained through the use of the Earth element. When you have a discrepancy within a creation where the elements are employed and one has a more dominant position than another, there is not a balancing. Then the manifestation either cannot fully come to its fruition, or it is stifled.

If you are trying to create and it is too rigid, possibly you might bring in an amount of the Water element because there is a fluidity to it Another consideration is that Water has stillness to it. There is a depth to it. There is a calm to it. You can move things around. And yet if it gets to be too much Water, the energy gets very hurried. It rushes like a raging river.

And then there's the Fire element! There's a passion in that Fire element. It has the ability to move things along. When you have too much Fire, it begins to be somewhat reckless in the creative process.

The exercise is: can you be clear and specific about how you create? As you choose which and how much of each element to use in your creation, you are actually using the fourth, fifth and sixth Rays of Creation to disassemble and reassemble until you have the perfect recipe for your success. You move the elements and the aspects of the elements onto your workbench, up to the

sixth Ray and down to the fourth to bring into form. Can you begin to see the possibilities?

Working with the Elementals

Many people ask, "What do the Elementals look like?" Like much of what the Teachers offer, there is no right or wrong answer to this question. There is no one way of seeing or experiencing the power of the Elementals. When the Elementals come to you, they will appear in a way unique to you. As you move through this work, how you experience this communication will evolve. For example, aspects such as their colour and size may change. This is true for every step on this path. As you practise and become, what you experience deepens and grows.

In your meditation space, call upon the Elementals and become friends. Get to know them as the playmates and co-creators they are. Begin to experiment with the energy words they each offer as tools in your daily life. Would you like a little more flexibility in your workout? Ask Undine to send Water to flow through your joints and muscles to lubricate them. Would you like inspiration for a work project? Ask Salamander and Fire to bring you more creative passion. As you re-acquaint yourself with your old friends, you will remember how to work and play with them to create results you both want.

When you have practised and are confident in your creative process with the elements and the Elementals, together you can direct your attention and intentions to Mother Earth. Yes, humanity is going through a tremendous transition as we move into the fifth-dimensional consciousness. So is planet Earth. As you are aware, Earth is now experiencing significant changes in its oceans, pollution, droughts, extinctions, sun spots, increased temperatures, hurricanes and earthquakes. These are but a few of the changes. It's therefore very necessary for Earth to heal and elevate herself into a higher state of consciousness, just as you are doing. The Elders have told us this can be done without significant disruption to humanity. But humanity must participate. You must participate. A co-creative focus with the Elementals will assist Earth's transition. The Elementals, Elders and you can join together to direct the elements of Fire, Air, Water and Earth to bring about an easier journey into the fifth dimension.

Enjoy the reunion with your old friends. It can be beautiful.

Online resources

Lecture about how to use the elements in practical ways (12:46)

Meditation to heal the waters of the Earth (32:43)

To access the online classroom,
visit www.masteringalchemy.com/book

Lesson 25

The Divine Feminine and Divine Masculine

The aspects of Divine Feminine and Divine Masculine are misunderstood and out of balance on the planet. Separation, third-dimensional beliefs and conditional programming have split humans according to gender and the divine aspect of each of us has been lost. For aeons there has been the duality: male and female, masculine and feminine. Such differences only exist in a third-dimensional reality. Separation, in all of its various forms, does not exist in the higher dimensions.

Some ancient and current spiritual practices do identify and speak of the Divine Feminine and Divine Masculine, however not always as a unified consciousness. Each archetype, deity, god or goddess has heavenly characteristics that humans want to embody, and humans believe that by understanding them, praying to them, merging with them or "channelling" them, they too will become divine. Gender, however, plays no part in this pathway to the Living Light Body that the Teachers have laid before us. Divine Feminine and Divine Masculine have no relation to the body or the rational mind (other than they each are created from Divine Feminine and Divine Masculine application).

This pathway is about our own internal, unified nature and our expression of creative energy. Regardless of our sex, gender or sexual orientation, we all have access to the masculine and feminine creative energies within ourselves. Most of us, however, are unconscious of the great treasure we have access to, and hence do not know how to recognize and use these energies for our own success and personal evolution.

Feminine creative energy is both simple and complex. It is multifocused, energized and fast, while masculine creative energy is uncomplicated, single-focused and slower than the feminine. When the Teachers talk about "feminine" or "masculine", they are referring to a set of characteristics and energetics within the creation process, not female or male qualities. Feminine energetics can be demonstrated as ease, patience, flow, smoothness and understanding. Masculine creative energy holds energetics such as stability, structure, focus and command. This is not to say that the masculine can't flow in ease, or that the feminine can't be stable and commanding, for example. Stability as a feminine energy demonstrates itself differently than stability as a masculine energy. Flow as a masculine energy demonstrates itself differently than the feminine flow. Take a moment and observe this for yourself.

To illustrate this in a visual way, masculine creative energy creates through structure, such as straight lines and angles. Feminine energy is made up of flowing curves and swirls. There are no straight lines and angles in feminine creative energy, and there are no curves and swirls in masculine creative energy. Both types of energy are essential to one another and are required for you to bring forth balanced creations. Masculine energy without feminine energy is not whole. It does not feel valued. It is not nurtured or appreciated. It is incomplete. I'm not talking about men and women or relationships, although this applies to those too. I'm talking about your personal, internal, masculine and feminine balance. Feminine energy without the masculine is incomplete – it feels unsupported and without focus; it is scattered, ungrounded and unstable; it is without structure; and as a result it has no sense of direction, completion or success.

Within the creation process the feminine energy is the first spark, the initial impulse. It's the first thought of a creative idea or desire. Masculine energy then takes that impulse and creates a structure for its manifestation: the scaffolding upon which to construct it. This co-creating occurs within each of us, in our individual expressions as well as our external relationships. For example, the feminine creative energy within you has the idea and impulse to garden. The masculine energy within you builds the raised garden beds. The feminine then plants and nurtures the vegetables and herbs. The result: you benefit by having fresh, delicious organic food. This is a unified creation process of flow and structure. Without both components, you would have no food.

Humans, whether we realize it or not, use both feminine and masculine creative energy with every thought we think and every action we take. More often than not, however, we do it through reactionary thoughts and unconscious actions. Balanced creations use a balanced, organic flow of both types of energy. Those who create dominantly in one energetic or the other end up with results that are off balance, incomplete, do not have longevity and are generally not successful.

It is of the utmost importance during this time of Shift to identify, experience and begin to anchor healthy masculine and feminine energy into your third-dimensional creative process. Increasing your awareness of how you create using these two powerful energies will allow you to use them in balance, intentionally and successfully. This awareness and practice will also allow the anchoring of the higher-dimensional equivalents to more easily move into your experiences

---

*Anna discusses the fracture between
the feminine and masculine*

I am very pleased to be enlisted and to be a presenter at this time. I withdrew when I left my lifetime as Anna, bound in embodiment, for a very long time and went into a collective of creation called the celestial realm. The celestial realm is

a massive realm, where there are many collectives operating within it. I have been in unity with this realm for quite some time.

I was enlisted by Prime Creator to come forth at this time, not through an embodiment but through my energy and my nature, to bring forth these teachings. I will be supported by, and also many teachings will come forth from, Mary Magdalene and Mother Mary.

Aeons ago, before Yeshua or I walked your Earth, there was a separation, a fracture that took place within the creative realms of form. There was a mutation that began to occur within the energetics of the creative process. The energies that held everything in operation, and held everything in unity, began to split and fracture. Part of that fracture was within the energetic positioning of the masculine–feminine unit. It was in that fracturing within the energetics that there came into the creative process an aspect of dominance and submissiveness. This was a polarity that began to creep into the energetics of the creative process.

Because of all the variances and mutations and anomalies that were created in this fracture, unity consciousness and the unity of the creative process were split. This took on many aspects, and as the creative process was further impacted by the realms of form and the realities of form, more deterioration took place. The Christed Matrix of planet Earth was greatly disturbed and began to be affected. The Christed Matrix could no longer sustain unity consciousness on all levels of its physicality. Not just mental–emotional, the physical, spiritual, Soul Spirit, the masculine–feminine, all were split. The electrical and magnetic fields became very imbalanced. The creative process began to further deteriorate because of this imbalance in the electromagnetic field. The creative process deteriorated eventually to such a state that the Christed Matrix had to be removed because it could not exist within the imbalanced electromagnetic field of Earth.

A new third-dimensional matrix was put in place to stabilize the deterioration and hold it very stably in that third dimension, so no further fragmentation could take place. The concept of God, of Prime Creator, the All That Is, however, was very much altered and disturbed in the physical realm, especially on Earth. When this new matrix was put into position, that split within the electromagnetic field caused a further split in the consciousness around many things. Over the aeons the positioning of the mother figure, the matriarchal representative, took dominance because it was all about fertility. It was all about survival: survival of the planet, survival of the species. The matriarchal position was called forth and put into play in that matrix. It took predominance because of the fear that was present in regards to survival. This was a very split positioning and did not allow for the masculine to be present in a strong position. The matriarchal image took on a very fragmented space within that third-dimensional matrix. It was one of dominance because it held the creative process, the regeneration so the species would continue to exist. And the masculine was positioned in a subservient position; it was in a position of being less-than and weaker-than.

That electrical component that is held in the essence of the Divine Masculine could not be positioned on Mother Earth because of that third-dimensional matrix. That electrical component, as you now know because of the presence of the yellow Coding, has to do with the mental body. The mental body did not have the opportunity to participate from a creative perspective with Prime Creator because of the fragmentation. The proper electrical stimulus was not available because the masculine could not function due to its subservient positioning in the creative process.

As the species evolved the power of the masculine began to assert itself, not from equal positioning, but from a place of dominance. The masculine usurped the power of the feminine and took dominance. A subservient position was assumed by the feminine, and it became less-than. Neither position was a position of the divine, of the original schematic. They were fragmented positions of masculine and feminine. The electrical and the magnetic fields were still greatly disrupted and unbalanced. You had the reverse in play on the planet. The mental body took dominance, while the emotional body became greatly fragmented. The electrical stimulation took dominance, while the magnetics became subservient. Because of this imbalance the only emotions that were available were of a negative nature. The imperfect charge within the magnetic field of the emotions could not create emotions that were more in balance and in unity with Prime Creator and the creative process. There was anger and fear. As the masculine began to come into a dominant position, you can see how that fracture within the mental–emotional body prevented a very smooth, powerful, creative presence on the Earth. This is demonstrated today in the third dimension on Earth.

It takes the electrical components of the masculine essence and the magnetic components of the feminine essence, merging and working as a unit, to co-create. The old archetypes of the masculine and the feminine, represented by many archetypal gods and goddesses that have come down to us through the aeons, have kept that separateness alive and well, not allowing a unit to operate within any part of the system. That matrix of the third dimension is all about separation and polarity.

A balanced positioning must take place for the fifth dimension to come into being on your planet and raise it to another level. A new positioning within the creation process, within the physical realm, is now being entered into and was prophesied aeons and aeons ago. It is a change in the state of consciousness. It is a change in the energetics that are present in the physical realm.

The masculine–feminine total balance is an integral part of your ability to shift into this new positioning in a very balanced way. Not only are all of the bodies coherent here, they also are merged, functioning as a unified unit. Your consciousness is also functioning at a different level. You have a different under-standing of Prime Creator and your relationship with that essence.

As that representative of the feminine, the matriarch, I have come to explain to you how those two aspects, the Divine Masculine and the Divine Feminine, are present within the greater realms of creation. Each particle, each section of this vast Christed Matrix which you have been experimenting with contains the perfect alignment that the Divine Feminine holds. It is one of fluidity, one of intuitiveness, of great Love with power, nurturing, compassionate. Unlimited potential. But within that realm of creation also must exist, simultaneously, that Divine Masculine that brings the stability in the fluidity, that brings the direction, the precision, and yes, the Love. Love with great power.

Balance restored

Due to the planetary Shift that is occurring and this path of the Teachers of Light, we have now reached a point in human evolution where the present masculine patriarchal phase is about to end. Instead of continuing as we have in the third dimension with alternating masculine and feminine cycles, we are moving into a new cycle of consciousness. This is one in which masculine and feminine become one balanced Unified Field of consciousness. In order to enter and hold yourself in the vibrations of a fifth-dimensional reality and bring the Unified Field into wholeness, the masculine and the feminine within you must first be in balance. When this is accomplished the structure of the masculine creative energy will begin to be the structure in which the feminine creative energy can flow, grow and expand. The feminine energy can then direct the masculine energy into an expanded structure or system, which in turn allows the feminine to create within that new space. It's an ongoing ebbing and flowing of masculine and feminine that allows for amazing opportunities and a joyful creative process. This new level of balanced masculine and feminine creative energies is where we are headed. It's what the Teachers present to you.

This unification and rebalancing requires the original essences of the feminine and masculine to be re-established within you, and therefore also upon the planet and within all of humanity. This original essence or template is what you lived and demonstrated but forgot at the Fall of Consciousness. This is the divine aspect of who you are. This is known as the Divine Feminine and Divine Masculine. You hold both within your fifth-dimensional experience. It is the divinity you share with All That Is.

The wise and knowing Divine Feminine nurtures and offers the life-giving safety of the crucible (symbolically and in reality), so it's that aspect of divinity that has to be re-established first. This original Divine Feminine aspect of Creator will open the space within the fifth dimension for the Divine Masculine to enter and be present in its full glory, as it was originally created. At that point the Divine Masculine will take its proper place in perfect unison with that feminine aspect. It's the Divine Feminine who does this because the Divine Masculine is not strongly present at this time in the third dimension. The masculine is still operating from that place of dominance, inequality and control. For that masculine structure to be dismantled and transformed into the divine, it takes the feminine to set the energetic balance, make it available for the divine image of the masculine to enter and take its proper positioning not only in the creative process in the physical realm, but also within the physical body and all of humanity and Earth.

Anna explains the rebalancing

To be the Christed being that you came here to experience, there must be within you the Divine Masculine and the Divine Feminine.

We bring in and show to you the importance of this unlimited well, or womb, of the Mother who holds all of the fullness of Creation in an energetic template that is ever moving, spinning, swirling. That chalice holds the image of the Divine Masculine, as well as the Feminine, in all of its aspects. Within that container there is a precision, a directness, a force that propels out of the container into all of creation and into the physical realm. It can always be penetrated, entered into and drawn from because of the masculine component that is within that womb, within that crucible. It holds the complete divine imaging of creation in precision and force and power. And it is the Feminine, the matriarch, the wise one, the teacher who will open up that space within the fifth dimension that allows for the Masculine to enter and to be present in full power. Never dominant over, but in perfect unity with, in perfected divine Love.

I cannot tell you how important this is. For if the Golden Age is to reign and there is to be peace and love and harmony on

your planet, as you desire, this presence must be here in the physical, in every energetic aspect of the fifth dimension and above.

That Sacred Heart space where the Christed Matrix resides is a good positioning to start from because that Christed Matrix is in perfection. It is in the unity of All That Is. To draw a geometry from that Matrix is what is needed. That tetrahedron already has balance in it. Bring that balance, then, in a very specific way. Bring the energetics into the first chakra, into the second, and into the third and loop it back into the Sacred Heart again. Do this in the presence of the Holy Spirit and the green Colour Codings. That energy begins to flow very consistently, very coherently, very balanced and yet dynamically. You will have the masculine and the feminine working together again.

Holy Grail

The Holy Grail has been sought after since before Yeshua walked upon the planet. It was written about in Arthurian literature, Christian and Celtic mythology. Medieval legends, tales of the Knights Templar and movies like *Indiana Jones and the Last Crusade* have identified the Holy Grail as the cup that Jesus drank from at the Last Supper, the cup that Joseph of Arimathea used to collect Jesus's blood at the Crucifixion. This vessel has been called the Universal Well, a crucible and a chalice. Within the third-dimensional reality, it was believed that the Holy Grail held miraculous powers that could provide happiness, eternal youth and infinite abundance. It was believed that it had the power to create, heal and give life. The search for the Holy Grail was important because it signified union with Creator, but it has never been physically discovered or excavated. Many do not believe it exists. The

Holy Grail does not exist in the third dimension. It only exists in the fifth and multidimensional realms. It exists as the balanced Divine Feminine and Divine Masculine held in Love.

Mother Mary comments on the Holy Grail

Since the time of Yeshua, many have searched for the Holy Grail. From a third- and fourth-dimensional perspective of imbalance and polarization, the masculine–feminine essence of the divine could not hold the consciousness of what the Grail was. I show it to you now. It is the womb of creation where Prime Creator fully exemplifies perfection in balance, having masculine expression and feminine expression. There is no separation. There is only unity. That space lies within you, within that first Triad. That crucible lies within your Sacred Heart. Within that Sacred Heart are the four God essences, from which you express your godliness, your wholeness, your completeness, your power, your grace.

The Holy Grail is within you. You have been very diligent in creating this Unified Field that is around and within you now. That Unified Field is this crucible of which I speak. From this day forward your consciousness will hold the Divine Masculine and the Divine Feminine, regardless of the body type that you occupy, or who you love. It is within you in perfect balance. The Love of the Father. The Love of the Mother. All in perfect harmony.

No longer will you think of yourself as feminine or masculine. But you will honour yourself for those aspects that are in complete unity within you. You will honour your Divine Masculine in its power. You will honour its ability to organize, to orchestrate, to direct. And you will honour that Divine Feminine:

the Mother, the nurturer, the great Love that is expressed from the heart, always providing a space to return to that eternal womb in perfect balance.

It is very difficult for those who want to go to their rational mind and figure this out. It will not happen. You have to be within that unlimited potential, within that crucible or womb that is ever-evolving, ever-moving, ever-creating, without limit and without end. The Christed template is within it, the perfect balance of the masculine–feminine essence of the divine. All potential is in this massive unit. And all is created from that unit in complete unity.

As we bring in this matriarchal image as transformed and resurrected, you can enter this realm, this womb, this crucible at any time, and know yourself from that divine image. You are being nurtured, refreshed, and can receive the power that is necessary to create that state within your physical expression. We are providing the space for that balance to begin to take place and the resurrection not only of the Divine Feminine, but also the resurrection of the Divine Masculine, which allows unity consciousness and all creation to be brought back into that Unified Field that you have created around yourself. It will take some time for these things to be fully accomplished.

The unification process

As this unification takes place, any unreleased baggage that has not been addressed will surface. That energy must be cleared out of your energetic system in order for you to accept and embrace yourself as the Divine Masculine and the Divine Feminine, that perfected image of the All That Is in the fifth dimension. This is a crucial point because for so long how you viewed yourself was responsible for a great portion of the fragmentation and pain that was present in the mental body and the emotional body, therefore manifesting in the physical body. The imprinting that took place over aeons, through many lifetimes, is now culminating during this Shift in Consciousness and upon this path to the Living Light Body. The complete unity of the mental, emotional and physical bodies, as well as the spiritual body, can now take place.

During and after the process of unifying and becoming the Divine Masculine and Divine Feminine, you will begin to notice where your expectations are out of alignment with that unity because of prior imprinting. That false imprinting is generated from third-dimensional masculine and feminine perspectives, beliefs and habits. These can be beliefs about gender roles, gender bias, homophobia or judgements about who and what males and females are, as bodies and as personalities. Religious doctrine and cultural norms that usurped your power and your divinity are also a cause of this false imprinting.

As those expectations and beliefs start to fall away, you will begin to see through the eyes of the Holy Spirit and of your Soul. You will begin to observe those expectations and imprinting clearly and objectively. You can then further release the whole of this third-dimensional matrix. The Teachers have given you specific tools to use in order to eliminate once and for all the third dimension and embrace yourself as that perfected divine image.

Suggestions for playing with masculine and feminine creative energies

- Create separate lists of masculine and feminine words and wear one word each day, just as you did previously with the Seven Living Words.
- Become consciously aware in your daily life of how you create, and which energies you use. Notice if one energetic is dominant or weaker than the other.

- Notice where any of your incomplete projects or creations stalled and consider what energetic was involved in the halting of it. What energetic is necessary to rekindle it?
- Watch others around you as they demonstrate balanced and imbalanced feminine and masculine creative energy. Notice the weakness or the dominance.

Online resources

Lecture to prepare for the meditation (04:06)

Meditation using the feminine attention point (44:00)

To access the online classroom,
visit www.masteringalchemy.com/book

Lesson 26

You are rewiring yourself

No journey to the Living Light Body is consistently easy or comfortable. This is a journey about change. It's a journey of realigning, rebuilding, re-creating, reconstructing and remembering yourself. This journey requires intention and attention. But it doesn't have to be a difficult journey because new choices and tools are now available to you. These choices and tools allow for an ease that leads to success.

This journey leads to a profound and personal awareness that most have lost along the way in their life-travels. This awareness is "I like myself. I have value." In re-creating and rewiring yourself, you will come to remember many

---

Success story

Today I had a great validation that I'm changing and rewiring myself. I went back home to visit my parents after about a year away. I'm certainly not the me I used to be! They are the same old Mom and Dad, with their prejudices and judgements, their complaining and arguing, but this time I didn't play the old game. I didn't match their pain. I neither argued or defended or yelled or cried. I honestly was entertained and amused. It was the first time since I left home five years ago that I enjoyed visiting with them. Good job, me!

KM, Switzerland

---

things, but most importantly you will remember and re-experience the vast range of vibrations held within Love, and held within you.

On this journey to the Living Light Body, many big changes will occur in your life. Many new personal insights will arise and old negative patterns will surface and fail away. As on any path of significant growth, there will be changes. The friends from the pub who you hang out with every Friday will, most likely, become less interesting. You'll find fast food doesn't taste as good and the mall is too noisy. Your tolerance for hate will lessen, but hate won't make you as angry as it used to. You will spend more time alone, and you'll enjoy it. You may feel a heightened sense of distraction, coupled with an emotional sense that something is "just not right". You will become aware of what has been in front of you all along, but that you somehow never noticed.

Two things will be useful to know: you are not alone, and there is no need to be alarmed. The old structures that have supported duality, maintained separation, allowed disrespect and greed and controlled the masses with fear are now crumbling. As these old patterns fall away, many of your old points of reference held within these patterns will fall away with them.

There is a saying, "If you always do what you've always done, you'll always get what you've always got." Walking the path with the Elders is not "what you've always done". Choices are now presented for you to shift; however, sometimes this is not comfortable. Where you have experienced uncertainty, hesitation or fear, alternative structures of stability and choice are offered. When you change your vibrational colour to something brighter and more dynamic, all the old dull hues disappear. As you remember beauty and laughter and get a sense of who you really are, the old reference points of resentment, doubt and anger cannot be maintained and will fall away

This is a journey of transformation. You are completely emptying your vessel, though you may not be fully aware of what to refill your cup with next. New reference points will come to you, piece by piece, as you re-create yourself and refill the vessel that is you. Yes, there will be a few speed bumps, potholes, dead ends and wrong turns along the way, but if you keep focused and committed you will indeed drain your cup to fill it later with purpose. You are rewiring yourself to hold greater levels of awareness, consciousness and Light. You are clearing the Veil of Ignorance and Forgetfulness and putting yourself back together as you were before you dived into the density of the third dimension. Here, though, you are neither a caterpillar nor a butterfly. You are in transition from the old to something new, something not yet defined.

This journey occurs on many levels of who you are simultaneously. This evolution doesn't end when you lay down this book or turn off your tablet. The changes you're making continue as you sleep, go to work and do your daily tasks. When you make the personal commitment to remember yourself, every aspect of you enthusiastically joins in the party. Mental, emotional, physical and nonphysical changes take place. As you sleep you are still very conscious on the etheric levels. Each night as you go "Home", you return to the full, higher, multidimensional consciousness that you are, and you work in a way that allows you, in the physical, to remember and to re-create yourself more quickly, fully and efficiently.

One of the many things that occur as you practise these tools and integrate this information is that you begin to merge your mental and emotional bodies into one. This allows you to choose a thought and then draw to it an emotion that is not unconscious or reactionary. With intentional purpose you draw to you a desired result. This is not difficult to do, but it does require that you skilfully align the aspects of your intention and manage your attention point in the process. It's impossible to create the Living Light Body from the third-dimensional, past–future time structure. It requires you to be in present-time, fully aware and focused.

If you have been practising the exercises in this book, you are definitely in the process both of recognizing the noise and resetting yourself to raise your vibration above the noise and drama. You are successfully beginning to reshape, rewire and realign yourself with your own truths and with who you really are. You are on your way to becoming aware of being aware instead of unconscious of being unconscious.

Success story

I finally understand something you've been telling me for years. I train with a teacher to improve my body awareness and posture. I now hold my body very differently (graceful, taller, at ease) and am not in as much back pain. Part of the programme includes days of rest, which are very hard for me because I really like to push myself and make an effort.

It's a difficult but important programme, just like what you and the Elders offer. What's funny is that my friends notice my results and want to know how they can get out of their pain. I tell them about my teacher, they try it once and never return. "I don't have time," they say, or "I'm too old." Like you say, they are fighting for their limitations.

This journey with you requires commitment and time too. It's sometimes not easy for me to see my old destructive patterns, but I like the me I am now. It's okay that my friends are stepping away from me so they can continue to keep their spiritual and physical pain. I love my life and I *am* happy. Thank you, Elders. Thank you, Jim.

Doug, Vermont, USA

A growth period

This new wiring takes a bit of time to integrate. I call this time a "growth period". During the brief period of adjustment, when your cup is being emptied and you're pausing before refilling it, there are specific things that will assist in creating greater ease.

- Understand that this period is not only temporary, it's actually a time to celebrate. Your commitment and focus are making huge changes in your ascension.
- Don't resist this process of transitioning from who you are not to who you are. A restructuring of reference points will happen regardless of

whether you resist or allow. Allowing makes the transition easier and faster.

- Be amused at what you're noticing and don't beat yourself up. Let yourself experience this time however it unfolds, even if it you find yourself drooling and staring off into space.
- Continue to use your tools to better assist in clearing out what might be preventing new reference points from finding you.
- Lastly, treat yourself well. You are taking huge leaps in your ascension. Your slower, denser physicality is working hard to keep up. Make it easy on your total self and treat the denser parts well. Go for walks, sleep in, pet your cat, lie around and do nothing, have more sex, watch movies, have less sex, eat something special, take a bath . . . take care of yourself. If you don't take care of yourself during this important time, the process will only become more uncomfortable.

Hurry up!

Western culture and the third dimension are fraught with the pressures to hurry up, go fast, achieve more and do it right. We are all familiar with over-achievers, perfectionists and what standing upon a platform of those words creates: stress, unhappiness and dis-ease. On the path to the Living Light Body, many bring those same expectations and self-pressures to keep up and accomplish quickly. It doesn't work that way. I've known students to practise their weekly sessions several times each day, take notes and listen to them while drifting off to sleep at night. They worry they might be falling behind, missing something or just not getting it. That pressure stands in the way of receiving the gifts from the Teachers and from creating a Living Light Body. It's important to remember that much more occurs in the *non-doing*. In other words, you will be more successful by simply *being* rather than thinking and efforting. It is in the allowing that all the energy flows into the Sacred

Heart and integrates into your bodies. The rewiring begins to occur in the field of awareness outside of the rational mind's ability to understand what is happening.

As tempting as it might be to hurry, you will accomplish more in a much shorter period of time if you can temper your impulse to go fast and have no *need* to figure it out. Be comfortable sitting with the information you're receiving without knowing what to do with it. Just allow the experience to flow through you. This isn't a race. The slower you go, the faster you will arrive. Rest.

Yeshua speaks on the subject of rest

Greetings. It is I, Yeshua. We stand here heart to heart, Soul to Soul, together in this beautiful state of rest where we rest together within the Sacred Heart. We breathe in that wholeness of our self, our Soul. We rest in the fullness of our spirits, whole and complete. Take my hand and enter this quiet space of rest.

It is essential that you visit here often, for you have slept and forgotten your essence. You have forgotten the purity of who you are. When you enter a body, such as the human form, this time of rest to recall and remember who you are in that divine image, whole and complete, is essential.

When I walked your beautiful Earth, it was required of me that I take these times of rest within the quiet often. I went into the desert, I went into the mountains, I went into the gardens. I did this so that I might rest within the divine, so I could hold very stably the full essence of myself as complete and whole. Just as it was essential for me, it is now essential for you. For you will be called upon in the coming months and years to provide a great service not only for humanity, but also for all of creation. And that is your role. Your role is to hold the stability

of the fifth dimension, of the Christed Matrix, of who you are as that individualized expression of All That Is in its fullness and completeness and wholeness.

In these coming years, as you hold the stability of that Christed Matrix so others might find their way into this state of rest that you are now sitting in with me, much will be asked of you, just as much was asked of me. To accomplish what I began over two thousand years ago, you must withdraw and rest within the wholeness of your divinity. Breathe in your graciousness. Breathe in your love and will. Breathe in your power. Nurture yourself. Know yourself. We are the issue of the All That Is.

Blessings.

Online resources

Meditation for daily use (20:34)

Question: Are we some of those who "ran off the rail"? (06:08)

To access the online classroom,
visit www.masteringalchemy.com/book

Part 4

Your Living Light Body

Lesson 27

What is a Living Light Body and do you really want one?

If you've jumped ahead to this lesson before practising previous ones, if you're looking for the "good stuff", you've just passed by all of what you are looking for. The "good stuff" is the information, exercises and tools that build the foundation to install and activate the Living Light Body. Mastering the foundational tools and the gifts from the Teachers is what will allow you to experience a balanced, fulfilling life and create the platform from which to achieve the Living Light Body. The following lessons will seem like a stretch – confusing or impossible – if you've skipped ahead.

The tools and skill sets provided in the previous lessons were designed to enhance your ability to become more conscious and aware of the circumstances and environments that surround you. This new awareness provides the insight to see what opportunities lie before you. From now on this course becomes a journey of mastery, not an intellectual gathering of information that satisfies the ego's need to be seen, be better than or find comfort in what it knows and what it thinks it knows. The purpose of these next lessons is to inform you about what is involved in creating your Living Light Body, not to instruct you in its creation step by step. The information from the Teachers is detailed for the purpose of assisting you to remember yourself and to re-create yourself. As you read, allow the embedded energetics to move through and around you.

A word about words

Language can sometimes be a great hindrance, especially the English language, which is heavily based in a third-dimensional matrix. Language carries a vibration (ninth Ray of Creation) throughout the physical realm and in the body, so precision is important on this path. There may be many new words here that you don't understand, or that you research and still have confusion about. It would be a distraction not to clarify some of them here. The following words are used in the explanations of the seven layers of the Living Light Body. Keep in mind there is not a hierarchy here. These are aspects of you and aspects of All That Is. Don't let your analyser get stuck on any of this.

- *Soul:* The Soul was created by Creator to go out and have experiences in physicality. Creator wanted to know itself and this was how it went about doing that. This is the part of you that ran to the front of the line to dive into the third dimension.
- *Higher Self:* The Higher Self relates to that portion of the Soul that takes on embodiment for certain experiences and for the Soul's evolution. It's

Reality versus myth

In many spiritual mystery schools, achieving the Light Body is thought to be the ultimate goal and destination. It's the finish line in the ascension race. Once achieved, you will sit at the right hand of God and you'll have a body made of translucent glowing Light. Many believe that once you have the Light Body, you can astral travel and walk through walls. They believe that the Light Body brings with it the health, vitality and appearance of a 20-year-old, and that you can live that way for ever. Actually, it doesn't work that way. Once you become one with the Living Light Body, you have arrived at the starting line not the finish line.

the highest vibrational part of you that can be in a physical body. With the presence of the Living Light Body becoming more conscious to you, the Higher Self is taking a more active role in your physicalness.

- *Over Soul:* The Over Soul oversees the physical body and the Higher Self, much like a foreman in a factory guides and watches the employees without doing their work for them. Some call this the Over Self. It has a potent relationship, energetically, to All That Is. The Over Soul is that part of you that directs light frequencies into the Living Light Body. The Over Soul stays with you even when the physical body is dropped and is no longer needed. The Over Soul oversees that transition into the nonphysical realm and remains with the Soul and the Higher Self until such decisions are made to return into the vaster collective of All That Is.
- *Soul Spirit:* As the Higher Self gains experiences and wisdom in physicality, the Soul matures and grows closer in alignment with Source. Soul Spirit is that aspect of you that is in complete alignment with Source.

The process of creating and then merging with your Living Light Body will transform your dense carbon-based physicality into a crystallized body that is less physically dense. However, transforming into that hot 20-year-old? That is not going to happen. That would be too disruptive to you and all those around you. Think about it. Waking up in a 20-year-old body and then having breakfast in a fear-based third-dimensional reality? You think Jesus had a difficult time? Try going to work and announcing, "I have become a fully Christed Being of Light. I can assist you in becoming one too." Good luck with that.

Some believe that with the Light Body they will miraculously transform – like a caterpillar metamorphosing into butterfly – from what they were into a beautiful form surrounded by glowing light in the blink of an eye. Beautiful? Yes. In the blink of an eye? No. The process does bring more Light into your cells and transform them into a higher vibration of living consciousness. Your skin may indeed smooth. Your presence and presentation will flow comfortably with more grace and ease. You will draw your awareness from the higher dimensions. The opportunity to experience life on your terms will become fully available. The Living Light of Source will flow through you. You will glow with that Living Light, uplifting all those who are near you by your presence. You will come to recognize that you are the Light on the candlestick; you are a Light that makes a difference in the darkness. Your Light will be calm, inspiring and focused. All around you will be held in ease.

The Living Light Body is a journey not an instant manifestation. As with all the tools and skills previously provided by the Teachers, this experience requires intention and a managed attention point. Some assembly is required. You'll sit at the table with the Teachers, the angels, the Masters and yes, even Creator. You will be who you came here to be. You'll walk in this noisy world, but not be affected by it.

Archangel Metatron welcomes you as you step into
the seventh and final layer of the Living Light Body

As this seventh layer is engaged and becomes very activated, all layers become aligned and fully engaged. It is this activation that allows decisions to be made at a spirit level. Decisions will be made by these individuals to express themselves in one of several ways. Some will choose to remain as way-showers from the Ascended Master realm. They will walk the Earth, show others the way and direct the energy on a multidimensional level that will draw many others into their own full expression. There will be some who choose to remain within the physical realm with a fully activated Light Body who are Angelic presences.

They will teach and guide and reflect that pure Undifferentiated Light in very usable states. Not just the fifth, sixth or seventh dimension, within the realm of form, but escalating that into the 12 dimensions. It does not stop there. It continues to grow and expand into a 24-dimensional system and beyond. Others will choose to leave their physical form and go into the pure Undifferentiated Light of Source. So you see, this activation is not only significant, it is the next step into another state of being: remembering fully and completely who you are as that Light being, negotiating realms within realms within realms.

What does the Living Light Body look like and where is it in respect to the physical body?

Let's keep this very simple. The physical body has an electrical system, which we generally call the nervous system. This system consists of all the nerves in your body together with your brain and spinal cord. Electrical impulses run through this complex web of systems to animate and communicate health and wellbeing to every part of your physical body.

The Living Light Body has a very similar electrical system: an intricate network of pathways that together create a radiant field. This fine mesh or web of pathways is comprised of what are called axiatonal lines. This system operates directly above the meridians of the physical body and the lines connect up through the eighth chakra and into the upper seven chakras, reaching up to the fourteenth. The Living Light Body connects into the physical body through axial spin points located on the axiatonal lines. These spin points are part of the electrical system of the Living Light Body. Physical cells have their own version of energetic spin points that vibrate at specific rates according to the dimension in which that body happens to be functioning.

The Living Light Body's axiatonal lines and spin points were disconnected during the Fall of Consciousness to prevent communication with the Over Soul, Higher Self and Soul Spirit, and also with Creator. As a person begins the ascension process and enters higher and higher levels of consciousness, the body's cells match that higher vibration and begin to hold greater levels of Light. The highly vibrating cells affect the entire physical body. As the axiatonal lines and the axial spin points upon them are integrated and activated, they have a direct connection to the meridian system and acupuncture points. You might imagine the Living Light Body as a fine open-woven mesh with tiny nodes at every intersection lying just above your skin. It is a garment of Light, a coat of many colours.

With the activation of your body of Light, the potential for change within the physical body is significant. The physical body regenerates cells at a regular pace. For example red blood cells renew in approximately four months, stomach cells in two to nine days. As the energy and Light connections are created between the Living Light Body's spin points and the spin points within the cells, a resonance between the two bodies develops. The denseness begins to be eliminated and cellular regeneration starts to occur from that more perfected state. Newly regenerated cells vibrate at the new higher level of Light.

It may go without saying that this interface between the Living Light Body system and the physical system is not possible while holding your attention in a third-dimensional state. No matter how many years one spends praying and working and studying, the only way to merge the Living Light Body with the physical body is in a consistent fifth-dimensional state of being. One must *become* a body of Light before *having* a Light Body.

Because of the work that we have done with the Elders (and particularly the work we have done with the brain, the Eye of Horus, the Christed body, merging the mental and emotional bodies, the Triads and using the Colour Codes and Rays of Creation), your ability to walk in the Living Light Body and therefore change the density of your physical body has increased significantly.

A conversation with Archangel Metatron about the Living Light Body

Metatron: I have come to continue this teaching and this energetic conversion. I speak of it in these terms because that is exactly what we are leading you to do. We have talked about changing the molecular structure of the body at various times and given you specific ways in which to begin to accomplish that. Now that we have begun this integration of the Light Body, several things are occurring within the consciousness of the Soul Spirit and the consciousness of the body.

As we begin to activate the Light Body and merge it within the physicality, there are several initiatory processes that occur. And there is more than one level of Light Body. There are seven layers of Light Body founded upon all the work that has been completed to date. I'm speaking here of the energetic composition of the Light Body. These seven layers of unique energetic components that are each composed of Light, colour, sound and the frequency ranges of each. This is an initiatory process that began in this last gathering of the students.

They are offering their service not only to raise their bodies to a higher state of being, but also to facilitate the raising of planet Earth out of the density of a third-dimensional matrix.

This upgrade takes place within the physical body, as well as the consciousness of the Soul Spirit. It can be then modelled and translated through the Elementals for a re-creation of the way in which Earth is held within energetic configurations. An alteration is made not only of the matter of the body, but the matter of the planet itself. But it first has to be taken and utilized at the personal level. Here is where you find yourself at this moment: holding a consciousness that was not available previously in regards to creation of Light within the body and within form.

When this conversion is translated by the Elementals and made usable within the Earth, the ley lines of the Earth begin to be activated, recharged and enlightened. They begin to operate as the meridian system does within the physical body. This takes the direction of the Elementals, just like it takes your conscious direction, to direct the Light through the various channels to accommodate this conversion.

Jim: As we absorb this and interact with the Elementals, we reflect it to them to absorb and begin to use in their own capacity. *Metatron:* Correct! All are served at every level. But have no doubt. Have certainty that this process is occurring. You can see it, feel it and know it.

As Earth begins to absorb and then reflect this upgrade that is being made within the physical expression of the individual, then many alterations can be made throughout the collective. Even those who are not involved with these teachings will be affected because of the templates of energetics that are being created, both from an individual standpoint and from the standpoint of the Elementals and the Earth itself. Other individuals who are not as consciously aware will find there is more health and wellbeing available to them, and a different state of consciousness begins to very slowly open.

So much is happening. Very subtly, but it is happening. And we have to find another name for these students because they have moved beyond that. They are entering more into their mastery. They are on a path of various initiations in the coming months.

Online resources

Question: What are the benefits of having a Light Body? (05:30)

To access the online classroom,
visit www.masteringalchemy.com/book

Lesson 28

The first two layers of the Living Light Body

In the final lessons of this course the Elders offer activations and transmissions for each of the seven layers of the Living Light Body. Some are short and simple and will make sense to your rational mind. Others are more complicated, multifaceted and will make no logical sense at all. Each step along the way must be experienced and integrated before the next step can be fully received and anchored. The Teachers suggest that you take this very slowly and deliberately. The saying "the slower you go, the faster you will arrive" is truer than ever. Allow the wisdom of your inner guidance system and physical sensations to dictate when to take the next step.

As you move forward with this work, the kind Elders also suggest that you return often and review the earlier lessons in the book, even as far back as Foundational Tools to Know Yourself. Refamiliarize yourself with what has come before. The you who reads these words today, ready to step into the Living Light Body, is not the you who began this journey. When you review the tools, you will be approaching them from a new higher level of understanding and alignment. The experiences you now have with even the most simple of the tools will be deeper and more profound. You will notice things and have experiences that you didn't have the first few times you played with these tools.

Now let's begin.

The first layer of the Living Light Body

Activating this first layer of the Living Light Body allows you to begin to configure the cells and alter the glands and fluids of the body so that it may begin to hold a greater level of Light. It also unifies the Higher Mind with the Mind of Creator, also known as the Universal Mind.

This activation unifies all the previously separate systems of the physical body, upgrading the functioning of the chakras, Triads and the Unified Field. It also creates a synergy within the morphic fields surrounding the physical, etheric, mental–emotional, causal and Christed bodies, allowing for the merging of those bodies.

Archangel Metatron explains the new energetics

There are many energetics being placed into the physical realm through you that not only will open the consciousness of the body, but also will set a new level of awareness for you to observe. The Mind of Source is now within your Higher Mind. The Holy Spirit is within your Soul Spirit and within your body. When you begin to fully acknowledge that the Mind of Source and your mind are one and the same, it allows that eighth chakra to begin to function at a much higher frequency range.

This Light is distributed throughout the system, down from the pineal, into the pituitary, the hippocampus and the hypothalamus, throughout the glandular system. It also engages with the cellular system. As that Light begins to spin and vibrate at a higher frequency range within the pineal, there is another aspect of that liquid Light that begins to take form. It is much thicker and has a viscosity. This nectar-like Light is flowed throughout the system. The liquids within the body's cellular system, glandular system and digestive system must all contain this liquid Light in order to have this conversion into the Light Body. This Light also runs through the meridian system and engages the axiatonal lines and spin points to further disperse these higher frequencies into the system.

This golden liquid Light adheres to the organs, glandular system and to the liquids of the body. The liquid Light is dispersed outside the body through sweat, saliva and urination. It then begins to alter the expression of the Earth itself, into the ethers and into all parts of the Elemental kingdom. It begins to be made usable to the Elementals in the restructuring and the conversion of the energetics of the planet.

We have never experimented with these energetics previously. At this refined frequency range, it has not been present on the Earth plane since much before the Fall of Consciousness. It is not something that is to be understood, but something that is to be absorbed.

We, and all the Teachers of Light, are pleased to be involved in this project with you.

Upgrading the second Triad

When each layer of the Living Light Body is awakened, many other layers and systems need to be upgraded or adjusted to function best with this higher level of Light. You'll upgrade the Colour Codes, Triads, pituitary gland, DNA and more (and hopefully you'll upgrade your amusement, neutrality and personal goals as well). Think of this as being similar to when you install a new operating system on your computer and some existing applications need to be updated.

A series of automatic functions within the second Triad become engaged with this activation. The second Triad is upgraded here. This automatic functioning allows your pineal gland to constantly create Light, and this magnifies one-hundredfold when you consciously place your attention in that second Triad, reinforcing the presence of the first layer Light Body.

Upgrading the red Colour Coding

This return to previous gifts and tools from the Teachers can be likened to the way we learn mathematics. You're taught arithmetic when you first go to school, then years later you encounter algebra, then sometime after that you master geometry and then trigonometry. As you grow and mature you develop the ability to understand and perform more complex levels of maths. It's as if you're ascending a spiral staircase. As you step higher you are prepared and able to receive more advanced levels of information and experience.

The Colour Codes are specific technologies that are very useful in integrating the first, second and third layers of the Living Light Body and anchoring them into all levels of the individualized expression that is you. At this higher level of consciousness, the Colour Codes begin to hold a much greater energetic function at a physical level, while maintaining their simplicity of use.

Even though we played with the red Coding in the past, accessing it while in the Living Light Body offers access to additional powers and applications. (Here you'll be playing with trigonometry instead of arithmetic.) This red Coding very much applies to the first layer of the Living Light Body. It applies to the physicalness of who you are and also who you are-becoming as you receive these initiations. The red Coding smooths out any energetic peaks that are not balanced, reducing tightness, irritation and impatience. It also smooths energetic spikes such as the excitement or expectation of what is yet to come as your Living Light Body is integrated. And it smooths out leftover limitations that reside in the mental–emotional body. When the red Coding is invoked into the energetic system from this lighter, less dense platform of the first layer, those hitches in the navigations of life are balanced. A calm and harmonious energetic playing field is created. It's not something that requires a lot of work. It requires paying attention.

The second layer of the Living Light Body

The autonomic (involuntary) functioning of the Triads has been greatly stabilized with the initiation of the first layer. This is then brought to a new higher level of functioning through the activation of the second layer of the Living Light Body. The second layer applies to the physical and nonphysical aspects of all of your bodies. The second layer is drawn and merged into the first layer through the golden liquid Light that is now continuously produced within the pineal gland. This second-layer activation does several things. Archangel Metatron believes the most significant upgrade with this activation is that you will find yourself unable to revert back to lower states of consciousness. You will be able to maintain a higher state of consciousness, more of the time.

Two-way communication

This second-layer activation turns on a two-way communication within the cellular system. All your cells become both receivers and transmitters rather than only experiencing a one-way transmission of receiving. (That one-way system has kept decline, deterioration and death functioning in the body.) This two-way communication is not only between the cells themselves, but also between the Over Soul, the Higher Self, the physical and the Soul Spirit. The physical you (cells) can now more fully communicate with and experience the Over Soul, Higher Self and Soul Spirit. Those individual aspects of you also have two-way communication between each other. It's as if the team that is building the Living Light Body can now talk to each other for greater success in the creation.

THE FIRST TWO LAYERS OF THE LIVING LIGHT BODY

Undifferentiated Light

This activation also includes a download of Undifferentiated Light from the Over Soul. This type of Light not only is of a higher frequency range, it also is whole and complete in itself. It has no one specific purpose as the golden liquid nectar does; however, it contains all possibilities. In order to be made usable within the dimensions and within your physical expression, the Undifferentiated Light has to be available to, made sense of and made usable by the Over Self, Higher Self and the consciousness of the Soul Spirit. This Undifferentiated Light is then carried into the cells of the physical body through the axiatonal system.

The Teachers return again and again to this Undifferentiated Light as they give the initiations for the next five layers of the Living Light Body. It is a powerful resource and tool for your ascension. As you continue to access this Light, it becomes more attuned to who you are and your particular desires. It begins to recognize you, making more of its possibilities and powers available to you.

Upgrading the DNA

Since the Fall of Consciousness, all but five to seven per cent of our DNA has been dormant. It became dormant in order to produce the denseness necessary to experience separation consciousness. This prevented you from knowing who you are as a powerful creator. Scientists call this dormant DNA "junk DNA".

The two-way communication of the second-layer initiation affects the body's RNA, which now begins to activate the DNA that is dormant. The newly activated RNA transmits information to the parts of the DNA that hold the imprints from all the previous dense physical bodies you've had. This expands the communication between the axiatonal lines and spin points in the cells to an even greater level. Even though you're in a slow dense body, the

What are DNA and RNA?

- DNA (deoxyribonucleic acid) is a molecule that carries the genetic characteristics and instructions used in the growth, development, functioning and reproduction of all living organisms.
- RNA (ribonucleic acid) is a molecule that is essential for the coding, decoding, regulation and expression of genes. It's present in all living cells. Its principal role is to act as a messenger carrying instructions to and from DNA.

Here's an easy way to remember the difference between DNA and RNA. DNA is like a set of guidelines that a living organism must follow to live and function. RNA helps carry out these guidelines. RNA is more versatile than DNA and can perform many diverse tasks, but DNA is more stable and holds more complex information for longer periods of time.

vibration is increased enough to allow this two-way communication into the DNA, overcoming the limits of the body. Although the functioning of the cells takes on an autonomic process with this activation, it is still important to be conscious that this process is occurring.

The upgraded DNA and RNA will affect the levels of ATP (adenosine triphosphate) and ADP (adenosine diphosphate) within your cells. ATP and ADP are molecules in cells that carry energy where and when it is needed. These two molecules exist in a very delicate ratio in a healthy cell. Certain conditions of the third dimension affect this ratio, such as oxidation, illness, sloppy breathing, neglect, acidosis and emotional, mental or physical stress. The longer a cell lives in these typical third-dimensional conditions, the more the ratio of ATP to ADP changes in ADP's favour. This is called aging.

As you now begin to engage and connect the axial spin points to the spin points within the cells, the RNA and DNA begin to function in an upgraded way. ATP is increased to a significantly higher level so it does not fall back into the third-dimensional ADP-dominant ratio. As this ATP becomes the dominant energy-carrier of the body, the process of illness, decay and death no longer has a strong platform to live upon.

As you merge with the Living Light Body, the physical body has the potential to return to greater balance and wellbeing. The second-layer activations upgrade the physical body's chemical composition and the way in which cells receive nutrition. Cells begin to recognize Light as food, as sustenance.

The first two strands of your DNA relate to the physical body, its genetic lineage, the actual way the body is constructed and its ability to maintain a state of health and wellbeing. The new relationship between you, the Soul Spirit, the Higher Self and the Over Soul now begins to awaken two additional strands of DNA. These two strands are structured to open up the communication between the Over Soul and you, as Soul Spirit in the body. These strands are beginning to reawaken but this doesn't happen automatically. They gradually develop as you begin to allow yourself to have a regular, consistent communication with the Undifferentiated Light and make it a part of who you are. Both strands are further activated and enhanced with subsequent initiations. The awakening of these two new strands kick-starts the unfolding of the other five strands of DNA.

Upgrading the blue Colour Coding

The blue Coding begins to be automatically upgraded and drawn in as other second-layer activations occur. The Soul Spirit starts to have a greater presence in your physicalness and your creative nature becomes explosive. When these layers of the Living Light Body are anchored precisely, the unique nature of you begins to vibrate radiantly. The blue Coding and its sound tone (ninth Ray of Creation) have a powerful, creative magnetism. It simply and powerfully draws pieces together. An example would be the process of putting together a jigsaw puzzle. You may sit for a while looking at all the pieces and suddenly you actually see them and intuitively know where they fit with each other. Another example would be in that creative space with a friend where one of you has an idea and the other adds to it. Then the first person has an "aha!" moment and adds to the creation again, and on and on, magnetically attracting the creation and the puzzle pieces into an optimal fit and balance. This space of easy unfolding is what you're beginning to experience. Some call such experiences being "in the zone", synchronicity or mini miracles.

This experience, however, occurs specifically from within the Sacred Heart. The Sacred Heart is no longer a location or a chakra. In the Living Light Body, the Sacred Heart is a consciousness. It's a state of being. In that Sacred Heart state of being, the magnetics and engagement begin to be something that simply happens, effortlessly. This happens only while you're in the sixth and seventh layers of thought. There's no thought and no thinking here. There are no words. You simply know. This is where the answer appears when the question is asked with regularity. Soul Spirit begins to know itself in the Sacred Heart state of being.

The process of absorbing

Merging with your Living Light Body is a systematic and gradual unfolding. It requires integration time because there is much more involved in the second layer than in the first layer. Long quiet times of stillness devoted to this second-layer integration will allow the process to anchor and to accelerate. This is a very conscious choice that has to be made by each one of us. It's not a minimal choice. You can't think, "Oh, I'll get around to doing this whenever I get around to it." As you proceed it's important that attention be placed on the very subtle alterations that are occurring within your consciousness, your physiology and your psychology. If paid attention to, great differences will be observed in the way in which you experience life now. This simple act of observation will trigger more shifts, changes and upgrades within your life.

The process of absorbing and knowing these layers of the Living Light Body is not done with words, though it is through words that you are receiving this information. You are also receiving the energetics of these initiations because the Teachers of Light embed the energy into their transmissions and into these lessons. As you read and listen, pause occasionally and notice what you feel internally.

Don't expect to draw the words in or make sense of the words. If you allow the energetics you receive to be absorbed, amplified and expanded, the knowledge and experience will be comprehended in a very different way than through words. And the grasp of that awareness will be much more beneficial and easy without trying to translate it. We have left the realms of the third and fourth dimensions, which are based in language, words and rational thought. We are now operating at a multidimensional level. The first layer of the Living Light Body relates to the fifth dimension. The second layer relates to the sixth and seventh dimensions.

At this point in the course, it is very important to review the previous work with the seven layers of thought. Receiving the transmissions and allowing the Living Light Body to live within and around you can only happen and be maintained at those higher layers of thought. It's also important to consciously be aware of the Universal Mind merged into the first layer and the I Am That I Am. Ahayah Asher Ahayah.

Archangel Metatron comments on the second layer of the Living Light Body

Greetings. It is I, Metatron. Much is occurring, beloveds. This second initiation establishes that multidimensional functioning of you as a Soul Spirit in a body. It allows you to traverse the limits of the body and enter into states of consciousness that are directed by your Higher Self. The thoughts and the emotions that are present in that fifth–sixth layer are very coherent and cohesive, and it is where they operate as a complete unit.

This mental–emotional body has no separation point in it. It becomes very in-tuned and in resonance with your Higher Self and comes under the direction of your Over Soul. Even though you are operating in a body that is slow and dense, you are able to increase the vibration of the body enough that it allows this two-way communication within the DNA. This is important, because it is a more direct interface with your Over Soul. It allows you to experience it without the hindrance of language. Here is where you step into the environment of the Holy Spirit, and that knowing is very present.

The information that then is transmitted comes in blocks of energy that are known and understood at a Soul level. Because of this two-way transmission that has been opened up within the DNA lattice, it is acceptable to the body. There is a resonance that has been established through the vibratory levels of the body. It is not yet at the frequency range or the vibration that it is fully established in that fifth-dimensional state. But there is this resonance, this energetic compatibility, that is now being established so that this interface can take place at all levels of yourself. This functioning within the DNA lattice becomes more established, viable and expansive.

It will be a slow process, much slower than what you would like, but much faster than what you think. So have no expectations here. Allow the process. How you do that more effectively is to put yourself in that sixth layer of thought, coming down to the fifth, and back up to the sixth, and resting in that sixth layer.

At first you may have limits on the amount of time that you can hold your focus and attention. When that starts to wane, allow it. Do not be concerned that you are not doing it right, or you have not prepared enough. Just allow. This is a very high frequency and rarefied energetic space. You will find yourself, at first, dropping in and out of it. But the more that you afford yourself the opportunity to be in it and be conscious, the less time you will notice that you've dropped out of it. You will be able to maintain it. This is the environment that must be established to move forward with the full integration of all layers of the Light Body.

Here again, be kind to yourself. And allow that process. It is engaged, and there is no reversal here. We have long since passed that. It is a given.

I thank you for receiving us.

Blessings.

Success story

I just have to tell you what I've been experiencing these couple of weeks, especially after the second-layer activations. My body feels different. I have never been an athletic type. I normally don't do any exercise except walking and occasionally stretching.

Lately my body wants to stretch, stretch, stretch. My arms, legs, neck, fingers, everything wants to stretch. I have suddenly started doing a lot of yoga-type of stretching. I can't help it. I have to stretch. My body is so excited. I feel a great excitement inside. It's visceral. I just know all the cells of my body, including the cells of my muscles and organs, are *so* happy when I stretch my body. I can imagine the Living Light and the nectar of Light flowing through my entire body and enlivening it.

It is truly very exciting. I don't have words. I just stay allowing. Thank you so much for the fantastic journey.

KK. New Zealand

Lesson 29

The third and fourth layers of the Living Light Body

As you reach significant transitional points throughout this course, you may experience new sensations and insights. This is one of those significant points. This process is not just an ascension of your consciousness, it is an ascension of your physical body and the physical planet into a much more rarefied energetic composition. This requires an extensive transformation of the body itself. As the dormant strands of DNA get activated one by one, your Soul Spirit, Over Soul and Christed Over Soul are drawn through the causal body into the Higher Self. The Higher Self can then upgrade the physical body to a higher level of functioning. This upgrade occurs throughout the brain, neurological system and cellular system, and it affects the production of chemicals and hormones. All of this is done under the guidance of the Soul Spirit moving through the Higher Self. This flow of Light not only transforms the physical vehicle, it interfaces with the Elementals and with the Earth itself to upgrade the Earth with the Christed template so it may return to being a Christed planet once again.

Because this point within the process of anchoring your Light Body is so significant, it's important to be kind to yourself. I suggest you return to Lesson 26. You are rewiring yourself.

The third layer of the Living Light Body

The activation of the third layer of the Living Light Body greatly reduces the third dimension's range of frequency. Even though there may be some leftover habits or residues that you pick up from mass consciousness, this will only be momentary because your body is now resonating in a totally different capacity, a capacity that allows the dust of the third dimension more quickly and permanently to demagnetize from your space. Taking the time to sit within and enjoy the first and second layers of the Living Light Body, with no agenda and no hurry, facilitates this.

This third-layer activation re-employs several of the Teachers' previous gifts at higher frequency. The Colour Codes are amped up and the Triads are engaged at a much higher vibration, plus the Unified Field expands exponentially and becomes unified with more of those higher aspects of you. More of Universal Mind becomes involved in the functioning of the physical body. You are able to bring more of who you are as a Soul Spirit into the body because of the energetic work with these various templates that are being put in place not only in your consciousness, but also within the body itself. The Teachers of Light have taken great care. Under their direction and tutelage, now you can set free the potential you've held in hiding so long.

Upgrading the yellow Colour Coding

The third and fourth layers of the Living Light Body are key because they set in motion the Soul Spirit operating in your body, in full communication with Universal Mind. The yellow Coding begins to amplify and bring forth knowledge and wisdom of who you are at the Christed Over Soul perspective. This allows you to create very consciously and precisely, and most importantly it allows you to create with intention. The yellow Coding further opens the brain to a higher frequency range and increases the two-way communication between the neurons and the cells within the brain. Within this layer of the

Living Light Body, the yellow Coding can be used with laser-like precision. It can be accessed also as a yellow energy that floods the body like a bath or gentle river.

This yellow Coding has a significant impact on the eighth chakra. It's within the eighth chakra that the Christed Mind exists. When you begin to use this yellow Coding from the Living Light Body platform, you will draw from the Christed Mind. You will begin to create a stability of thought that is within the Christed Mind and begin to draw from the Christed Over Soul. This is the step that starts to create the possibility of a Christ being in a physical body.

Coupling the yellow Coding with the blue Coding and the sound tones in both, you will begin to create a stability within all aspects of the physical body. The cells understand the sound tones in the blue and yellow Codings. This allows the cells to shift and creates stability within the production of ATP. The triangle that holds the yellow Coding becomes a tetrahedron when accessed from the Living Light Body.

A conversation with Archangel Uriel about the Sacred Heart and the fourth strand of DNA

Uriel: **I am here today to continue this process of integrating the Light Body. We have built the bridge between the second and first layers because of all of the preparation that these students have made over the last two years. We are ready now to enter this third layer-Light Body.**

You will see, as we continue this Light Body process, much of this energetic work that was given over the last years is again being touched on. If that work had not been done previously or deeply enough, those two DNA strands could not have been awakened to the level in which they were in the second layer initiation. It would have been a much slower process.

Most beings who enter this second and third layer have to do extensive work, which is a lengthy process. That's already been taken care of with the work you've done. This group can now very effectively and proficiently glide through these first three layers, which many take years and years to accomplish.

Jim: I understand what you're saying. My observation is there's a consciousness that's in the Sacred Heart. When noticed and chosen, it actually has a more rapid and a more beneficial experience attached to it. And the key to it is, as you step into the Sacred Heart, the old habit really is now falling away much faster.

Uriel: Correct! First of all this Sacred Heart state of being is crucial to the Light Body process. For it is within the Sacred Heart where you come more into unity with the Holy Spirit and you come into a knowing of yourself as a Soul Spirit. There are two components that make up a fifth-dimensional state of consciousness. One component is the element of Love, which we have worked with and will expand with the fourth-layer activations. The second is this unity consciousness which we have also worked with. Unity and Love are the primary components of the fifth-dimensional consciousness. And so it stands to reason that what you are seeing and perceiving is very accurate.

You have to stay centred within the Sacred Heart, where your actions, your thoughts and your emotions are directed and guided from that state of being. In your everyday life you are constantly bumping up against the fragmentation and what you call noise. In some instances this still has an effect on your ability to stay automatically and naturally within that Sacred Heart state of being. It is not an automatic function! You have to draw your attention back consistently into that space because of the highly charged electromagnetics of fear, separation and survival which you are surrounded by. That automatic function of the Sacred Heart cannot always be sustained without your attention.

That is why Michael, some time back, reminded anyone willing to listen of the importance of creating that collective mass of Light, of consciousness, so that in these particular times, those gathered together holding enough Light could offset what could be a potential problem.

The memory of who you are from the perspective of Soul Spirit is very accessible now. And that requires certain DNA strands to be activated, in addition to these seven layers of Light Body. The further activating of one of those strands of DNA is part of the third layer. This fourth strand of DNA allows the Memory Codes held within the causal body to be recognized in such a way that you are that Christed being operating within a physical body. As you begin to access those memories, the rational mind has a tendency to want to categorize them as past-life occurrences. You are not accessing past lives when you access these memories.

Many like to focus on if they were a king or a queen, or a this or a that, and they forget that lives had a purpose in their conscious evolving. Those lives affect this current ascension. Those lives were about the experience and what was to be gained from that life occurrence. It is here that you start to have a greater access to circular time, the simultaneous nature of who you are. As you begin to play in the memories of the causal body, you begin to have reference points that are very valuable, if they are viewed as information that is being drawn for your utilization in this now moment. Not as a past life. The life is, in a way, really insignificant. It is the experience that becomes very valuable in the moment. So when we say it helps you to draw forth the memory, it is not the memory of a past event. It is an event that is currently occurring. And those layers of evolving have to do with that causal body. It is all imprinted in that causal body.

As this DNA strand gets more integrated in the physicality, you become aware of more of what resides in that causal body. And because you are able to interface with that causal body through a Christed Mind (which is drawn from the Over Soul and the Christed Over Soul, and interfaces through that eighth chakra) it becomes a more conscious, viable and accessible remembrance, a remembrance not of a specific event or a specific life experience, but as a whole, as an interweaving unit.

Accessing those Memory Codes is one of the most important steps that you take in this Light Body activation. Those Memory Codes that were disengaged and prevented you from seeing your true nature are now being reconnected so that a greater unity is established, not only within the body, but also within all of who you are. These newly activated Memory Codes also draw knowledge and information from your Soul Extensions.

These Soul Extensions are not what some refer to as soul mates. Soul Extensions are other expressions of the Soul. Some are in physicalness and some are not in physicalness. As this activation occurs, and as this fourth-level Light Body begins to become very usable, you are going to begin to find that you have awareness of those Soul Extensions. You will begin to draw the knowledge that those Soul Extensions have. You will also begin to share your knowledge with those Soul Extensions. It is not important who or where they are, what their names are or what their life experiences are. What is important is that you begin to have a greater range of capacity available to you within this fifth-dimensional body that you are creating.

You have just put the key in the door to opening that consciousness a little further. You are beginning to access some of these Memory Codes through the causal body, the Christed Mind and the Over Soul. I hesitate to say, "You have just begun," but this is true!

The fourth layer of the Living Light Body

Archangel Raphael gives the installation of the fourth layer of the Living Light Body

This level of Light Body is the base where everything flows in and out, just as the Heart Triad is the base that holds the Unified Field. This level of Light Body also begins a conscious awareness of the self in the fifth, sixth, seventh dimensions. Just as we have talked about conscious remembering and conscious receiving, this is consciously knowing when you are operating in, and when you are receiving from, that sixth- or seventh-dimensional flow. You still have experiences that are related to the body and the physicality, but you are also receiving energetic information and a knowing of the you operating in the sixth and seventh dimensions.

At first it will be only snippets of awarenesses that you are able to hold on to for very short periods of time. But as more of this fourth layer is anchored, and as you train yourself to become very aware, then the bringing back of knowing into the body is a possibility. This allows you to navigate the fifth, sixth and seventh dimensions simultaneously, and use those experiences when you bring them back into the fifth-dimensional body. Consistency and paying very close attention is what is required.

Success story

This rewiring and electrical upgrade we are all going through is apparently now affecting other things around me as well. This morning I woke up at 3am to find the house way too quiet and totally dark, except for one small light downstairs in the kitchen that I leave on overnight. I had no electric power. Neighbours' houses had lights so it looked like it was just me. No fuses were tripped, yet there was somehow power for only one small light. Odd. That's never happened before, not to me or to anyone I know.

I called the power company at 5am and several hours later they had to rewire and upgrade the underground electric connection at the edge of the road to my house. The connectors were corroded and not letting power through, except for the tiny trickle that kept that one small light in the kitchen lit. How did the electricity know to go to that one small light and not to anything else? But now all is well, power is restored and I am no longer in the dark.

There are of course some synchronicities in this event to my own being. I've always felt I had a small pilot light hidden deep in my Sacred Heart that nothing could affect. It was "on" even when everything else was "off". The rest of my connections to the energies of Source were pretty damaged and nonfunctional for a good part of my life. But now that this work has greatly upgraded, cleared and restored my personal power system I enjoy a big and clear energetic connection to the higher Light and Power of Source.

LR, Connecticut, USA

This fourth-layer Light Body is the most important of layers. The first three layers merge into that fourth layer, as do the fifth, sixth and seventh layers. All layers fold into that fourth-layer Light Body and into the heart. It is in this fourth layer where you take on the power of the Christ. Not only the power but also the element of Love to be expressed consistently and continuously without any reservation. This fourth layer expands around the body and outward into the fields of Spirit and Soul Spirit. It is a merged energetic vehicle now. It expands far beyond the body, but is not separate from it, because the body is still being used. This energetic field in this fourth layer is most important because of this expansiveness to all levels of each individual as a Soul Spirit using a physical body.

Until this fourth layer is engaged and integrated at a more conscious level and that massive expanding Sacred Heart is engaged, we cannot give you the information on the fifth, sixth and the seventh layers that we are wishing to discuss with you. We want to make this very clear. This group is a very unique collective consciousness. We have chosen to divide these layers of Light Body into seven layers for this grouping, however there are 12 layers. Much of those other five are interwoven within the previous teachings. These participants, through the guidance they have been given and the evolution that has taken place, require only seven activation points within the completion of the activation of a Light Body.

Upgrading the green Colour Coding and the element of Love

In the fourth layer of the Living Light Body, the element of Love can be understood as empowerment within self: self-empowerment, self-awareness and most importantly, self-Love, self-recognition, self-approval and self-value. Archangel Metatron mentions that feelings and emotions surface with great Love for the planet and for humanity. This is very easily recognized. But when you are asked to recognize that heartfelt Love of self as a divine essence, that individualized expression of All That Is, there can be resistance. There's still a remnant of disbelief within the ego. The sense of unworthiness has been taken care of to a great extent through all this work, but there still is that underlying doubt, a feeling of "well, maybe not". This is due to the massive collective belief system that still plays in the ego.

Now is the time that all of that resistance to self-love can, and must, be eliminated. It is eliminated through conscious awareness, through the greater levels of the green Coding and through accepting the knowing that comes through the Higher Self into the energetic system. Green originates at the Godhead level of the Holy Spirit and allows the knowing of self and self-love. If allowed, this is a great, extensive Love that begins to wash through the emotions and through the Higher Self. If allowed, the mind accepts it because the Christed Mind knows it.

This green Coding, drawn into the Sacred Heart, begins to instigate changes in the way you think and in your emotions. It makes changes in the way you react and the way you view yourself. It provides the impetus to begin to create differently. As you notice these misalignments, you can more easily transmute them and deliberately create different thoughts, different emotions and different reactions. This allows for a much larger range of appreciation and respect for yourself. Humanity has pushed this away since the Fall of Consciousness. And it has been unavailable because of personal and cultural programming and the dense matrix that many have operated under, lifetime after lifetime. Because it is based in the element of Love, this green Coding is instrumental in creating an energetic template that allows self-love to come more fully into the forefront of your consciousness.

Green also tempers what is not Love. Green tempers inhuman treatment of animals and others, bigotry and hate: all that does not vibrate at the element of Love. For example, your thoughts and emotions of "What they're doing is terribly inappropriate/hurtful/cruel/hateful" are tempered and become a very calm understanding: "I understand who they are and the pain they hold. Pain speaks very loud. They are demonstrating their self-hatred and their own separation."

Archangel Raphael comments on the element of Love

Self-love is a more extensive dynamic of the element of Love. When it is taken into the consciousness, into the mind, into the emotions, into the very core of your being, it allows some of this inappropriateness to dissipate. If you do not accept yourself completely and wholly and Love yourself unconditionally as that individualized being of Light, you cannot truly understand humanity. You will judge them as you judge yourself. You will project onto them all of the anomalies that you hold within yourself, whether they be conscious or unconscious. These are residuals of the ego that have yet to be transformed.

This is the teaching and the design of this fourth-layer Light Body: to transform all those pieces within the ego's operation of the body and the mental capacity of the body, as well as the emotions that they evoke. The ego can then rest in its own divinity. That inappropriateness within the interactions of humanity itself is also tempered because this new energetic template of the fourth-layer Light Body is physically held by you. It is modelled for others as you integrate it for yourself personally.

This higher element of Love and the green Colour Coding have a maturity because they emanate from Prime Creator and the Holy Spirit. As such this brings forth that mature state of Love that is not just an emotion or a reaction. It is mature, and it is wise. It brings a wholeness and completeness to the individual through this wise and nurturing aspect. This element of Love does not dissipate. It is solid, stable and very powerful. As you begin to work with it, and the green Coding, it brings in a reverence of self that was not available previously. As Love seats itself more fully, the power within it begins to be recognized.

We have worked a great deal on the many levels of you, unifying the system, holding, creating drawing Light in various ways, using the Higher Mind, accessing the upper chakras and unifying the entire system. Now is the time to complete this process through this element of Love, completing the unity process.

Success story

I want to share with you my recent Higher Self whisper experience. I recognized it very clearly, and I am certain that it is because of all the work we have been doing together to build a Light Body.

Last night on the way back from work (I teach Spanish to adults at night in Los Angeles), I waited at the crosswalk for the light to change as usual. The light changed, but instead of stepping down onto the crosswalk right away (as I usually do), I sensed some kind of energy above my head on the left side and I waited another moment after the traffic stopped. As I took one step onto the crosswalk, a car came out of nowhere, went over the crosswalk and stopped right in front of me, blocking my path. If I hadn't waited that one second, it would have hit me.

As I continued to cross the street, I realized that the energy I sensed was a Higher Self whisper. Everything had happened outside of time. There was no thinking. This was an important experience for me because I became aware of what had just transpired. It's very exciting that I am, and we are, together, building a more coherent multidimensional body!

Thank you so much for all you do with the Archangels and Teachers, and more!

CK, Los Angeles, California, USA

LESSON 29

DNA and the fourth Eye

All the strands of DNA that are activated through these initiations are very important in establishing your consciousness as a Christed being and as a physical expression of All That Is. As you activate more of the Living Light Body and more of these DNA strands, you will be able to see yourself more accurately as that Soul Spirit; not just from the perspective of an evolving Soul in a physical body, but as a part of All That Is. The fifth strand of DNA is awakened with the fourth layer initiation.

The process of activating the fourth eye also activates this fifth strand of DNA. The fourth eye resides a few inches above the crown chakra, below the eighth chakra. This fourth eye is in the geometry of a star tetrahedron, just like the golden Christed Matrix on the altar within the Sanctuary of the Pink Diamond in the Sacred Heart. It is a brilliant sapphire-blue colour and has a specific emanation of Light coming from Universal Mind in the eighth chakra.

The activation of the fourth eye is structured as a looping of Light and there are distinct energy points that have to be consciously recognized, entered and paid attention to. The Light loops through the energy points in the following sequence:

1. The Christed Mind in the eighth chakra holds a perfectly balanced image of unlimited possibility.
2. The Undifferentiated Light is drawn through the Universal Mind and Christed Mind in the eighth chakra and is brought into the fourth eye.
3. The brilliant sapphire-blue star tetrahedron in the fourth eye begins to ignite and shape the possibilities of what the Undifferentiated Light's purpose is for us in this layer.
4. The Undifferentiated Light passes to the Eye of Horus in the crown chakra. The individual expression of Soul Spirit in physicalness

begins to get formed through that Eye of Horus. The Eye of Horus also has the ability to draw that Light through the Eternal Eye/the Eye of All That Is.

5. The Undifferentiated Light passes to the pineal gland aspect of the Eye of Horus. Undifferentiated Light then flows into the pineal centre. Here this Light adjusts so it can be used in the body. This is possible because of that unification of Soul Spirit that's now in the body in a much greater capacity. The capacity to create in a physical body as a multidimensional Christed being is what you are about to experience – fully conscious, very capable, very focused.

6. Finally the Undifferentiated Light flows into the Sacred Heart, into the Unified Field of the first Triad and then returns to the Christed Mind, creating a loop. This looping enables interdimensional consciousness to begin to take place at a more aware level and it turns on the fifth strand of DNA.

As you loop this Light through these energy points several times, notice what you notice. As this fourth eye opens, it's now as if you're using a very expanded camera lens that provides a much greater reference point that is not yet familiar. This is occurring simultaneously within you and within the Earth. There's a tremendous amount that's going to be noticed. From that standpoint, journalling, paying attention and sitting quietly without having to make sense of this is very valuable.

Archangel Raphael teaches about the fourth eye

Greetings, beloveds! It is I, Raphael! We are all with you this session as you begin to open your Heart more fully and receive the fullness of who you are in a more experiential way. So if you will now take a deep breath, and be very conscious of yourself in your Sacred Heart, and allow me to show you the extent of what

you have absorbed with the green Coding that you have been working with. I wish to show you all of the Codes, the energetic Codes of Love, as they emanate and are distributed through that green, that magnificent green Coding that expresses itself in a much more rarefied vibration.

As you sit within your Sacred Heart and absorb this Code that I am now showing to you, there is a realization of yourself as Soul Spirit in a way that you have not seen previously. It is very unified and powerful. The Light is magnificent, and the Love that is present is beyond description in your language. Rest in this place of unification within the Sacred Heart that is the base for all of who you are. Through these various templates that are held in that green Code within the Heart, all separation begins to be displaced: you separate from Soul Spirit; Light separate from Love; physical expressions separate from the creative realms. All of this begins to fall away! And there is a strong knowing as you absorb these Codes of unification. You know yourself as indivisible from All That Is.

It is from this state of consciousness, beloveds, that you know yourself as a powerful creator. You know yourself as Living Light and Love that is emanating through matter and is exemplifying itself simultaneously within that matter, as well as within all realms of creation. You, as a being of Light filled with Love, begin to recognize yourself from this perspective.

When you create and activate that compression mechanism in the second Triad, in the pineal, that Undifferentiated Light is drawn in through Universal Mind and through that fourth eye. There is a recognition of yourself from the perspective of the fourth eye as Undifferentiated Light expressing itself in the physical form. That complete cycle is activated and is in play continuously, drawing in from Universal Mind, through you as Undifferentiated Light. Through the crown into the pineal, where it is compressed and then made usable in the physical realm.

All the while this is occurring, you are aware of yourself simultaneously in the Sacred Heart within the Christed Matrix, vibrating at a very high frequency range in a unified state. Here there is no separation whatsoever with any part of your consciousness. The Codes that you are given that reside in that green template, those rarefied vibrations, allow you to know yourself as the Living Light in complete unification. Every aspect of yourself is drawn into the Sacred Heart. Every aspect from the you as that Undifferentiated Light from the eighth chakra, to the you as an embodied being expressing itself through the first four chakras that are also anchored and drawn into that Sacred Heart. All parts of you in that physical expression begin to vibrate with this green Code of unification, this green of Living Undifferentiated Light. The physical body is transitioning and making adjustments to bring itself further into this unification, into the unified Light that is necessary for the you, in a body, to express yourself as Soul Spirit.

Much is occurring! It is important for you to rest in these states of consciousness. Acknowledge the flow of energy that is transpiring within every part of your being, within every part of your physical body. In this state of consciousness, you have no trouble loving yourself. For you are not separate from the All That Is because you are the Living Light and Love in an undifferentiated form. And you have the power to compress that undifferentiated form of Light and create its expression within matter, within your body and within the realms of form.

There is an exhilaration that you feel coming out of your emotional body. Some may experience this as an ecstasy they have never felt before. Some may experience this as a joy that they have looked for and sought after their entire life. This is real! This is your first step into the multidimensional realms of reality, where all parts of you are expressed and known. The presence of the Holy Spirit in this space is unmistakable. The knowing is solid, not from the perspective of form, but from the perspective of stable unification. And what has been unknowable to you previously is now known.

You have begun to know yourself as you have never seen yourself previously. This is a path, a journey that you have entered into very consciously and intentionally to know yourself. The gates are open! You are now seeing yourself, knowing yourself as the Living Light. We are honoured to witness this evolving of your consciousness. We support you. And most importantly, we share our Light and our Love with you, as we are part of that unification of all parts of creation.

We welcome you into this awareness. We stand with you, as we have said many times, shoulder to shoulder, heart to heart. But now that has a deeper meaning, for we are one!

Blessings

Online resources

Meditation to establish an expanded space in the Sacred Heart and begin to live in the body differently than before (33:27)

To access the online classroom,
visit www.masteringalchemy.com/book

Lesson 30

The fifth layer of the Living Light Body

As with previous layers of the Living Light Body, a series of activations occur that together turn on and bring in the fifth layer. Although it isn't complicated, the rational mind does have a tendency to attempt to figure it out and understand it. As you move through this next series of initiations, allow the words and energetics simply to flow through, around and within you. Give your rational mind a vacation.

Archangel Metatron comments on the activation process

Every activation that is taken, at every layer of this Light Body, is dependent on another. And they all function as a unit simultaneously. This must be understood, because not one layer is more valuable or relevant than another. In the activation process we approach it in a numbered, sequential process for ease and assimilation in the consciousness and in the body. But they all have great value and eventually, in this activation process, operate within the Unified Field of who you are.

The emphasis of the fifth layer is to create a state of consciousness where you are aware of being in the physical form and in the collective consciousness simultaneously. After it has been activated, the fifth layer is merged with the fourth layer. This activation is given by a group of Teachers. Several other Elders offer enthusiastic comments and welcome us into the collective.

Archangel Metatron talks about merging
the eighth, ninth and tenth chakras and bridging the eleventh

Greetings. We are here, beloveds, as a collective configuration. We are much more than just Michael, Metatron and Melchizedek. There is a grand collection of beings gathered in a collective state to be with you, to set the energy for this transmission and model where you are going. Although we come as a collective, we also retain our individual expressions of All That Is. At an energetic level you will also begin to receive templates that are involved in developing a collective consciousness, as we do, without diminishing your individualized expression.

We would like to talk about the chakras that are important in engaging this layer Light Body. They are the eighth, ninth, tenth and eleventh chakras. You are already very well aware of the function of the eighth chakra. The function of the ninth chakra relates to the collective realm, the collective of us as Teachers, Lords of Light, Elohim, Archangels and Masters, as co-creators of consciousness at a physical level. You have begun to create an interface already and a merging with these Great Beings.

The tenth chakra relates to your Higher Mind and the Mind of All That Is. This is the Mind of Prime Creator as it relates to the nonphysical state of who you are as spirit, plus that collective nature of who you are. Can you see the advantages of having a fully operational tenth chakra available to you to use at

a physical level? This interface between you at a physical level and you at a collective level, a nonphysical state, is important. We will work with you in the coming weeks creating that interface.

The energetics within the eleventh chakra are needed in creating this fifth-layer Light Body. Understand here that this fifth-layer Light Body is your creation. We give you the information. We support you in creating the energetics that are necessary. But it is you who use the energetics within your system to create the fifth-layer Light Body. You are the creators now.

The eighth and the ninth and the tenth chakras are first elevated and activated, then there is a bridging of the eleventh chakra. This bridging begins to allow the Over Soul to operate within the physicalness of the body, bringing that consciousness of the collective nature of the nonphysical into the physical expression.

As you begin to construct a bridging into the eleventh chakra, there is the opportunity and necessity to activate a sixth strand of your DNA. The energetics of the eleventh chakra are dependent on that sixth strand of DNA to be usable. The eleventh chakra is where the energy components of yourself as Soul Spirit and the physical body reside and are then manifested in the world of form and in your life. This strand relates to your physical body and allows you, at a physical level, to know yourself in this collective consciousness. This is the collective consciousness in which we Teachers are all participating with you at this moment. That sixth strand of DNA begins to enable the drawing from this collective nature, fully consciously, with every thought thought, experiencing yourself consciously with the Thought that thought you into existence.

To maintain this state of recognizing yourself as an individual and a member of the greater collective requires a focused awareness in your day-to-day activities. This does not mean that as you move through your day you have to be only present in that vast collective consciousness. It also does not mean you seek out sensory communication with any particular Teacher. This "mediumship" or "channelling" is a distraction, and the collective seldom uses words. Any communication or transmission is a subtle, quiet knowing. As you navigate your day-to-day life experience, you begin to recognize that you are much more than only an individual. You have available to you a very expansive collective nature to use in your daily life. That collective is a key resource in your ability to create and express yourself in a potent, certain and powerful way. Not for the sake of power itself, but for manifestation in the physical realm. You now have available to you a grand fount of information on how, for example, to create delicious and beautiful meals. Tapped into the collective consciousness, you are now able to successfully, intuitively create incredible meals with little effort. Another example would be as a director of volunteers in a nonprofit organization. Now you have the wisdom from the collective of Elders to inspire good leadership. This is a knowing. This is not something you actively search for.

The Teachers are now asking us to focus more intentionally throughout our daily life experience. There can be many, many distractions in the world that keep us from this. Returning to and practising previous tools from the Teachers will help you to better maintain the state of being that allows this knowing to flow to you. As this layer becomes more integrated in the physical body through the presence of that sixth strand of DNA, you will notice there are fewer disruptions in the energetic flow of your day. Fear, which is the biggest energetic template of the third dimension, begins to be eliminated and is no longer a consideration as you operate from this fifth-layer Light Body. You are operating at a state of consciousness and a physical state that is blended and is no longer affected by the rigid physical template of fear.

Yeshua comments on this blended state of being

This blended, merged state was very difficult for me in my embodiment as the divine individual and the divine collective. And some will find the same difficulties. It takes a while to seat this massive consciousness in your body because of the limitations of the body, the dimension in which the body was configured and the density of the consciousness of the body. So do not be concerned when you are not able to hold this state continually in your life expression. There is an ebb and a flow that occurs in the beginning, where you are able to be that consciousness simultaneously: the divine individual and the divine collective.

It was only near the end of my embodiment that I was able to merge these two states very significantly. I could then operate simultaneously, without effort, in focusing any part of my attention as I existed in my body. This allowed me to operate in the last days of my embodiment without stress or pain of any kind. During the time that I remained with my companions in my Light Body, my physical body was transformed fully and completely into my Light Body. Yet I remained in the physical realm of a third dimension. I could very easily, then, transcend that state and move fully and completely into the collectiveness of the I Am, where I reside and am present with you at this moment.

I come with an open Heart, my Sacred Heart, and I merge with you at that collective state so that you might gain from my experience. This merging of self as the divine individual and the divine collective is seated through your Sacred Heart and very specifically anchored in that eleventh chakra, so you may draw this consciousness to you and in your body at will. When you realize you can draw that merged consciousness at will through that eleventh chakra into your physical state, it will then only take a moment to shift your attention to the spinning vortex of that eleventh chakra and the consciousness that is held there, to be made usable in your physical, day-to-day life. No longer will you view yourself as separate. You will view yourself as a unit with all life in form. As this anchors more fully in your body, in your awareness, you will know yourself as the Christ. And there will be no doubt.

Success story

The Teachers have told us so often to "pay attention" and one of the things I have been noticing with the Living Light Body is the effect of food and how that can affect (to an extreme) my mental–emotional body. It has always been important but now it's really crucial. Food can throw me off balance more than people or situations do.

This morning I wanted to eat some homemade jam but I couldn't open the bottle. I tried and tried, and I kept seeing this image of the Archangels holding the cover closed and hearing them say, "Think twice." I smiled and thought, "You really don't want me to eat this then?" So I put it back into the refrigerator with a bit of disappointment and a feeling of contradiction because, "Hey, I have free will."

But the moment I put it back into the refrigerator I saw a bowl with two pieces of fruit, cut and ready to eat. This time I laughed and I ate them instead of the sugary jam. I feel good now. And I am in balance. If I had eaten the jam I would not feel this good, and in the end I would have regretted it.

So I am paying attention more than ever, feeling and hearing more, improving my senses and finding it a really great contribution to building the Living Light Body. When I am in balance, I live the most amazing experience of inner joy. Thank you again for this amazing journey.

FM, Macau, China

Mother Mary comments on this aspect of the fifth layer

As you merge the eighth, ninth and tenth chakras, something significant happens in the consciousness of who you are. The eighth chakra is where you begin to think from the Universal Mind. The rational mind drops away. And Universal thought, the divine thought, through that eighth chakra, is very present.

As you merge into the ninth chakra's fuller expression within yourself, you not only access the Lords of Light, the Elohim, the Masters and the Archangels, but also you are one and the same. You are one! You operate in a vast collective consciousness. And there is no separation. Here is where you begin to enter into the field of that Undifferentiated Light.

As you merge into that tenth chakra of a fuller expression, this is where you begin to draw into yourself the Undifferentiated Light. The creative will and power become a very dynamic force within you. And that complete balance of the Divine Masculine and Divine Feminine becomes known to you from that state of unity. As you sit in that Undifferentiated Light, you can know and see what those divine aspects of the force are within you, without separation. This is enhanced in that Universal Mind through the presence of that fourth eye.

Then you merge into that eleventh chakra. This is where that Undifferentiated Light is held within your energetic field and is drawn upon at will in full alignment with the thought of Universal Mind, through the presence of the Holy Spirit and through the presence of that Christed Over Soul. Full expression in complete unity. Will and power, thought, emotion and the dynamics of your mental–emotional body come now into a full merged state. And the consciousness of that body is now able to hold the Christ Consciousness of the Christed Over Soul.

LESSON 30

Elevating will and power in the fifth chakra and Sacred Heart respectively

Power and will are applications (eighth Ray of Creation) in your third- and fourth-dimensional creation process. Creator's Will is held within the throat chakra, and Power within the Sacred Heart. As the layers of the Living Light Body are merged, however, power and will have a much more expansive ability to add to your creations. Will and power are held within the Undifferentiated Light that is now generated within the pineal centre and drawn from the eleventh chakra.

We are at a very significant point here. This is a birthing process. It is like the moment when a baby bird pecks its way out of its shell. You have been a caterpillar in its chrysalis, and now is the moment for you to decide, "I'm leaving the chrysalis. I will become a butterfly." And the only choice you have now is *how* (not *if*) you'll express your power and alter the energetics and the dynamics of form on Earth. That has been the focus all along. Not to escape the form, or the body, or the Earth, but to alter it substantially so that the divine expression of you, as creator, can be fully expressed, easily and consistently. This alters the energetics of the Earth and the physical body.

There is a deep core knowing of the power that you hold within you, and the will to establish it very precisely. You've always had this will to alter the Earth and the power to bring this about. This is where it's been said, "You're big. You've never been small. You're significant. You've never been insignificant." You came here to alter.

This is your personal will and personal power coupled with the element of Love. Those seven Living Words that you learned many pages back are not just words any longer. Those simple words are now a state of consciousness. Those words are a state of being. How many times in your life experience have you had to stand firmly for what you believed and what you knew to be true? Regardless of the disagreement or opinions of others, you held strongly to that knowing. That was your power and will. It took your will to hold the energy of Certain and Capable, regardless of what was being expressed or thrown at you. There is an underlying knowing, a feeling of the quiet power that you, as an individual creator, possess and can direct to create precisely what is wanted in a moment. It is quiet, it is centred and it is known.

The divine will and power within the fifth layer of the Living Light Body are balanced. They work within that unity consciousness of Source and are undivided and undifferentiated in their expression. Not only is there unlimited potential, there also is unlimited momentum. In the movement of the Undifferentiated Light through the eleventh chakra and the creation of it within the pineal centre, you begin to experience the divine version of will and power. This will be known and felt within the emotions. This is the creative force that you hold within you and have always held, although up to this moment, had very little experience with.

The only direction that is required energetically is the further creating of Undifferentiated Light and directing it into the first Triad's throat chakra and the Sacred Heart. This Undifferentiated Light must be felt, recognized and allowed. It's expressed through the power and the will within you. This is the Light of Creation. You hold the power and will to create. It's not your power and will plus Source's. It is divine will and power operating as a unit.

Eliminating separation, victimization and unworthiness held within the first two strands of DNA

Programming of separation, victimization and unworthiness were placed into the physical DNA at the Fall of Consciousness. They were then unconsciously reinforced and solidified through the repetition of genetic lineages and cultural agreements for aeons. These energetic programmes and the corresponding thoughts and emotions prevent you, as Soul Spirit, from experiencing freedom within the physical form. They are held within the first two strands of DNA. Metatron is very clear when presenting this. It's not about eliminating the two strands of DNA, or even clearing everything from them. Those patterns of separation, victimization and unworthiness are removed by creating a very focused, intentional, precise laser beam of Undifferentiated Light and directing it from the consciousness you hold in the third Triad. Divine will and power from the unified collective state of being are important in this dismantling.

As the consciousness in the third Triad is drawn into the Undifferentiated Light from that eleventh chakra and organized very precisely, you will bring it down, drawing it through the fourth eye and into the pineal centre. That brilliant flame will then magnify the Undifferentiated Light into a precision laser beam. You will then direct it into the thymus centre in the etheric body and, with clear, focused Intention, draw it into the physicalness of the first two strands of DNA. This eliminates the separation, victimization, unworthiness and rigidity that prevents the Soul Spirit from operating fully and freely within the physical form.

Archangel Metatron instructs us

This session is completely devoted to eliminating those parts of the first two strands of DNA that relate to separation, victimization and unworthiness, which are huge energetic blocks within the Christed Matrix. You have many tools at your command to disengage and eliminate this structure. A big portion of this is through the use of Undifferentiated Light and through the use of the Triadic system.

Recognize your mind as divine and have access to that divine expression through the eighth and tenth chakras. From the ninth chakra have the ability to connect with the Lords of Light and the Elohim more directly and with the intention of Unity, rather than division. This will take a little focused attention within that ninth chakra to sit in that collective consciousness and direct

the Undifferentiated Light into the DNA structure to eliminate the energetics of separation, victimization and unworthiness.

You are engaging your divine will and power as the Christed being that you are. It is not power over or divided power. It is a unified will and power that allows for this elimination of that portion of the DNA structure that is no longer compatible with the state of consciousness you have developed through the activation of the layers of the Living Light Body. These structures are a hindrance to your ability to begin to activate other parts of the Living Light Body.

The fourth-layer Light Body was very significant in opening the heart further. Now, that said, this fifth-layer Light Body is very connected to that fourth layer and enhances its expression, as you can very well see. By altering the first two strands of DNA, coming into that unified consciousness and accepting the will and power within yourself, that fourth-layer Light Body expands exponentially. The fifth layer accelerates and expands the fourth layer. The first layer, the second, the third, the fourth are enhanced and magnified by the presence and activation of the fifth layer.

Upgrading the pituitary gland to match your new fifth-dimensional physical body

What will be required at this next step will be to create a new balance within the physical body. Those levels of thought and emotion that have instructed the hormones, chemicals, fluids of the body and cellular system how to function are no longer there. They have been upgraded. There will be an opportunity now to bring balance within the waters, the blood, the fluids, the hormones, the oxygen and the hydrogen. When that victimization, separation and worthlessness are removed, there is an opportunity to use the Undifferentiated Light to bring about balance in the messaging structure of the pituitary gland.

Archangel Uriel comments on this process

The reason we want to pay attention now to the pituitary gland is because it is a master gland that alters the chemical balance within all parts of the physical body. To have the consciousness and the physical body function at a more multidimensional level requires a reformulation of how hormones are used and the chemical system itself operates. This is an important thing to understand. In the disengagement of the two strands of DNA relating to the physical body, a rebalancing of the chemicals is required so that the operations and the communications within the body are brought up to the new level of fifth-dimensional functioning.

It is through the use of the flowing Undifferentiated Light that a rebalancing can occur.

As the Light of Creator is drawn into the pituitary gland from the eleventh chakra, it is brought into the pineal and the second Triad. Because of the flame that burns there very brightly, it is immediately, through your intention, directed into the neurons of the entire cellular system elevating and balancing the production of hormones that support a fifth-dimensional body. Here you will begin to balance the chemicals in the body that are present in each cell. The fluids, the waters, the blood, the hormones, the secretions, all become perfectly attuned in the element of Love. The air, the gasses, the oxygen, the hydrogen, are raised in vibration and balanced with all the elements. The element of Fire enhances the elevation and

the passion of a perfectly balanced fifth-dimensional physical form unfolding.

Here again it requires attention, specific intention and time for absorption and complete utilization. So patience and continual revisitation. Not long periods. Just stay aware and notice how these activations affect the functioning of the physical body as it moves into a fifth-dimensional level.

It is within that noticing that you absorb even more awareness of yourself. Recognize yourself as whole and complete unto yourself through divine imaging within the Undifferentiated Light, merged through your intention and your will and power.

Lesson 31

The sixth layer of the Living Light Body

At this point in the work, the Teachers have a very specific request. Be quiet unto yourself. Really hold this energy close to you and don't go out and tell your friends and family about it. Can you remember who you were before you began this course? There was a noisiness, a non-focus, a scatteredness and probably much more. That you is not the you who you are today. Notice the gap between the today-you and the then-you. Many of those not following the teachings with you are still in that noisy, disruptive place. Keep this work and the transformation you've achieved close to your heart and cherish it as a precious thing that is vulnerable to the opinions and judgements of others. It is. What you have accomplished thus far, most have no clue about and they don't have the commitment or focus to create it for themselves. They are not bad or less-than. You are better than none. And the Teachers are very clear. Staying quiet in this space will be extremely valuable to you as we continue. This is the time when managing yourself makes a significant difference in what you can achieve and how your life unfolds.

As with the other layers of the Light Body, the sixth layer includes several activations, tools and energetics. Yeshua and Archangel Metatron are the primary teachers for this layer.

The Arc of the Covenant

The Arc of the Covenant is not a gold-covered box sitting in a dusty tent, covered in skins and cloth. It doesn't hold the Ten Commandments and it wasn't carried through the desert for 40 wandering years. The Arc of the Covenant is much more.

What will be accomplished in the activations for the sixth layer is the opening of the brain and the neurological system in order to turn on the spiritual autonomic system in the physical body and the spiritual bodies. We're mechanically rewiring the electrical system, so the sixth-layer (and later the seventh-layer) Light Body can be anchored.

To refresh your memory, the medulla oblongata is a component of the second Triad and it is located at the back of the brain at the top of the spinal cord. Its third-dimensional job is to control the autonomic functions of the physical body, such as sneezing, swallowing, circulating blood and breathing. The medulla oblongata is a critical element in the second Triad and it assists in creating the autonomic functioning of the first Triad in the Sacred Heart. The medulla oblongata will now assist the third Triad to operate autonomically. It is a key component in the creation of the Arc of the Covenant. This activation also further unifies the left and the right hemispheres of the brain.

"Ark" vs "Arc"

The Teachers have purposely used the spelling "Arc" instead of "Ark". Their intention is two-fold: to make a distinction between this energetic and the biblical references to a golden box or a big boat filled with animals; and to describe how this energetic domes or curves over the head.

Yeshua gives the activation for the Arc of the Covenant

I would like to address the medulla oblongata and the reason why this centre has to be activated consciously in your body at this time. You have taken great steps in many activations. The work that you have done with your pineal centre, the work that you have done in your Sacred Heart, and in opening the higher chakras is quite extensive. If you had not activated the pineal centre and the pituitary gland to the extent that you have, you would be unable to use this centre in a way that I am going to direct you to use it.

There is a very important part of this medulla centre that you have to understand. It creates an arc over your head. Many call this the "Arc of the Covenant". Some call it the "Arc of Light". This magnificent Arc arcs over your physical head and connects the fourth eye, the pineal part of the Eye of Horus, down through the central channel and into your Sacred Heart. This Arc has many specific purposes. It begins the ascension process. This ascension process has to take place in your head, because the head represents the functioning of the brain. The brain then becomes the receiver and the transmitter of communication between you and Prime Creator and all realms of creation, of which you are a part. You are the All That Is.

This communication has to flow through the electrical, neurological functioning of the brain for it to be made usable at a physical level. For is not that what this ascension is all about? Not only ascending your consciousness, but ascending the physical realm, the physical body and the physical Earth. You have to use the components of the brain to achieve this and more of the brain is made usable because of this activation in the medulla centre. You begin to commune with Source in a much different way. This has nothing to do with talking with a separate being. It has much more to do with consciously coming into unity with the All That Is. Mainstream religion could not understand this. It did not have the capacity to understand as you understand.

This is the Arc of the Covenant and I know that many of you have heard that this is a box where the Ten Commandments were placed. That was because, at that time of denseness, people could not understand that that container was your brain: your mental body unified with Divine Mind. They did not understand, so they thought of it as an exterior container.

Now let us talk about the Ten Commandments, so you have a little better understanding here. Those Commandments were necessary in those dense times of separation because the ego was in charge. The ego had to be controlled, so it had to have laws from which to operate. This is no longer the case. Through this course, you have transformed a great portion of that ego into a more unified, Light-filled state. You are not operating in an ego state. You are operating in the holiness of your Soul Spirit. The laws were written for your ego and they are not necessary now. Your ego lives by grace, enlightenment and Christ Consciousness now. You have brought this into being and you set that template for the rest of humanity, for the collective consciousness.

As you engage in the activation, the ascension template then flows through the blood and every fluid of your body. This ascension template is present in every chakra. This radiant Light is composed of brilliant colours that you have never seen before. The coding of those colours will become very available to you for your use.

As you continue to experience this Arc of the Covenant, you will discover it is not just a single line moving from the back to the front of your head. It is a dome with no base. You might imagine it as a helmet that extends down to your shoulders. The Light energetics of the Arc of the Covenant flow into your Sacred Heart.

Success story

I am in a place beyond words with our new space helmet. Way fun!

I recently tripped and fell hard on a cement surface, deeply bruising the inside of my left knee. Honouring the healing process with my herbal remedies and Reiki, I continued to experience a painful knee. I was taking ibuprofen to sleep at night.

A few nights ago, in a meditative state, playing in the new space helmet, aligned with the Undifferentiated Light and the element of Love in the Unified Field, I sent this powerful healing energy into my aching knee. The pain was immediately gone. And it hasn't come back after several days and a long-distance drive.

The interesting thing about pain is that once it's gone we don't give it much thought and just go about our business. In my life experience, with the tools I have learned and cultivated through A Course in Mastering Alchemy, I have effected some wonderful changes/healing within my body. This, however, is the most dramatic physical change I have ever experienced. Wow!

Dianne B, Washington, USA

Seed Crystals

Another activation within the sixth layer that the Teachers of Light present is Seed Crystals. There are three significant crystalline seed energies that are located within the etheric body. They provide more coherence and communication from the Soul Spirit and from that connection with Source. These Seed Crystals are able to translate various tones and sound vibrations that are not heard with the human ear, sometimes known as Light Language.

Many have worked with Light Language, although without fully understanding nor having an ability to translate it. This Light Language is more than a spoken language. It's an energetic format from which the higher-dimensional levels of thought are translated and made usable from one dimension to another. This provides a coherency within the fifth, sixth and seventh dimensions.

These waves, or unheard sound vibrations, contain Undifferentiated Light. This not only allows the language to be spoken, understood and heard, but also carries energetics similar to some of the Colour Codes that were introduced previously. These sound vibrations, however, are of a much higher, more refined frequency range and emanate from the seventh-dimensional frequency band.

Archangel Metatron steps up to offer us this

There is a configuration of Seed Crystals within the etheric body that make a triangle. There is one above each eye, just above the eyebrow, and one just below the hairline, right in line with the nose. This triangle is significant because the Eye of Horus is in that third eye, the pineal and the crown. These Seed Crystals activate that Eye of Horus at a more expansive bandwidth of frequencies. The Arc of the Covenant further enables you to decipher this language.

In that etheric body there is also a column of Light that runs from the eleventh chakra into the Earth's Christed Matrix, passing through the Sacred Heart. The seed triangle is not only a triangle, it is also a tetrahedron and has an anchor point held within that column of Light.

That tetrahedron draws from the Undifferentiated Light moving through that column, creating an interrelationship within the etheric body and the physical body. It is also creating an interrelationship with the merged Christed Over Soul as it is becoming anchored into the body, all operating as one vehicle.

There is another separate Seed Crystal located above the right ear, in a lobe of the brain of the etheric body. This one enables you to hear tones, sounds and patterns that cannot be heard by the physical ear but are present in the Creation realms. This one also enables you to activate more memory of experiences in other star systems, planetary systems and dimensions. The Memory Code in the causal body relates to your mastery and this Memory Code relates to your experiences in the many existences that you have had.

Ze and On particles

Much occurs in the Arc of the Covenant. Within this dome exist electrical components, and once the dome is seated it becomes more expansive and encompasses more of your individual and collective state. There is an automatic electrical arcing within the dome that amplifies the life force of the body through the neurological system, thus altering the performance of the body itself. The Light that is activated around and within the head begins to extend from there, around the entire auric field. These electrical charges also begin to alter the capacity of the brain to communicate thoughts that come in from the realms of Light, as well as various star systems.

Through the Unified Field and the merging with All That Is, your ability to think as one with the Universal Mind is enhanced. You can now, as the individualized expression of Creator, create the Ze particles with the

Undifferentiated Light that you intentionally draw from your eleventh chakra. Ze particles enter the Arc of the Covenant and move electrically through it. The Ze particles exist in the Undifferentiated Light and are the expanded aspects of your own consciousness that are not accessible or knowable while in the third dimension and the lower levels of thought. Ze particles are what your thoughts are in the higher realms and in your Higher Mind. These thoughts don't contain words and words can't describe them. They mediate between the body's consciousness and your divine consciousness and allow you greater access to the you in the higher dimensions.

Seed Crystals and Ze

The Seed Crystals must be activated by the Ze particles in order for changes to take place in the electromagnetic field of the body and in the electrical components of the neurological system. This allows the brain to open more fully to the broader range of communications that are possible. The Seed Crystals also act as transmitters into the brain. They transmit the Undifferentiated Light and electrical impulses, altering the neurological structure of the brain. It's only in the fifth and sixth layers of thought that you can observe this.

As these Seed Crystals become more efficient, the electrical transmission into the brain begins to move into the cells of the body, altering the molecules of the cells. As this alteration occurs, the ability for the merging of the Soul Spirit, the Christed Over Soul and Over Soul, through the Ze particles, is again increased and expanded. More knowledge and awareness flow into the cells.

This higher-functioning electrical system was disengaged at the Fall of Consciousness. Through this electrical stimulus, a magnification takes place in the third Triad, which also stimulates the second and the first Triads to further expand the vibration of the Unified Field. This process also alters the functioning of the electrical components of the cells to enable the cell to hold and create more ATP.

LESSON 31

On particles

The Universal Mind and the Mind of Source function together as one massive consciousness, which is only now accessible to you as this sixth layer is anchored. You've done all the preparatory work to merge now with those Minds. You've anchored the Eye of Horus; become skilled at using the Undifferentiated Light and the Colour Codes; activated five layers of the Living Light Body; upgraded the pituitary gland, medulla oblongata, Triads and pineal centre; and you've awakened four additional strands of DNA.

The consciousness and thoughts of these two all-encompassing minds create On particles, which are also held and accessed within the Undifferentiated Light. The Ze particles (your higher consciousness) can merge with the On particles (the consciousness of Universal Mind and Mind of Source) within the Arc of the Covenant. Just as you drew the Ze particles into the electrical arcing function of the Arc, draw in the On particles from the vastness of the Undifferentiated Light through the eleventh chakra.

Your mind and the Universal Mind and Mind of Source merge and are accessible as electrified Ze-On particles within your doming Arc of the Covenant. This unified function of the three minds establishes the domain of the Christed Over Soul, which begins to direct your consciousness. Your consciousness, at a Soul Spirit level, is no longer hindered by the functioning of your third-dimensional vehicle. You are now better able to sit within the seventh layer of thought. You and the Thought that thought you into existence can now think together. Again, "thought" is not in words or concepts. It is a great knowing. You access and "know" from an expanded consciousness. This sixth-layer activation allows you access to a unity that has not been available.

The Undifferentiated Light of Creator is absolutely key in this process. It is the way and means of unifying the spiritual body, the physical body, the etheric body, and most importantly, enabling that Christed body to take the dominant position in the functioning of the physicality as a divine being of Light.

THE SIXTH LAYER OF THE LIVING LIGHT BODY

The triad of Archangels Metatron and Michael and Lord Melchizedek comment on this initiation

We have all gathered together to recode the consciousness of the human body. And by that we mean you could be in a state of consciousness, knowing yourself as that divine being of Light, and very easily slip out of it, depending on how that third-dimensional matrix of humanity bumps up against you. With this activation there is a stability in the energetic fields and in the consciousness of the body that holds an equilibrium and does not allow the variance or the slipping in and out of states of consciousness. It allows you to maintain that Light energy within all parts of yourself and begin to function energetically through your thoughts that are very much merged with Universal Mind and the Mind of Source.

Your rational mind cannot participate in this. It is unnecessary for you to research the physics of it. Yes, you can find some relationships in that exploration, but, we ask you, does it serve that higher purpose of you transforming yourself into Light? Even though you have not had this technology for aeons of your time, there is a portion of you that will remember these things. You have to allow the opportunity for the experience and the remembrance. This sixth-layer activation is extensive. It brings an amplification to the Unified Field. It amplifies exponentially the functioning of the Triadic system in the body and most importantly, that third Triad, which hasn't really been fully understood or fully activated. Yes, it has been functioning, but the amplification that is taking place in that third Triad because of these electrical charges and arcing is extensive.

This is one of the very few times where we will encourage you into that state of aloneness, to disengage from collective consciousness and fully immerse yourself in this individualized experience of these energetics.

Disengaging the lower tiers of the emotional body with the tenth Ray of Creation

There are three tiers to the mental–emotional body. The first tier is third-dimensional thought and emotion – anger, rage, jealousy, resentment, etc. That tier is very dense and rigid. You've been dismantling this tier for a long time, but that structure still has a presence. The second tier has an electromagnetic field that supports the first tier of thought and emotion. Additionally, the second tier has a relationship to the third tier. The third tier is of the higher mental–emotional state of Spirit. This is the place you're moving to and will live in always. An important action occurs with the activation of the sixth layer of the Living Light Body: the first tier of the mental–emotional body is disengaged.

You've used the Rose tool and the fourth, fifth, sixth and eighth Rays of Creation to decharge and alter the strong magnetic field of the emotions. You've brought it into a refined state that is more compatible with the electrical Ze-On particles and you've begun to access thoughts from the merged Universal Mind and Mind of Source.

Archangel Metatron comments on the lower tiers

Now, with this sixth-layer Light Body, you will not experience the ranges of emotion that you experience at a third-dimensional level. As you enter into that fifth-, sixth-, seventh-dimensional functioning of your Soul Spirit embodied, you begin to use the emotions in a little different way. There is a neutrality in this expression and there is not any variance, no spikes of highs and lows. This emotional body carries a heavy, heavy magnetic force that has to be further altered so the entire functioning of the mental–emotional body can begin to alter the capacity of the body to hold the more refined states of Spirit. We can do this together with the tenth Ray of Creation.

It is with your intention and direction that you will begin to access the tenth Ray. There is a huge, magnetic set of refined templates in the tenth Ray. It is going to be through the Higher Mind and the electrical arcing in the brain that you can begin to call on this Ray. You begin to draw this tenth Ray and its magnetics into the mental–emotional body. Then direct it specifically into the emotions. It is the electrical component of the Ze-On particles and the directing of the tenth Ray that begin to disengage the restricted rigidity of the lower two tiers of the third-dimensional emotional expression. In the presence of this refined tenth-Ray energy, the magnetics and the electrical components of the lower emotions are no longer compatible with the sixth-layer Light Body.

The emotional body begins to function only from those more refined emotions. It becomes a consistent state of harmony between the mind and the emotions. And there are no spikes. There are no lows. There are no highs. There is a consistent harmonic resonance that is established between the electrical components of the mental state and the magnetic components of the emotional state. This has to be established to create at a Spirit level.

We want to add that those lower tiers of the mental–emotional body are not instantaneously removed when you do this, as some might think or hope or believe. The continued application of redrawing that tenth Ray into this space and establishing that bandwidth of frequencies at a refined level is what will dismantle this. That aspect of slipping back into those old patterns has been significantly removed. Some may believe that it is all complete, but there is still some assembly required here in this process.

Merging the Over Soul and Christed Over Soul

All the sixth-layer activations now allow for the merging of the Over Soul and the Christed Over Soul. In the sixth and seventh dimension, these aspects of you begin to function as one consciousness. They then can be drawn into the Sacred Heart and the physical body. From that merged state of the Over Soul and Christed Over Soul the doming effect of the Arc of the Covenant is significantly enhanced. The Arc becomes much more vibrant and brings the consciousness from the nonphysical state of being to within the functions of the physical body. This merging also creates tiny electrical arcs within the Arc of the Covenant and within the physical brain, which stimulate and refine the electrical system within the neurology. This begins to draw vaster, wider levels of communication and awareness into the experience of the physical body.

---

*Yeshua comments on the merging of the Over Soul
and Christed Over Soul*

This merging of your Over Soul and your Christed Over Soul is a significant step that you take. It has many, many factors within it. It begins to amplify your physical body at all levels. It sets in motion this medulla oblongata and begins to create the spin within it, just like you created the spin within your Triadic system. This spin is very significant because it begins to help all of your bodies operate at a more refined and unified level within this sixth-layer Light Body. The bodies begin to operate autonomically with the merged Over Soul and Christed Over Soul, just as your breath functions, just as the blood circulates in the body.

This autonomic function helps you function as that Christed being, without having to make continuous conscious choices. This was invaluable to me when I walked the Earth as Yeshua. In those times, when I sequestered myself in the desert, this activation of my sixth-layer Light Body took place. This enabled me to go out into a very dense world and function as the Christ and not be disturbed by my environment, or disturbed by others' opinions, but to function with focus and purpose for what I had come to do.

So you can see, this activation of the medulla oblongata and the merging of your Over Soul and your Christed Over Soul is quite a significant step that you take.

Upgrade the axiatonal lines

The axiatonal lines and spin points need to be upgraded with this sixth-layer initiation. These are very important pathways that assist you to begin to use this Living Light Body more effectively. They also relate to your ability to step into that seventh and final layer. Much attention and work has been done with seating the axiatonal lines within your physical body through the spin points and the meridian system during the first-layer activations. The Teachers present this by design, so the body can very gradually be upgraded. With the merging of the Over Soul and Christed Over Soul, no aspects of the cellular system or neurological function of the body are disturbed; they are enhanced exponentially. All the layers of the Living Light Body are put into place very precisely by this collaboration between you and the Teachers of Light. These axiatonal lines are not only connected from the first layer to your physicality, they also extend through all the layers of the Living Light Body and assist in precisely aligning those layers with each other.

Success story

For ten years I have felt like I have had one foot in the spiritual realm and one foot in the physical realm – if that. Since we brought in the Over Soul and the Christed Over Soul, I feel like I've brought both together and am able to be totally present in both the physical and nonphysical at the same time. I am excited about life again. I'm making art and just enjoy being in the world.

Yes, things come up to be released and are released very quickly and without suffering or holding on. This, for me, is amazing and I am very thankful. I see glimpses of other worlds while I am walking around and they are coming into focus slowly, not yet accessible. I'm able to go outward and come back very quickly.

In this time of Thanksgiving, I am so grateful and appreciative of all the time and effort both of you and all our Masters and Archangels and Teachers have invested in me. And I am grateful to myself for choosing this path.

Susie H, Virginia, USA

Through the axiatonal pathways and the Ze-On particles, you can also connect to other parts of creation and other dimensional realms. They help maintain stability within the physical body, which is necessary as you navigate these realms. These lines of communication with the Christed realms were disrupted at the Fall of Consciousness in order for the third-dimensional matrix to function, and so there would be no outside influences to stop separation. As the disconnection of the lines took place, your ability to have direct communication with Creator halted. The disconnection limited your ability to have energetic, conceptual or knowledge-based communications with the Teachers of Light and others who did not fall as humanity did.

Now it's time to bring back coherence and unity. It is through extending and re-establishing these axiatonal lines into the more rarefied realms of creation that you can create a line of communication with the residents there. By participating in the previous initiations you can now re-establish these connective lines and make them available to all in form to connect also to the Christed realms.

This is the time to use all the tools available to you, all the tools you've learned in this course. Command the extension of these axiatonal lines from the meridian system of the physical body through the layers of the Living Light Body and out to connect with the realms of Creator and the Christed Beings of Light.

---

*Archangel Metatron comments on re-establishing
these lines of communication*

We mentioned a time or two ago that you must stop thinking of your body as a third-dimensional vehicle and re-establish a conscious awareness that the body has been altered substantially and is now in the higher ranges of a fourth-dimensional functioning. This is important for you to continue to keep in your consciousness. Doing so facilitates the seating of these more extended axiatonal lines to the Godhead.

Re-establishing these lines of communication will have vast effect on the physicality. But most importantly, it will have great effect on your conscious ability to communicate outside of a familiar realm of the Earth's atmosphere and communicate directly with we Lords of Light, Elohim, Archangels and most importantly, with Prime Creator.

Begin to spin those axial spin points that you configured a while back. Spin them with the new consciousness that is now being derived from a re-establishment of the axiatonal lines into these other star systems that have not fallen, and most importantly, to the creative realms, the celestial realms that have not fallen into the third dimension.

By paying attention to these lines and points, the axiatonal connections will seat with a greater resonance in the body. It is more effective and fast-acting with your participation, while we Teachers make these reconnections and make these advanced sound templates and Colour Codes more available to you. You are in a body that is transitioning very quickly now.

The other point that we wish to make here is: with this reconnection a template is set forth that can be used in the seventh-layer Light Body. This is where you are not limited in your communication to individuals within this Christed realm. So when some of the gifts from the Holy Spirit begin to manifest, you will have a response that is open, receiving and quickly adaptable to your experience. You will not fear when various languages are heard through the clairaudient channels, or feelings felt through the clairsentient channels. When you notice a presence of beings that you are unfamiliar with, there will be no fear. With the reconnection of these axiatonal lines to these vaster realms, there is no possibility of reverting back to old templates of third dimension. The re-establishment of these lines ensures that your consciousness remains very coherently engaged within your physicality, but most importantly, engaged with your Over Soul, the presence of the Holy Spirit Shekinah and the Christed Over Soul.

The sixth layer of the Living Light Body

Some common experiences we've observed with this sixth-layer activation, and particularly the Arc of the Covenant, include a slight, not-uncomfortable pressure in the head, a feeling of being empty, tingling sensations, a spaciousness that is not spacy and indefinable emotions. Some people experience the body as being cold from the inside out. All of this can be expected as the physical body adjusts to this higher level of energy and Light.

Archangel Metatron comments on this sixth-layer activation

There is a massive expansion going on within you. There are really two things happening simultaneously. We are actively building a Light Body. And you are becoming conscious of being conscious as a Christed being within a physical body. What we have taught, guided and supported in this last year of Light-body activation has been what you might term in your languaging a "crash course", where we moved very quickly, even though it did not seem like that to some. We moved quickly from one layer to the next, so that we could get this Light Body positioned, at some level, in the physicality. This is all about redeeming the physical realm and raising it to a more multidimensional state. Everything has a sequence to it and brings, one by one, these very beautiful refined templates into the body to make the energetics usable again. The body is altered and shifted into that multidimensional vehicle. Because of the relationship that humanity has begun to establish with the Elementals, the Earth itself is being raised. That raising affects the entire universe. Not just the galaxy where Earth resides, but the entire universe. Every planet, every star system, every being that has some semblance of form benefits and is changed.

Some on this path operate in the illusion that they have taken care of everything and that they are ready to fully use this Light Body and alter their life experience. That is true and it is a continual journey of refining, using, creating, applying, adjusting, altering. This applies mostly to the physical realm and to the physical body, because that is what you came here to do this with us. The Soul Spirit is also constantly evolving, constantly in states of evolution, ascension, refinement.

We think it is important for these beings to understand why we have been pushing so hard with them to get this seated at the level in which it is seated. It is like anything else that has transpired in this series of teachings over the last many years of your time – there are levels. We teach a level. We move on. We may come back and add to it and expand it. So, too, it is with this Light Body. You have the basics. You have the power to make alterations. But by no means is it complete. You have to create more of that completion by using it and creating with it. That will be a very individual process, as well as a collective one.

Lesson 32

The seventh layer
of the Living Light Body

This seventh-layer initiation is where you put all the pieces you've learned in this book into a concise configuration to be used more completely. You will merge all of the layers of the Living Light Body into one within the physical body, while fully connecting with Creator using the axiatonal lines, axial spin points, Undifferentiated Light and all the previous activations. This is where you begin to *be* that Light being you've dreamed and prayed about.

Your vehicle of Light

The activations in the seventh layer are personal and unique to you. In this course, which the Elders designed for us, you have accomplished much. Among those many, many things, you have connected all of the axiatonal lines within the body, within the meridian system and within the layers of the Living Light Body, thus connecting you, as physical and as nonphysical, to all realms, all planetary systems, All That Is. This is a key achievement. In this final activation you will create a fine network of Light around, through and within you that can be fully anchored, activated, recognized, used and explored. This activation unifies your fine network of Light into a single vehicle. This new vehicle offers a smooth, fast, sleek ride to wherever you wish to travel.

The concept of a vehicle of Light is not a New-Age Lightworker concept. It's very, very old and spans several mystery schools and ancient religions. The Teachers of Light tell us our Light vehicle surrounds the physical body like a three-dimensional geometric web. It appears to most as a geometric configuration that is uniquely yours. There is no right or wrong geometry or shape. It is ever-changing as you continue to live and evolve within it. It's dormant and nonfunctional until the human has the intention, attention and commitment to take the steps and make many changes in all aspects of who they think they are. You are doing that now. You are remembering who you are.

Archangel Metatron comments on the vehicle of Light

Many have experimented with this field. It is a field of consciousness. It is a field of energy. The field of energy that we are now helping you step into is one that is built on that crystalline structure that you have created within your physical body and the crystalline structure that you have created in your consciousness. It is important for you to notice how it is built through your ability to create the Unified Field and continually expand it and refine it. For it is the building of that Unified Field – at that expansive level and within the vibratory level of refinement that you have achieved – that stimulates the vehicle of Light to come into a greater position. When in position you actually have use of it to navigate all realms of creation and planetary systems. This dramatically changes your perspective on time and space. You actually drop the concept of linear time and begin to operate more fully in a simultaneous time. This is now more possible. It is not just a concept.

For a while yet you will notice that sometimes you fluctuate between that linear perspective and the simultaneous perspective. This is what we call a time–space overlap, because you are in a space of matter that still requires some of your attention to be held in a linear perspective. But that will soon fall away, and you will operate in this crystalline vehicle of yours without the limitations of linear time.

This is your Light structure in an individualized expression. It allows you to navigate and pass through space, time and dimensions completely, in your totality. It has a consciousness and as you begin to use it, you have a greater perspective of who you are as a Light being, a being of Light.

The final layer

This layer of the Living Light Body is a process that is unfolding. And this process has to be done by each individual. You can gather together with others for discussion and support but, at the end of the day, it is you as that individual expression who begins to use all of who you are, activate it and bring it more fully into your consciousness. Experiment. As you approach this with curiosity and enthusiasm for what you are going to create, you will then be able to draw to you more precisely what is your intention. And your intention is not limited to your physicality or the physical world. Your intention is much more expansive than that. Your intention is knowing yourself as that divine image without any limitation and seeking out avenues to express it and explore it. This takes individual time to experience.

This is why the Elders suggested that, at this juncture, they temporarily pause this course to allow each participant to navigate and step into the fullness of who they are as the Living Light Body without any influence of others.

It will take a quiet time of introspection and a quiet time of experimenting. There will be things that you remember and know from a Spirit level that will come more fully into your awareness during this process. The memory, not just from your causal body, but the memory that is seated in the Seed Crystal above your right ear, will become much more accessible because of the activation of this seventh-layer Light Body. That memory of who you are at a Soul level and at an eternal level will become more evident to you as this quiet space is allowed for this complete activation.

Archangel Metatron comments on this activation

All is in place now to alter the physical body into Light and to add to the process of reclaiming humanity and raising the planet. You are being asked to gather as an individual form within All That Is so that we might imprint the world with such a consciousness that can never again be divided or limited in its expression.

Understand that this collective consciousness remains. It is eternal. It does not end because a session ends, a lesson ends. The connection, the state of being, remains and has always been there. Your ability to perceive it and know it, until now, was limited because of the state of consciousness which you inhabited. These next steps are up to you. You have all the tools and activations necessary to live in your body of Light.

Know yourself as an individual, know yourself as Spirit, and know yourself as divine.

Success story

I've been doing some experiments with the Light vehicle and want to share one with you. I choose the vibration of 12 words (one for each side of my geometry) that I wish to experience during my day and, gosh, do they work. It's automatic. I can see them happening through the day. So amazing. All it takes is some quiet moments of intention and attention and that's it.

I've also created a protocol and officially invited Michael, Metatron, Melchizedek and Uriel to join me on this ride, create vibrations together and hold them with balance and stability. In this process we get to know each other better and work in unity.

Basically anything can be invited inside this space. And even better is that my Light vehicle breathes like an alive being and is completely permeable to Light and everything that vibrates in the Light of Creator. Infinite possibilities.

I am loving it because I see very fast results (and I like speed).

Faith, Montana, USA

Collective energy of Source introduces the seventh layer
of the Living Light Body

Greetings! We come as a massive collective energy of Source. Many of us have gathered in this magnificent collective state. Lord Metatron steps forth to be the spokesperson, as this being has been the guide through this process. But understand that there is a collective energy of Source that is engaged wholly and completely in this transmission.

It is I, Metatron. I step forth now to lead this communication of this vast Source collective to present to you the beginning stages of the seventh layer of Light Body. The presence of this collective Source energy radiates with the Undifferentiated Light that is necessary for this beginning activation.

Great merges have occurred within all of your bodies and, most importantly, the Soul Spirit is very present within your physicality. In that presence, there has been a descent and merging of the Over Soul into the body; a descent and merging of the Holy Spirit Shekinah into the body; a descent and merging of that Christed Over Soul into the body. These are most significant events that have occurred.

There are three significant levels within the dynamics of the collective consciousness of this group. There are states of being aligned with, and part of, the Archangelic realm. There are states of being that are part of and aligned with the Ascended Master realm. And there are some in this collective who are a part of and aligned with the return to the unlimited pure energy of Source. As this seventh layer is engaged and becomes very activated, all layers become aligned and fully engaged. It is this activation that allows decisions to be made at a Spirit level. Decisions will be made by the individuals within this group to express themselves in one of several ways. Some will choose to remain as way-showers from the Ascended Master realm. They will walk the Earth, show others the way and direct the energy on a multidimensional level that will draw many others into their own full expression. There will be some who choose to remain within the physical realm with a fully activated Light Body who are Angelic presences. They will teach and guide and reflect that pure Undifferentiated Light in very usable states. Not just in the fifth, sixth, seventh dimensions, within the realm of form, but escalating that into the 12 dimensions. It does not stop there. It continues to grow and expand into a 24-dimensional system and beyond. Others will choose to leave their physical form and go into the pure Undifferentiated Light of Source. So you see, this activation is not only significant, it is the next step into another state of being, remembering fully and completely who you are as that Light being, negotiating realms within realms within realms.

This will take some integration, some contemplation and some time of absorption. How we would like to progress with this is very simple, and it requires very little of your participation, just a level of practice. Know and have confidence in yourself that you are now Light Bodies. This is a gathering of Angelics, Masters, ultra-terrestrials, extra-terrestrials. Each of you in form and within this collective has alignments with many realms within the realm of Source. Sit with us. We show and offer you these energetics of the seventh layer. No words. No thoughts. Only you and us, sitting together in this layer. We are you, and you and we.

Activation of the seventh strand of DNA

As you well know, the numbering of these DNA strands, just like the numbering of the Rays of Creation and the Triads, is for your benefit while you operate in a physical body. These DNA strands are actually templates of energetics that hold various Light Codes, Colour Codes and Sound Codes that relate to you as a Soul Spirit embodied in the physical realm.

You have already activated what the Teachers term the third, fourth, fifth and sixth strands of DNA. They each serve specific purposes. This seventh strand allows you to step into the multidimensional state at a more physical level, not just a consciousness level. This strand runs through the centre of the helix of DNA. It upgrades the physical body to a fifth-dimensional vehicle. The body will not have the limitation of a dense physical expression.

"Multidimensional" here relates to the fifth, sixth and seventh dimensions. This activation is a foundational piece that you will use when going beyond the seventh dimension, all the while having a body of form. This is a significant activation. The activation of a seventh strand of DNA is brought about in a co-creation between you as an individual, as a member of a physical collective, and the Teachers of Light. The Teachers will assist you to activate and direct this energetic template. They won't do it for you.

This initiation involves, once again, the Undifferentiated Light. It flows and spirals through all the physical and nonphysical bodies, unifying and joining them into the Sacred Heart. It moves into all layers of the Living Light Body, aligning them and merging them into the fourth layer. This Light of Creator also moves into and through the DNA of the physical body, the glands and organs, the heart and pineal gland. This spiralling Undifferentiated Light connects the Christed Matrix within the Earth and the Sacred Heart to the Over Soul, anchoring unity with All That Is.

Archangel Metatron closes this final layer

These are the beginning steps of a much larger process, where you begin to see all areas, all planes, all dimensions merging back into the realm of Source. You begin to know yourself from that perspective and know yourself without limit. And you bring it forth continually. This crystalline structure allows you to be the navigator and the director of your experience while you are in a physical body. And as you begin to step into that and experience it, it continually expands your knowing of you as that divine image without limit. This is a process that cannot be rushed, and must be worked with, used, experimented with, created with. As I have said, it is just the beginning that opens worlds and realms that you have not even imagined.

Conclusion

Beginning your personal journey

Archangel Metatron leads you into the unlimited consciousness

Greetings! It is I, Metatron! I come today as the individual expression of myself and the representative of the many who have guided and taught over the last several years of your time to lead you into this space of unlimited consciousness. Each participant who is embodied in this gathering can begin to know yourself as that individual expression of the divine and also know yourself as that unlimited being of Light that has no boundary, is not restricted in any way.

All of us who have gathered in the realm of creation, who have been a part of this magnificent course, encourage you to explore the part of yourself that is unlimited. As you step through the doorway into the collective nature of yourself, you will begin to uncover the vastness of who you are, while still being grounded within your body and within the Earth. This is essential.

You have come here not only to transform yourself on every level, but also to be of service, to uplift the Earth and humanity.

CONCLUSION

You are the way-showers and we are in such gratitude for your choice to work with us so that we might show you the beautiful schematic from which you were created and you might know it at the very core of your being. You are providing an opening for the descension of Spirit into form.

We want you to know this, and we want you to know yourself intimately at all levels. This is your personal journey in the next many months and years. We encourage you to take private quiet time for this exploration and to hold it very close, so that you might know the holiness of your being. This time now is for you! It is a time of ascension that will continue for quite some time for each of you personally, for all of us collectively and most importantly, for you as that individual Christed nature.

As we close this particular teaching, it is much more than a graduation. It is a stepping into a state of being where your Light shines in a magnificent way. It is an integral part in the expansion of all creation because of what you have accomplished at a personal level and what you have achieved at a collective state. There will be more to come as time passes and further integrations take place for and within you. This is not a farewell by any means, but a shift in a process that is ongoing. We ask that at the close of these remarks that all sit in the magnificent collective consciousness that we have created together and sit in the beauty of this creation for five or ten minutes . . . knowing full well that you can enter into this state any time that you focus your attention in your Sacred Heart space.

As we have said, this is not the end by any means. It is the beginning of a co-creative force that the Earth has not seen. Ever! Now we will all sit within this crucible that we have created in silence and fully present and engaged in the energies that we are creating together.

We will withdraw at this time and we look forward to participating with you in the coming state of unlimited expansion.

Blessings.

Your continuing journey

As I have said often, this is a journey, not a destination or a completion. This is now just the beginning of your journey to the Living Light Body. The information, guidance and tools presented in this book are given by the Teachers to assist you on your personal journey to ascension. Their gifts – the tools, skills and wisdom – are intended to enhance your abilities to become conscious of being more conscious and aware of becoming more aware.

As Archangel Metatron told me when we first met, the Teachers and their activations offer an opportunity for us to know ourselves as fifth- and multi-dimensional beings of Light. Simultaneously we can return the Earth to its intended twelfth-dimensional, fully Christed state of being. The Teachers of Light are friends you know intimately but have temporarily forgotten. Perhaps their words, printed here, have reintroduced you to them and them to you. It is the request of these great Elders to present this information in a manner that may stimulate you to explore further the fullness of what is possible, leading you through your own personal evolutionary journey within the Living Light Body.

Although this is an individual journey, it is also a journey as one with Creator. We are each the Light of Creator and we are one with all aspects of Creator. Having a physical form we are also the individual reflection of Creator reflecting back to Creator what Creator is. The simple intention of Creator is to know Itself in Its fullness. As you realign, rewire, remember and know yourself, Creator more fully knows Its own completeness and possibility.

CONCLUSION

Return again and again to this book. Each time you do you will access deeper and more profound energetics. Many say it is as if they never really read the book the first time. New energetics, tools and insights reveal themselves with every read. Take notes of your experiences to chronicle your growth.

If there were only one aspect of this work that we wished you to remember and integrate into who you are, the Sanctuary of the Pink Diamond within the Sacred Heart would be that aspect. This is more than a tool or a place to sit in meditation. The Sanctuary is a state of being. It is a place or platform from which to create your walking-around daily life. All questions are answered there and all unification begins there. It is within the Sacred Heart that the crucible exists, the crucible that holds your connection with All That Is. Within that crucible there are channels of communication that begin to flow through all parts of your being and into the vast ranges of this Unified Field, where nothing is left out.

The crucible you find within the Sanctuary of the Pink Diamond holds that unity consciousness. It holds that vast Undifferentiated Love and Light that extends so far beyond your comprehension at this time. As you continue to sit within the Sacred Heart and appreciate all that you have created there, you will begin to see far beyond what you have ever seen before. And you will become truly the unlimited creator that you are.

Archangel Metatron concludes the course

Sit with us in this unified state of consciousness emanating from your Sacred Heart. Observe yourself in that very refined energy created through the presence of the Undifferentiated Light of Source and brought into manifestation into the physical cellular system. Observe how that alters you exponentially. Be in this grand state of consciousness! Recognize that you can never, ever be separate from this collective energy. The Sacred Heart reflects this vast consciousness of your Spirit.

346

We will assist you in holding this level of vibration ... expanding, directing, integrating, embodying all aspects of your divine Spirit. And we will be with you as you experience yourself as divine, as Spirit.

Blessings

Online resources

Meditation that combines several tools and holds powerful energy. (33:59)

To access the online classroom,
visit www.masteringalchemy.com/book

Glossary

alchemy Alchemy is the process and path of creating a life with awareness and intention and returning to a conscious relationship with *Creator*. It is transforming the density of your physicality into the *Living Light Body*. The process of alchemy changes the frequency of thought, alters the harmonics of matter and applies the element of Love to create a desired result.

All That Is Everything that exists. All the creations of *Creator*.

Arc of the Covenant The Arc of the Covenant is one of several *energetics* and tools presented during the activations of the sixth layer of the *Living Light Body*. It appears as an arc or dome over the top of one's head and opens the brain and the neurological system so as to turn on the spiritual autonomic system in the physical and spiritual bodies.

Ascended Masters The Ascended Masters were once embodied on Earth as ordinary humans. They chose to do the focused work required – over many lifetimes – to become spiritually enlightened. Many of the Ascended Masters are now choosing to return to Earth in a physical form to direct and guide the uplifting of the planet and her inhabitants during this transition. Included among them are some of the new children who are currently being born.

Atlantis The *Teachers of Light* have described Atlantis as the ancient civilization that was instrumental in the *Fall of Consciousness*. It was here that the *creator gods* reached the apex of their mis-creations and mutations that caused Earth to fall into the density we call the third dimension. Jim was intimately involved in the final days of Atlantis and this was what called him to say

"Yes" when the ***Teachers of Light*** asked him to participate in this experiment. A resident of Atlantis is called an Atlantean.

avatars Members of the collective called the ***Teachers of Light***. At the time of writing this book, the avatars have not identified themselves as actively participating in this project.

causal body The causal body is the nonphysical body that holds the accumulation of the ***Soul***'s positive experiences and converts them into wisdom for the Soul. These experiences are also called ***Memory Codes***.

Centre of Your Head The Centre of Your Head is the initial place to put your attention in order to establish a "command centre" for operating your life. It's an area directly behind your eyes. Being there brings you into present-time and neutral observation, both very important qualities for navigating these chaotic times of transition. To deeply experience the Centre of Your Head, you might imagine it as a special room or a place in nature within which to sit comfortably and observe the world through closed eyes.

Christ Consciousness An aspect of ***Creator***.

Christed A state of being where you are one with the ***All That Is***. A Christed planet is a planet that is fully in alignment with, unified with and demonstrating the ***Christ Consciousness*** of ***Creator***. The Christed Matrix (within the ***Sacred Heart*** and within the planet) is a tool to bring that Christ Consciousness into our lives and into Mother Earth.

The Collective *See **Teachers of Light***.

Colour Codes Enormous energetic patterns that contain many applications. During the activations of the ***Living Light Body*** these Colour Codes add opportunity and expand the capacity within the 12 strands of DNA.

Creator The Creator is the source of all creation.

creator gods Creator gods were created by ***Creator*** to go off into ***All That Is*** to have experiences and create in alignment with Creator's desires and power. During the ***Fall of Consciousness***, the creator gods began creating with their own power and will and in less alignment with Creator. Soon the creator gods were not creating in alignment with Creator's ***Light***, which caused misalignments, glitches and mutations. Eventually this mis-creating brought us to the situation in which humanity now finds itself.

dimensions Dimensions are states of consciousness that are available to anyone who vibrates in resonance with the specific frequencies inherent within each dimension. These dimensions or levels of consciousness each have their own characteristics and ways of thinking, feeling and interacting. They also each have unique structures, qualities and aspects that contain a variety of experiences.

Earth goddesses Members of the angelic kingdom. These wonderful beings oversee and guide the ***Elementals*** upon their journey back to Love and purpose. Tara is one such Earth goddess.

El Shaddai A powerful sound template within the ninth ***Ray of Creation***. The El Shaddai is used as a clearing mechanism. Where the eighth Ray releases more dense and known programming or energy, the El Shaddai is the broom that can reach into the hidden corners to release the smaller bits of stuck energy – the dust. It's usually used in combination with the eighth Ray of Creation.

Elders An alternative way to describe the ***Teachers of Light***. Our understanding and experience of the word "Elders" is less distant to the programmed human mind than the word "Teacher", a term that for some can be fraught with old patterns of control and domination. The Teachers realize this and sometimes refer to themselves as Elders in order to bridge the gap and develop a closer relationship with the participants. An Elder can be equated to a kindly grandparent.

Elementals The Elementals are a group of four simple beings. Each Elemental represents and works with one of the four elements: Undine works with Water, Salamander works with Fire, Gnome works with Earth, Sylth works with Air. The Elementals have the ability to take what humanity sends them (Love, for example), and send it back to humanity in a more pure, amplified form.

GLOSSARY

Elohim Members of the collective called the *Teachers of Light*. As of now they have not identified themselves as actively participating in this project; however, other Teachers have mentioned their presence occasionally. They tend to be present at conferences, lectures and meditations.

emotional body *See four-body system*.

energetics Energetics are combinations of vibrations and frequencies (light, sound, colour, thoughts and emotions) that are organized in a manner that allows a human being to create its experience and environment.

Eye of Horus An energy template configured within the brain. When activated it opens access to higher levels of consciousness and greater aspects of intuition. Working with the Eye of Horus allows greater integration of the information and *energetics* offered on this path.

Fall of Consciousness The Fall of Consciousness was a devolution that took place over aeons. The Fall was set in motion when the *creator gods* began to use their own *Light* instead of the Light of *Creator* to create things. This turning away from the Light of Creator has ultimately created the chaotic and hurtful world we now experience all around us. The *Teachers of Light* offer us a way to return to a life of unification with Creator.

four-body system Humans have four bodies: a physical body, an emotional body, a mental body and a spiritual body. The first three are anchored in the third dimension but the spiritual body is not. Many of us are dominated by one or two of these bodies. The physical body is the most solid and dense and it is the slowest to make personal evolutionary changes. The emotional body is slightly less dense and is more flexible. The mental body has even more capacity to change and transmute into something more expansive. The spiritual body is the layer between us and our ultimate higher selves. All four bodies greatly influence each other. We need them to be integrated and balanced if we want to achieve life-balance and eventually wear the *Living Light Body*. As you work through the teachings in this course your mental and emotional bodies will become merged into one body.

Great Beings of Light A respectful term that refers to all members of the collective known as the *Teachers of Light*.

Higher Mind The Higher Mind is 2.5cm (1 inch) up and 4cm (1½ inches) back from the *Centre of Your Head*. Once you're familiar and comfortable with being in the Centre of Your Head, you can put your attention in the Higher Mind as you continue to build a life experience of quiet observation, personal power and unification with *Creator*. The difference between existing here and in the Centre of Your Head is an experience that is unique to everyone. Many describe the Higher Mind as an observation platform that includes the higher aspects of who they are, whereas the Centre of Your Head is primarily for navigating the third dimension while still anchored in it. The Centre of Your Head is an excellent segue to existing in the Higher Mind.

Higher Self The Higher Self relates to the portion of the *Soul* that takes on embodiment for certain experiences for the Soul's evolution.

Holy Spirit The aspect of *Creator* that creates.

Holy Spirit Shekinah As we anchor and incorporate greater levels and layers of the *Living Light Body*, we are able to deepen and expand our relationship with the *Holy Spirit*. One of these deeper layers of the Holy Spirit is referred to as Shekinah.

Home The teachings of the *Elders* refer to Home (with a capital "H") as the place we return to when we unite with *Creator*. It is a sacred and affectionate term that many participants can viscerally feel and remember. Home is what we forgot when we volunteered to jump into the density of the third dimension.

I AM Presence A term first coined in 1875 by the Theosophical Society and used in the 1930s by Alice Bailey, Saint Germain in the *Ascended Master Teachings*, and various other organizations. Currently it can be defined as who you are as divine; who you really are when you ascend from the third to higher dimensions; who you are when unified with *Creator*.

Infinite Intelligence Usually used in relationship with *Creator*. The Infinite Intelligence of Creator is all that Creator knows. This intelligence is infinite and unlimited.

inner smile The inner smile exists within the *Sacred Heart* and within every aspect of you. It is a feeling and a state of being that may be described as joy, ecstasy, reverence and inner peace, although those words are too small to truly define it. Once experienced and anchored, the inner smile can be used as a reference point that allows you to return to those higher states of consciousness.

Law of Attraction The Law of Attraction is one of several universal laws (like gravity). It states that whatever we hold our attention upon, we draw into our life experience. Much of this occurs unconsciously rather than deliberately. The transition humanity is currently in (the *Shift of Consciousness*) is bringing this law into greater awareness, and consequently more of us are able to understand and leverage it for our personal comfort and growth.

Lemurian As Earth began slowly to recover from the *Fall of Consciousness*, higher aspects of consciousness began to become infused and seeded into the planet. This new consciousness was called Lemurian. Lemurians were simple beings that did not have dense physical bodies. They were the first step in the experiment to return Earth to its *Christed* state.

Light Light carries the vibration of wisdom, intelligence and consciousness through the layers and dimensions of *All That Is*. It can be used as a direct connection to *Creator* and as a tool for our personal guidance and wellbeing.

Light Language This is more than a spoken language. It's an energetic format from which the higher-dimensional levels of thought are translated and made usable from one dimension to another. It provides coherence within the fifth, sixth and seventh dimensions.

Living Light Body Many mystical traditions offer definitions of the Light Body. In this course the Living Light Body is the form we are building that will allow us to re-merge with the *Unified Field* of *Creator* and *All That Is*. "Living" refers to the fact that we can now experience this body while alive and moving about our daily life. To activate a Living Light Body is no longer just the work of secluded gurus, sages, monks and masters. It's a way of being available to all who wish to pursue it.

Lords of Light Members of the collective called the *Teachers of Light*. Lord Metatron and Lord Melchizedek are Lords of Light.

Memory Codes Memories of positive experiences from past lives that are stored within the *causal body*. These are used as wisdom on your path *Home*. They are introduced during the activations of the third layer of the *Living Light Body*.

mental body *See four-body system.*

Mind of Creator *See Universal Mind of Source.*

Mind of Source *See Universal Mind of Source.*

On particles Thoughts that are thought by the *Universal Mind* and *Mind of Source*. These can be accessed within the *Arc of the Covenant* and drawn from the *Undifferentiated Light* through the eleventh chakra.

Over Soul The Over Soul oversees the physical body and the *Higher Self*, much like a foreman in a factory guides and watches the employees without doing their work for them. Some call this the Over Self. It has a potent relationship, energetically, to *All That Is*. The Over Soul is that part of you that directs light frequencies into the *Living Light Body*. The Over Soul stays with you even when the physical body is dropped and is no longer needed. The Over Soul oversees that transition into the nonphysical realm and remains with the *Soul* and the Higher Self until decisions are made to return to the vaster collective of All That Is.

Personal Power Field One of the first tools the *Teachers of Light* teach is how to establish your Personal Power Field. This is a field of energy that when built, and with regular use, offers an increase not only in your personal power but also your ability to manage the noise and drama of the third dimension. The ability to step into a *Unified Field* with *Creator* and *All That Is* also becomes possible.

present-time Present-time is the now moment. It is a moment of nonreaction that, when cultivated, helps you step out of the noise and drama of the third dimension and leads to a life of greater awareness and connection with who you came here to be.

Rays of Creation The Rays of Creation are taught during the unfolding of this project by the *Teachers of Light*. These are powerful tools and part of the pathway to bring humanity and Earth back into alignment with *Creator*. Each Ray of Creation is designed for a specific application or purpose.

Sacred Heart The Sacred Heart is the place where you can interface and connect with *Creator*, the higher aspects of yourself (such as your *Soul*) and *All That Is*. It is located in the area of the thymus gland in the centre of your chest, but is not the thymus gland itself.

Sanctuary of the Pink Diamond A room within the *Sacred Heart*. Within this sanctuary there exists a glowing pink diamond and an altar, both of which appear differently to everyone. As you enter and remain in the sanctuary, your awareness expands more and more into the fullness of what the Sacred Heart is. This is your sacred place where you can sit at the table and communicate with the higher aspects of yourself, the *Elders* and *Creator*. It's a place of doing nothing and experiencing everything, allowing all things to come to you. Much occurs within this sacred space. It is the place from which to observe the world around you, and it is the room where each of the lessons in this book is best enjoyed.

Seed Crystals Crystalline seed energies are located within the etheric body. These Seed Crystals are able to translate various tones and sound vibrations (sometimes known as *Light Language*) that are not audible to the human ear.

Shift of Consciousness Humanity and Earth are currently in a transition known as the Shift of Consciousness. This may be one of the most, if not *the* most, important times in human evolution. We are transitioning from the dense, noisy, dull life of the third dimension into the higher awareness, ease and community of the fifth dimension and beyond. We are transitioning from separation to unity with *All That Is*.

sleep space Sleep space is the time when the physical body is fully at rest. During this time the mental and emotional bodies become one (the astral body), allowing the spiritual body to have adventures and experiences. This is the time when you meet the ***Teachers of Light*** at the table in the ***Sanctuary of the Pink Diamond***. Most of us don't remember this time when we return to our bodies; however, Jim is able to remember and bring the teachings back from his sleep space and share them with us.

Soul The Soul was created by ***Creator*** to go out and have experiences in physicality. Creator wanted to know Itself and this was how It went about doing that.

Soul Extensions Each ***Soul*** is comprised of Soul Extensions. You might imagine them like this: the parent (Soul) takes all the children (Soul Extensions) to the park (***All That Is***). "Go off and explore," says the parent, "When you've explored and experienced all the games and toys (life's adventures), return to me and we can all share and learn what you've learned. Then together we can go ***Home*** (back to ***Creator***)." While incarnated it's highly unlikely you will meet your Soul Extensions. They are scattered throughout All That Is, busy having new experiences. Some Soul Extensions have physical bodies, but many do not. Once all the Soul Extensions, including you, have experienced all there is to experience in the realm where you live, you all return Home, as one Soul, to the heart of Creator.

Soul Spirit The aspect of you that is in complete alignment with ***Source***.

Soul Star One of the three centres within the third ***Triad***. It is located above the eighth chakra and slightly to the left.

Source Another word for ***Creator***. It is the creator and source of all things. The source of all wisdom and knowledge.

spiritual body *See **four-body system***.

Teachers of Light The Teachers of Light have identified themselves as a collective of beings whose common intention is to create a pathway, called A Course in Mastering Alchemy. Their purpose is to offer tools, information and activations that, when applied, will uplift the individual participant, humanity and Earth to their full capacity to live in the fifth dimension and beyond. Members of this collective include Archangels, *Ascended Masters* and other significant players such as the *Elohim* and *Lords of Light*. Consider each one of these as a job title.

Triads The three Triads are your higher-dimensional chakra system. They create a *Unified Field* that opens realms of awareness, knowledge and wisdom that you have access to but had no knowledge of prior to working with the Triads. The first Triad is a sphere that surrounds the fourth chakra, thymus gland and fifth chakra. The second Triad is a sphere that surrounds the sixth chakra, pineal gland and medulla oblongata. The third Triad is a sphere that surrounds the seventh and eighth chakras and the *Soul Star*. These Triads are an unexpected gift of *Creator*.

Undifferentiated Light Light *energetics* that originate from *Creator* and are streamed through the eleventh chakra for our use within this ascension process. Undifferentiated Light is whole and pure with no predetermined purpose or direction, unlike the *Rays of Creation*, which were designed for specific purposes. Undifferentiated Light is able to flow freely, move and be used for any creation. It is accessible only while living in the higher dimensions and within the fifth and higher layers of thought.

Unified Field All living creatures have an electromagnetic field (aura) surrounding them; sometimes it's coherent; many times it's disjointed. Using the *Triads* we are able to create an energy field that is unified and surrounds us in a full, stable and coherent manner. As we continue along this path we further activate it, anchor it and expand it. Our personal *Unified Field* becomes unified with (one with, conjoined with) *Creator* and *All That Is*.

Universal Mind of Source The Universal Mind of Source is accessed within the eighth, ninth and tenth chakras. The *Teachers of Light* offer a pathway to connect with (unify with) this all-encompassing library of experience, wisdom and creative power. It is also known as the Mind of Source and the Mind of Creator.

Veil of Ignorance and Forgetfulness A vertical nonphysical partition, perpendicular to the corpus callosum and located between the temples. It is an electromagnetic field of energy that significantly minimizes the function of the hypothalamus, medulla oblongata, pineal gland and the seventh and eight chakras. It restricts us to a narrow field of logic, duality and rigid rules. When the veil is neutralized or dismantled, observation from the *Higher Mind* is possible, as is awareness of multidimensional consciousness.

Ze-On particles Electrical in nature, Ze-On particles are your *Higher Mind* thoughts (Ze) merged with the thoughts of the *Mind of Source* (On).

Ze particles These are your thoughts that are thought in the higher realms and in your *Higher Mind*. They exist in the *Undifferentiated Light* and are not accessible or knowable while in the third dimension and the lower levels of thought.

Index

INDEX

WATKINS
Sharing Wisdom Since 1893

The story of Watkins began in 1893, when scholar of esotericism John Watkins founded our bookshop, inspired by the lament of his friend and teacher Madame Blavatsky that there was nowhere in London to buy books on mysticism, occultism or metaphysics. That moment marked the birth of Watkins, soon to become the publisher of many of the leading lights of spiritual literature, including Carl Jung, Rudolf Steiner, Alice Bailey and Chögyam Trungpa.

Today, the passion at Watkins Publishing for vigorous questioning is still resolute. Our stimulating and groundbreaking list ranges from ancient traditions and complementary medicine to the latest ideas about personal development, holistic wellbeing and consciousness exploration. We remain at the cutting edge, committed to publishing books that change lives.

DISCOVER MORE AT:
www.watkinspublishing.com

Read our blog   Watch and listen to   Sign up to
our authors in action   our mailing list

We celebrate conscious, passionate, wise and happy living.
Be part of that community by visiting

 /watkinspublishing    @watkinswisdom

 /watkinsbooks    @watkinswisdom